IMAGES
of America

CHENEY

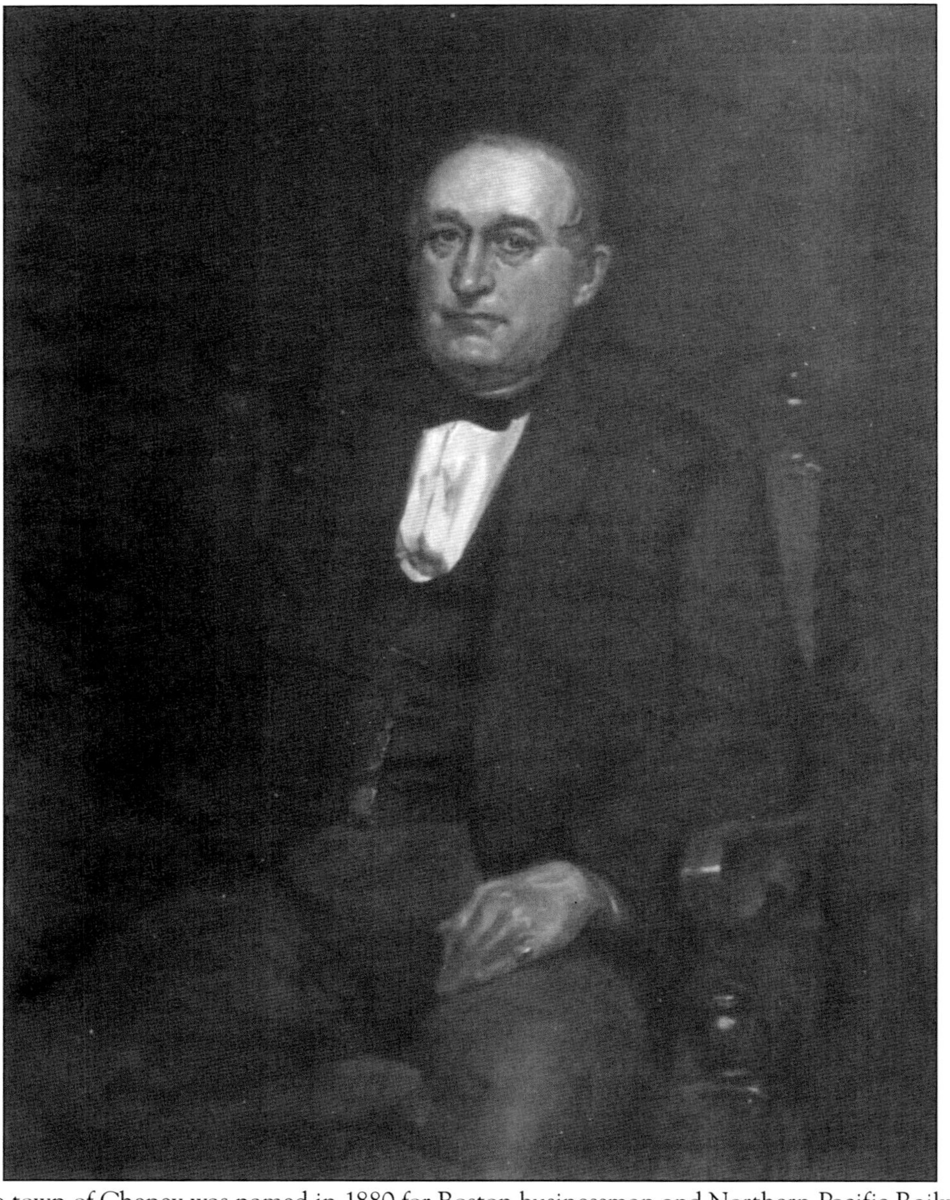

The town of Cheney was named in 1880 for Boston businessman and Northern Pacific Railway director Benjamin Pierce Cheney. Flattered by the honor, Cheney provided money, teachers, and books to start a school upon a request from the citizens. That school evolved into Eastern Washington University. In September 1883, Cheney and his wife made their only visit to his namesake town. (Cheney Historical Museum.)

On the Cover: The annual May Day Festival, held from 1910 to the start of World War II, brought crowds of visitors to Cheney each year. Horse-drawn floats, bands, and decorated automobiles, like those shown here, wound through the streets from downtown to City Park. Visitors enjoyed the crowning of the May Queen, a Normal School faculty versus alumni baseball game, and an evening dance. (Cheney Historical Museum.)

IMAGES
of America

CHENEY

Joan Mamanakis and the Southwest
Spokane County Historical Society

ARCADIA
PUBLISHING

ISBN 978-1-4671-3348-7

Published by Arcadia Publishing
Charleston, South Carolina

Printed in the United States of America

Library of Congress Control Number: 2015932860

For all general information, please contact Arcadia Publishing:
Telephone 843-853-2070
Fax 843-853-0044
E-mail sales@arcadiapublishing.com
For customer service and orders:
Toll-Free 1-888-313-2665

Visit us on the Internet at www.arcadiapublishing.com

Contents

ACKNOWLEDGMENTS

I want to thank the many people who have donated their family photographs to our collection so that we may share a more complete story of our history.

I especially want to thank Dr. Charles V. Mutschler, Eastern Washington University archivist, for his generous assistance, without whom this volume would be impoverished. I also offer special thanks to Kyle Pugh Jr., Nancy Rueppel, Margit Johnson, Barbara Curtis, and Marietta McGourin, who all helped to make sure I had the images I needed for this publication.

A number of our historical society volunteers assisted in the proofing of this book. It is a difficult, detailed, and tedious task. I am especially grateful to Carolyn Wall who worked with me to make sure my sentences were complete, my punctuation made the text readable, and my typos were corrected. I hope I have not reintroduced too many errors.

Finally, I want to thank my husband, Steve Fabre, for his advice, assistance, and, especially, his patience as I worked on this project.

Unless otherwise noted, images are from the Cheney Historical Museum collection. Other sources are identified as follows:

EWU	Eastern Washington University
EWU-SPC	Eastern Washington University Library Special Collections
EWU-SPC-WWP	Eastern Washington University Library Special Collections Warren Westerman Papers
EWU-SPC-BFSC	Eastern Washington University Library Special Collections Benjamin Franklin Stephenson Collection

INTRODUCTION

A spring bubbled up from the ground, feeding a year-round pond where Native Americans had a winter camp at the base of a group of hills in Section 13. It was the highest point on the surveyed route for the transcontinental Northern Pacific Railway line between the Idaho border and the Columbia River crossing near modern-day Tri-Cities. This was a natural place for the railroad to build a section station.

A handful of homesteaders were in the area, including Thomas Philleo, who arrived in 1869 with a stock of horses and cattle to locate near the lake that bears his name. Civil War veteran Daniel F. Percival homesteaded land along Rock Creek in 1872. George W. Cook settled to the north, where his wife and daughter joined him in the autumn of 1878. The Cooks' elder daughter, Sarah Jane, soon arrived with her husband, Samuel Showalter, to homestead land to the west.

These settlers knew the railroad was coming, so they set to work building the enterprises the new community would need. Charles Carreau built a log structure that he dubbed the St. Charles Hotel. Stephen Harris set up the first blacksmith shop. By the end of 1878, the settlers had established the first school on a hill in a log building, with Mary Cook walking over from her father's homestead to teach 15 students. Foreseeing the demand for supplies by the railroad and pioneers, Isaac Ballinger entered into the freight business, making month-long trips to Walla Walla while his wife took care of their infant alone in the sparsely populated country.

In 1880, Gen. John W. Sprague, a superintendent for the Northern Pacific Railway, named the town site on Section 13 Cheney, though it was formerly known as Billings, Big Springs, and Depot Springs. Naming towns after railroad company officers was a common practice of the period, and Boston businessman Benjamin Pierce Cheney was a major stockholder and a director of the company. When the first plat of Cheney was laid out in 1880, the streets ran parallel to the rail line rather than the compass. This gave the town its oddly angled streets and pie shape of today. In November 1880, Cheney became the Spokane County seat in a hotly disputed election. The town that had started the year with a population numbering in the tens ended the year with several hundred residents and the county government.

Cheney was also at the center of the temperance movement in the Pacific Northwest with the arrival of Lucy Robbins Switzer in 1880. Switzer traveled throughout Washington Territory establishing temperance unions. She had a regular column in the newspaper and the temperance journal, and was a featured speaker at several regional and national temperance conventions. She was also a strong advocate for women's suffrage and lived to see Washington women win the right to vote in 1910.

In 1881, the businessmen of Cheney embarked on their most enduring project for the town, establishing an educational institution. They wrote to Benjamin Cheney asking for his assistance, and he gave $10,000, persuaded the railroad to give over eight acres of land, and sent a pair of teachers to start the Benjamin P. Cheney Academy, which opened April 3, 1882.

Cheney incorporated as a city in 1883, the same year that Benjamin Pierce Cheney and his wife, Elizabeth, made their only visit to the town and academy. The couple, along with other dignitaries on the inaugural trip of the Northern Pacific transcontinental line, stopped for a few hours on September 18, 1883. The citizens put on a celebration with food, song, a parade, and many speeches to honor their benefactor.

Spokane won back the county seat in 1886, and Cheney then pinned its dreams on agriculture and education. The Benjamin P. Cheney Academy became Washington's first state Normal School on March 22, 1890. Those early years of the school were rocky. Twice it burned to the ground, and three times Washington governors vetoed funding for the school. Each time though, citizens, teachers, and students fought back, keeping the school going and overcoming government skeptics.

The Cheney School District set up its own school in 1887 with William J. Sutton as its principal. Sutton, a charismatic speaker and teacher, went on to head the Normal School and was one of its most passionate advocates. As a state senator, he served on the education committee, helping to build a robust educational system for Washington. Through consolidation, the Cheney public school district grew to be one of the largest geographic districts in the state.

Cheney endured early trials as major fires nearly swept the town away in 1883, 1889, and 1890. It has been home to many kinds of business; a few have endured, but most have vanished. It was home to one of the earliest breweries, as well as a number of creameries processing and selling milk and cheese. Fred Reuter opened the Cheney Cheese Factory just south of town in 1903. At the turn of the 20th century, one-third of the cheese made in Washington came from Cheney creameries. The rotary rod weeder, a farm tillage implement, was invented by local men Kyle and Cleve Wolfe. The Cheney Weeder Company manufactured and shipped weeders all over the country and beyond from 1912 to 1953.

Lumber mills provided materials for building the business district and homes, as well as wagons, furniture, and the furniture makers' second business of supplying coffins and grave markers. In the early 1900s, there were eight sawmills within a 10-mile radius of Cheney.

The farmers in the district also needed gristmills to grind their wheat into flour. The first flour mill opened in 1880. The longest operating business in Cheney is its current flour mill, opened in 1907 by Frank M. Martin and now operated by Archer Daniels Midland.

Cheney's most prominent native son, Clarence D. Martin, graduated from the Cheney Normal School in 1903. He became Washington's first native-born governor in 1933. Among his many accomplishments as governor, Martin was instrumental in securing the Grand Coulee Dam project, which was one of the most successful jobs projects of the Great Depression and for the state industry and agriculture.

Into the 1960s, Cheney straddled the main east-west highway of the state and hosted a thriving business district. At one time, there were 13 gas stations, a movie theater, three motels, two hardware stores, a department store, a jeweler, two pharmacies, dry cleaners, three grocery stores, a clothing store, two banks, and numerous restaurants. When the freeway bypassed the town in 1965, Cheney's struggle began against the easy access to goods and services in the much larger Spokane.

With Eastern Washington University as its hub, Cheney continues to strive to build its niche as a gateway to recreation and the channeled scablands of the ice-age floods, as well as capitalize on its friendly rural, small-town atmosphere.

One

Early Years

The future city of Cheney was the highest point along the surveyed route of the Northern Pacific Railway in Washington Territory. It had a year-round spring to water the locomotives, and was a good location for commerce at the edge of the fertile Palouse hills, timberlands, and the broad plains of the Big Bend country. The earliest pioneers named the lakes and creeks, raised stock for the military, and set up businesses in anticipation of the railroad and the immigrants who would follow.

Section 13, Big Springs, Willow Springs, Depot Springs, and Billings were early names of the community. In September 1880, railroad superintendent Gen. John Sprague declared the town would be called Cheney after Northern Pacific Railway Company director Benjamin P. Cheney.

In November 1880, Cheney won the vote to become the Spokane County seat, but the election was disputed by rival Spokane Falls, which refused to give up the books. Cheney called this stealing the election. In March 1881, a group of Cheney men rode into Spokane Falls to recount the ballots and collect the county books. Spokane called this "the big steal." Cheney held the starring role for six years before losing the county seat to Spokane in an election rematch in 1886.

On September 18, 1883, Benjamin Pierce Cheney and his wife, Elizabeth, made their only visit to his namesake town and academy on their way home to Boston from the Northern Pacific Railway "last spike" celebrations in Montana and Portland, Oregon. The whole town came out to meet his train. A procession, headed by a band and students, walked the crowd up to the academy, where Cheney gave a speech and a grand celebration was held.

The early settlers were people with a progressive vision who established a school and a bustling downtown business district, which stretched from Pine to Union Streets. Cheney incorporated on November 11, 1883, with Daniel F. Percival as its first mayor. The town survived and rebuilt after devastating fires in 1883 and 1889. Those early years established education and agriculture as the foundations on which Cheney developed.

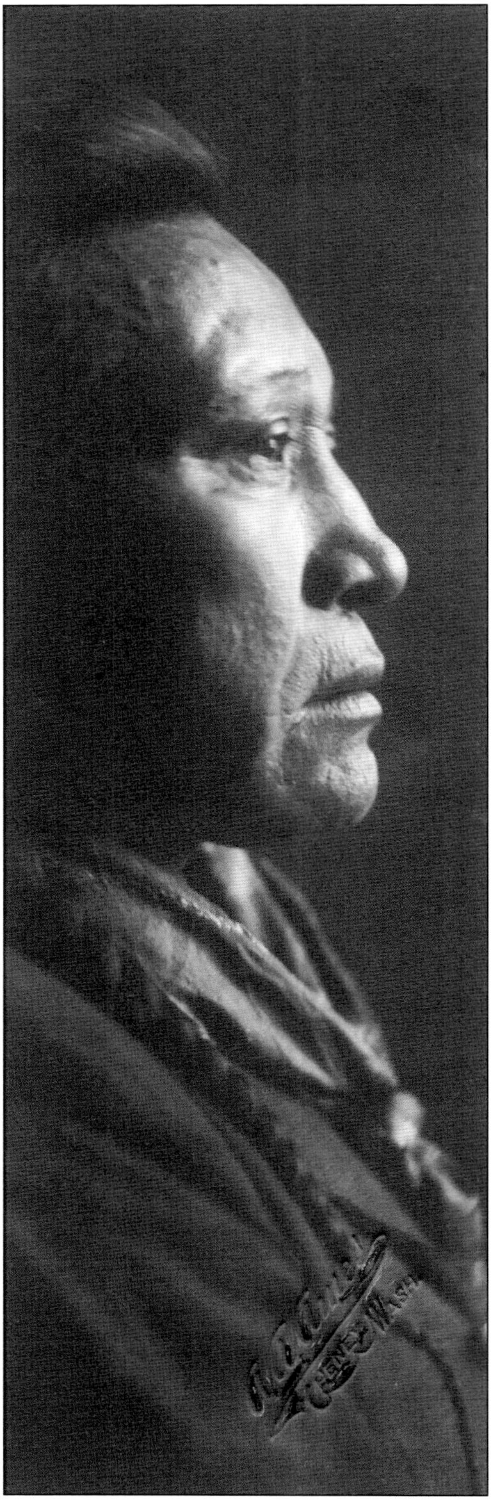

The native Salish-speaking people of the region had seasonal camps at the site of the future Cheney. Their more permanent encampments were near the Spokane River. In the spring, families congregated near the wetlands to harvest and process Camas root, an onion-like bulb. They hunted deer in the woods, fished the lakes, and grazed their horses on the bunch grass of the plains and hills. South of Cheney, on the plain near Stubblefield Lake, was a regular gathering spot for meetings and games. Their relations with the new white settlers were ambivalent. The Native Americans were met with fear and antagonism as they tried to continue their traditional activities and were slowly pushed out of the area. A few white settlers came to know and even have warm relations with them. Pioneer Fred Campbell recalled that Indians would often come and "borrow" the dugout canoe his father made, but they always returned it when they were done fishing in Williams Lake.

Thomas A.E. Philleo arrived in 1869. He filed for homestead land south of Cheney that had a good spring to provide water and a grove of aspen trees for shelter and fuel. He was known for his skill in treating sick animals, which earned him the nickname of "Doc." In the early years, he raised horses and cattle for the Army. Philleo's descendants still farm the homestead land.

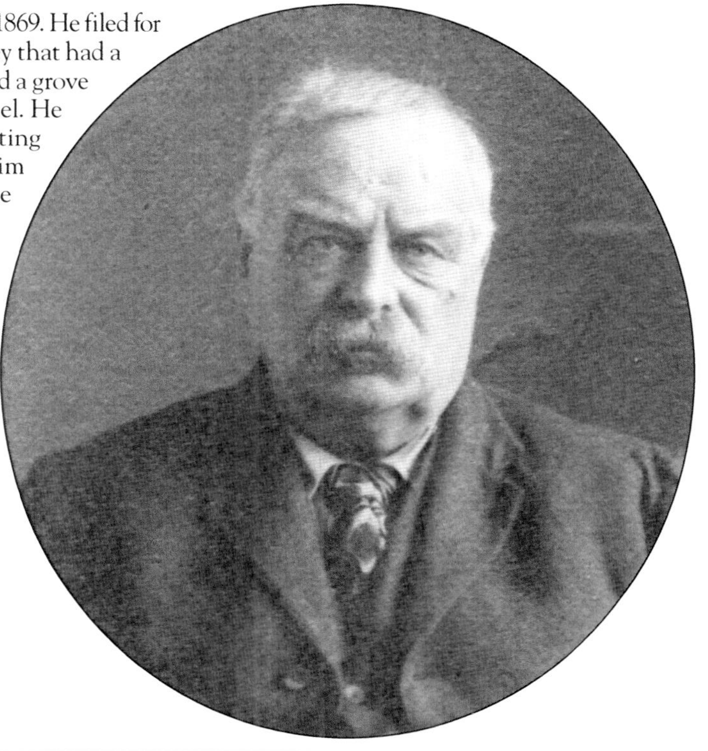

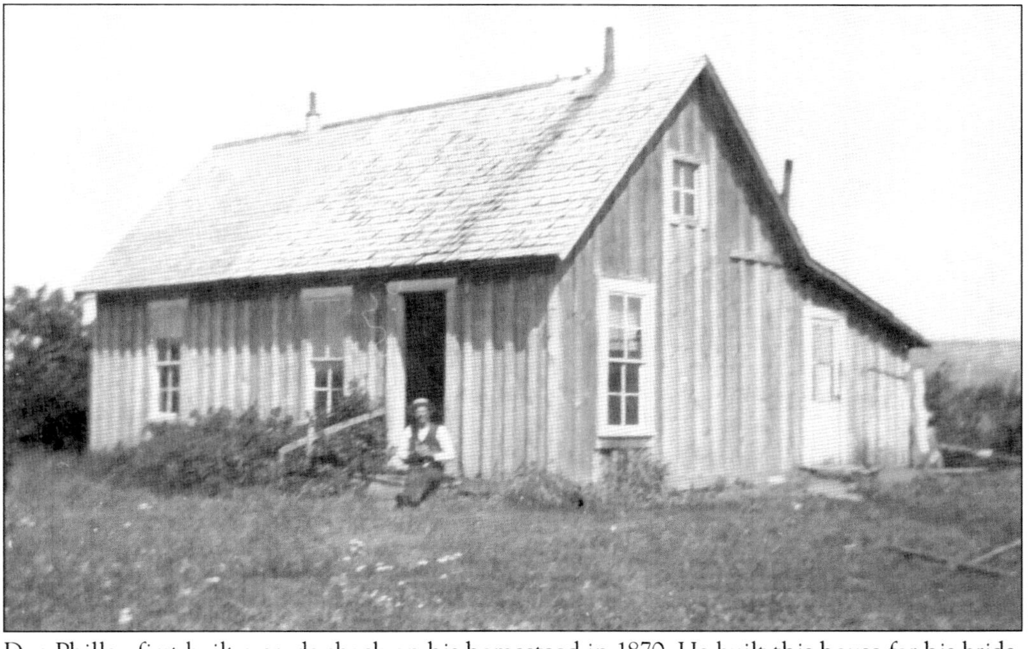

Doc Philleo first built a crude shack on his homestead in 1870. He built this house for his bride, Margaret Kime, in 1879. In 1896, the family moved into a two-story brick home built nearby. The photograph shows neighbor Pete Anderson sitting in the doorway of the homestead house in the early 1900s.

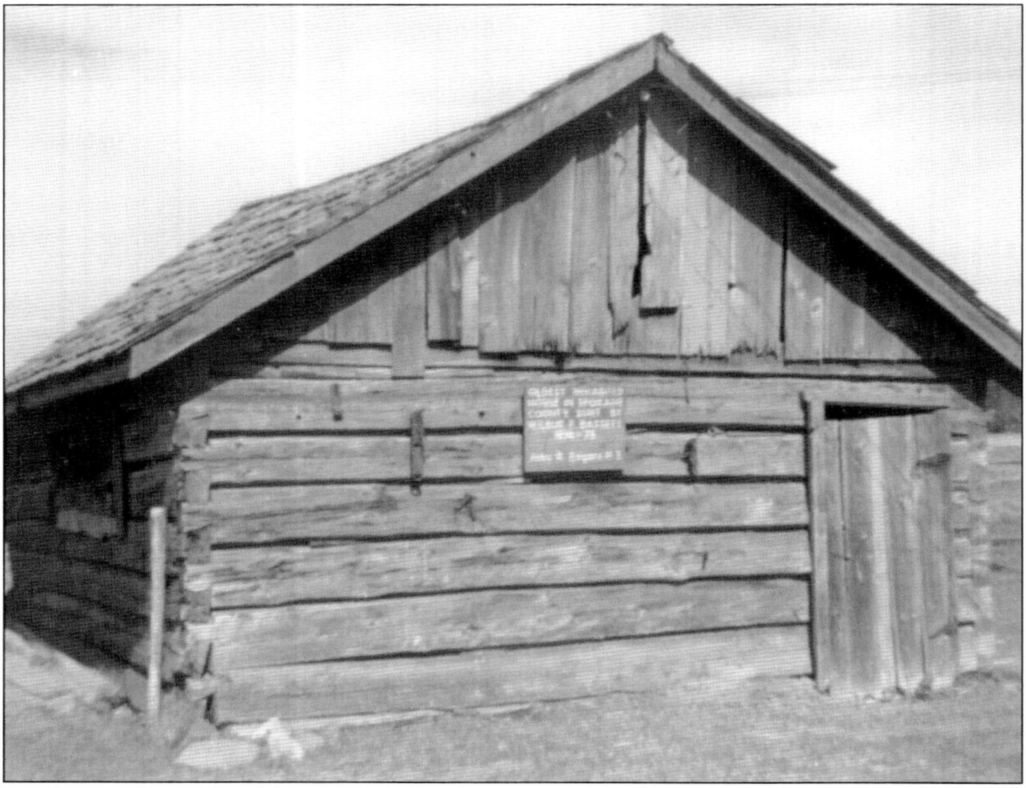

In 1871, Wilbur and Adele Bassett arrived at Spokane Falls, where he helped to establish the first sawmill. In the spring of 1872, the family, which included son Herman and baby Minnie, homesteaded in the Four Lakes district, where Wilbur gave names to Granite, Silver, and Clear Lakes. The Bassett house, built in 1874, still stands near Granite Lake Road.

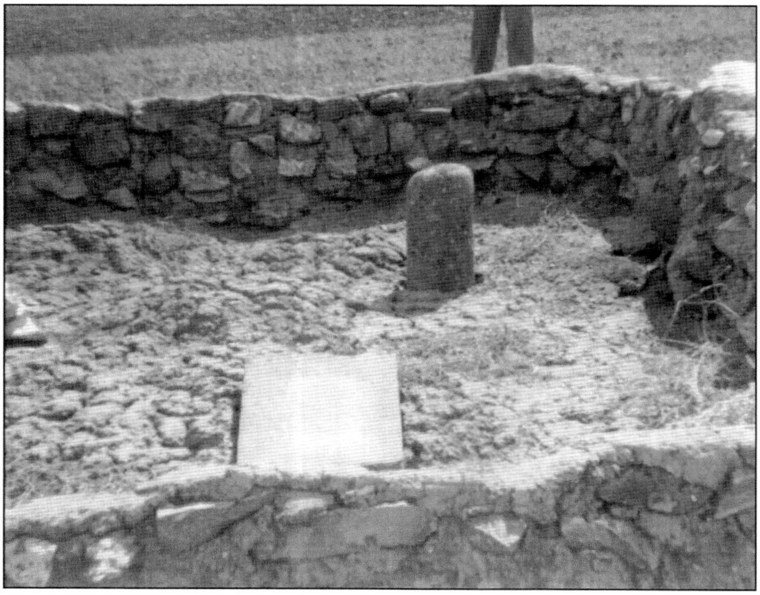

Minnie Marie Bassett was the first white child born in Spokane Falls on January 2, 1872. Young Minnie slipped away from the hired girl and drowned in the creek near the family cabin on July 19, 1873. She was buried on the hillside with a stone carved by her father. A baby brother was interred beside her in 1884. The landowners care for the graves to this day.

Civil War veteran Daniel F. Percival started a stock ranch on Rock Creek in 1872. He served as a county commissioner, and also served two terms in the Washington territorial legislature. He introduced the bill to create Spokane County in 1879, and is remembered as the principal advocate for creating a Normal School out of the Cheney Academy. Percival was a successful banker and served as Cheney's first mayor.

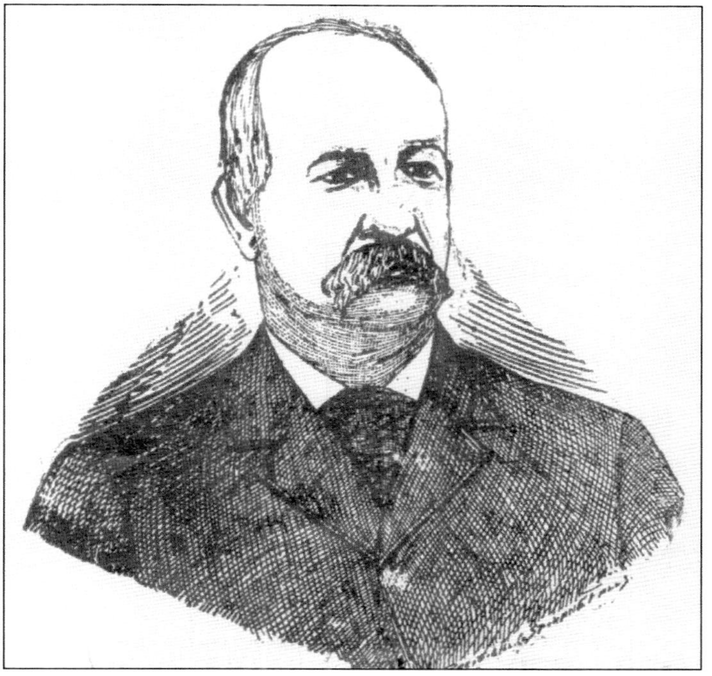

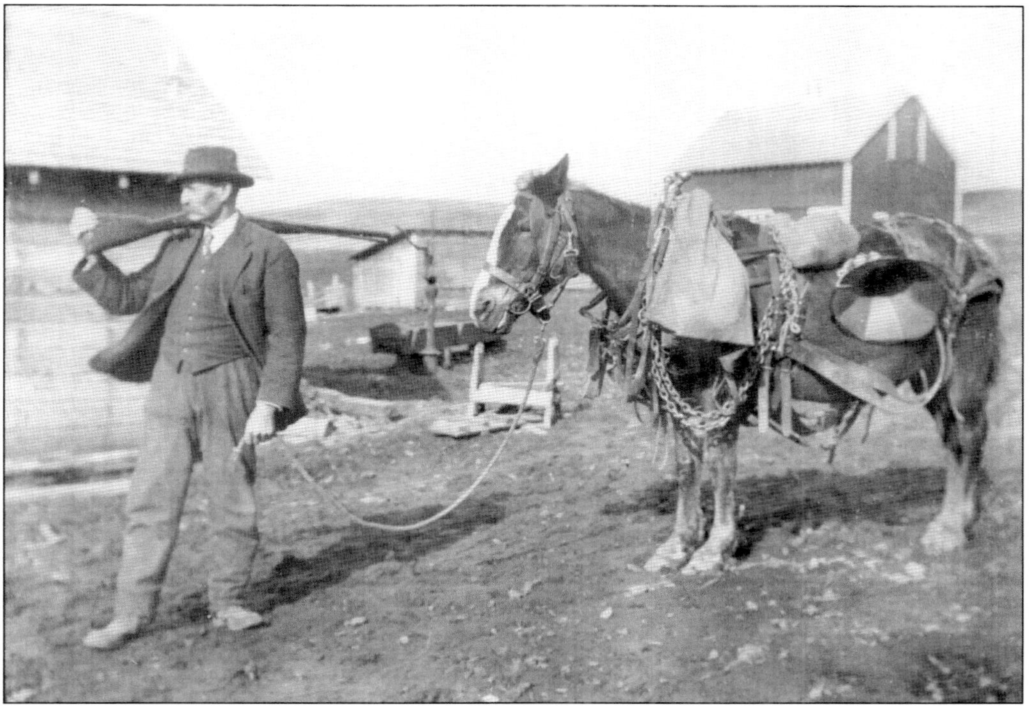

Traveling salesmen, such as the fellow pictured here on the Babb homestead, brought goods and services to the isolated farm families. Violet Thompson Ash recalled that a traveling tailor visited each winter when she was a girl. He sewed clothes for all the family. Her mother had a basque and skirt made of cloth she had spun and woven herself.

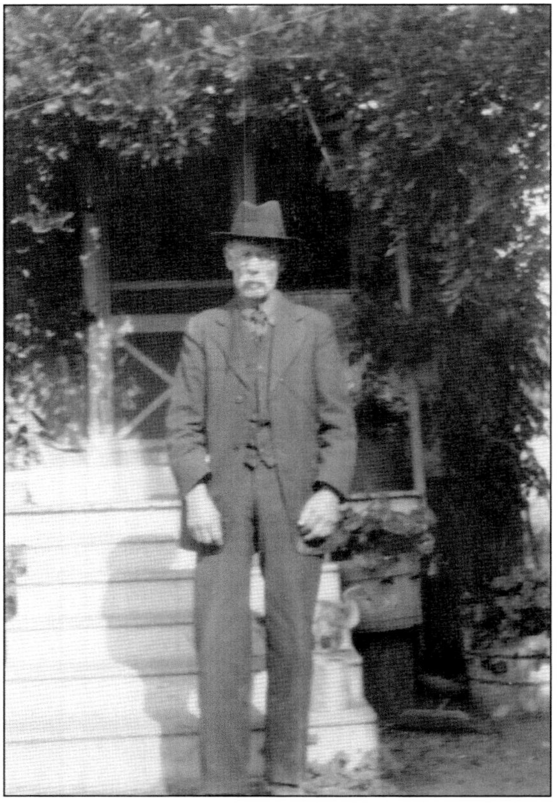

John Lemon built a log cabin in 1878 on the hillside of what would become Cheney. His home was the site of the political meeting that put Cheney in contention with Spokane Falls for the new Spokane County seat in 1880. His residence was also the precinct polling station for that November's election. This photograph was taken in Watsonville, California, in 1927, shortly before his death at age 80.

Cheney won the vote for the Spokane County seat in 1880 and erected a two-story courthouse at Fourth and D Streets. The county jail was located on the opposite corner of the block. When Spokane took the county seat in a new election in 1886, the courthouse became the public school. This drawing shows the Baptist church below the courthouse.

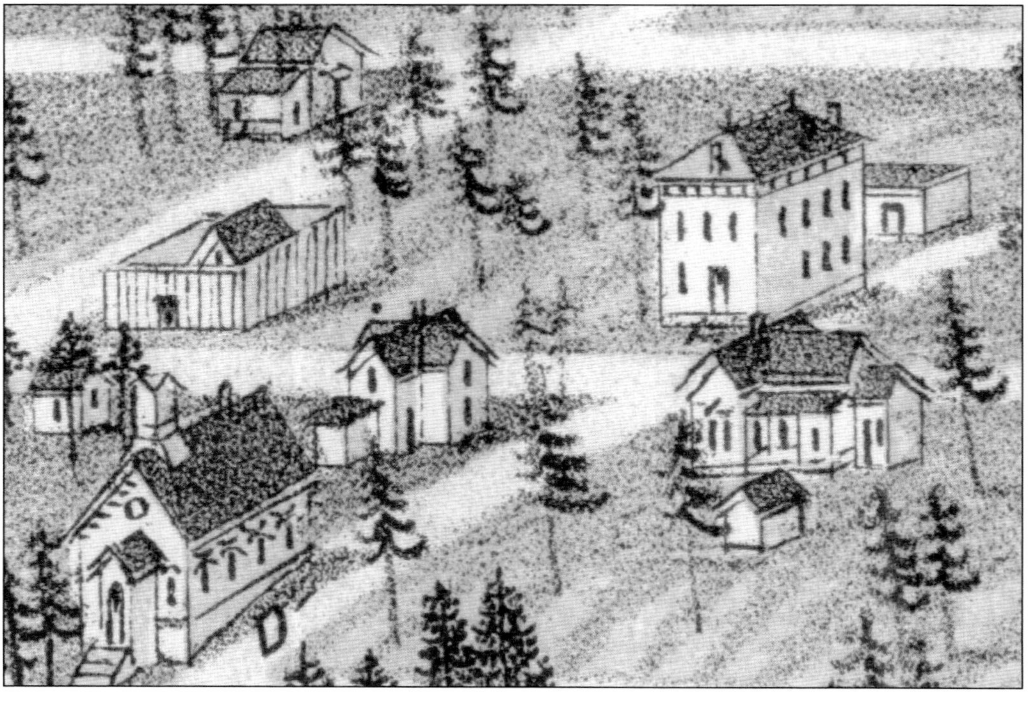

Mary Elizabeth Nealey and Albert Barton Babb headed west shortly after their marriage in 1867. Eleven years later, the couple and their five children homesteaded south of Cheney. Four more children were born there. The original homestead is still farmed by their descendants and has now been in the family for over 135 years. Babb poses with his granddaughter, Clara Belle Wood, in this 1906 photograph.

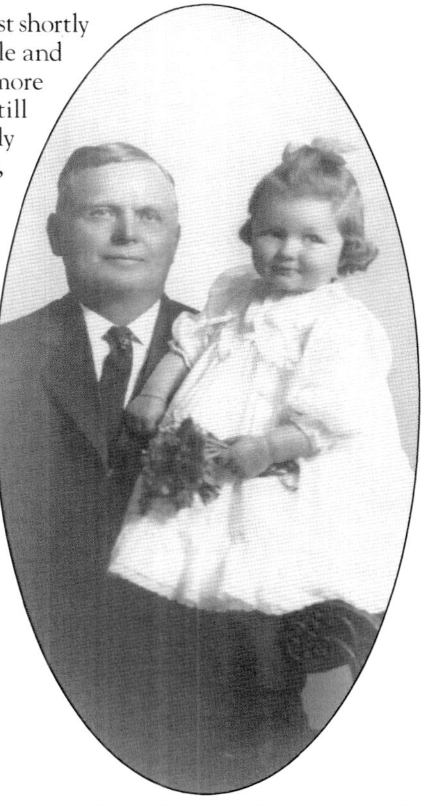

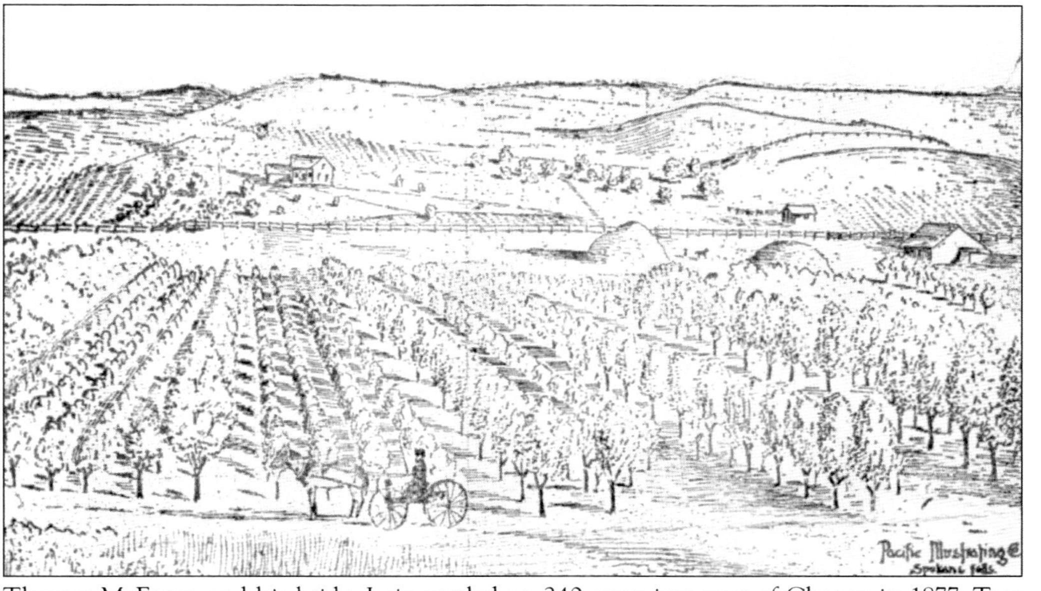

Thomas McFeron and his bride, Lois, settled on 240 acres just west of Cheney in 1877. Tom established the Fairview Fruit Farm, a large fruit orchard and tree nursery that supplied the early orchard industry. Seventeen acres of the southeast corner of his farm were used to establish the Fairview Cemetery in 1883. Some of Tom's original fruit trees are still growing in the cemetery.

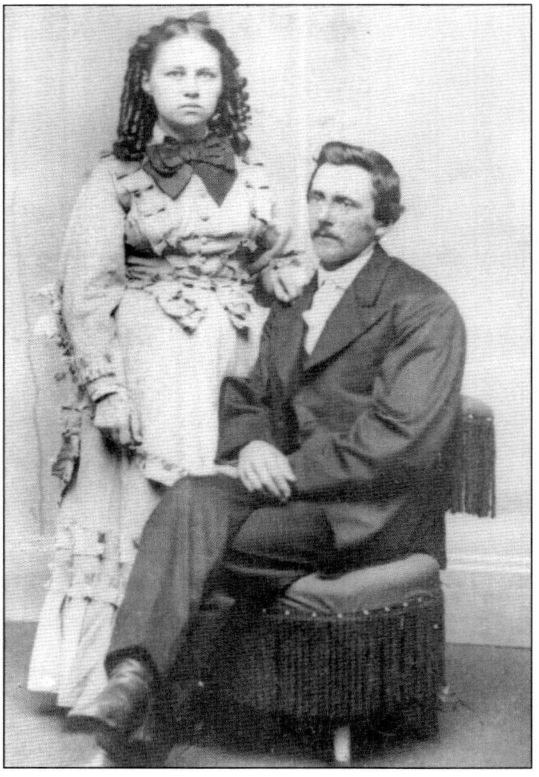

Samuel Showalter and his wife, Sarah Jane Cook, came to the Cheney area by wagon with their young family along the Mullan Road from Oregon. The 23-year-old Samuel filed a homestead claim near Tyler in 1881. He built a straw-roof barn and a house with a dirt floor. The couple had 10 children. Their descendants still farm and ranch in the region.

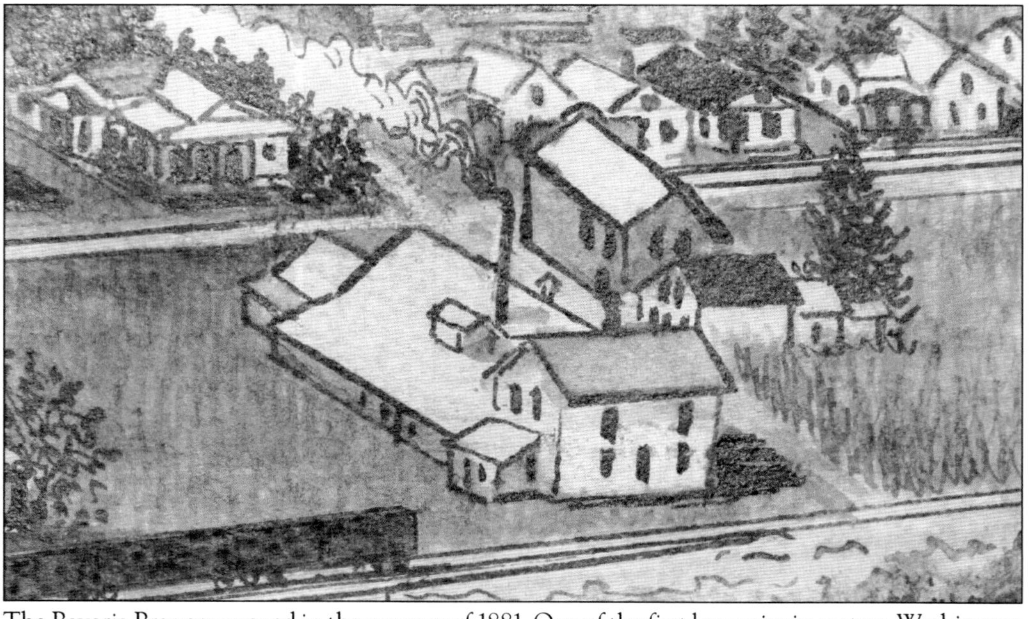

The Bavaria Brewery opened in the summer of 1881. One of the first breweries in eastern Washington Territory, it controlled the beer trade throughout the Coeur d'Alene mining district. Soon after Alois Schmidt took over the business, citizens voted for a local prohibition, and he was forced to close in 1910. He turned the building into a boarding house, but it burned down in July 1916.

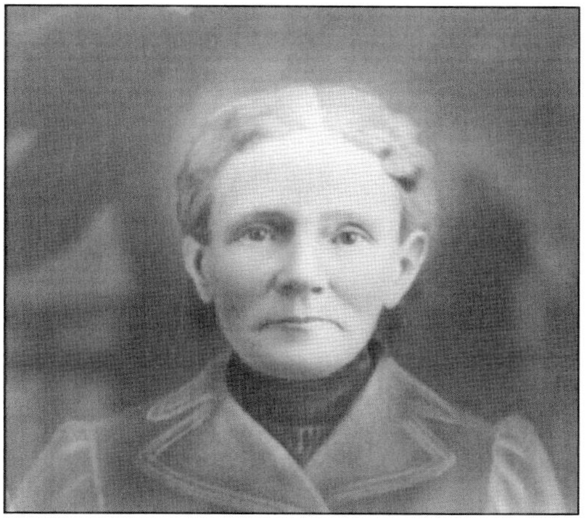

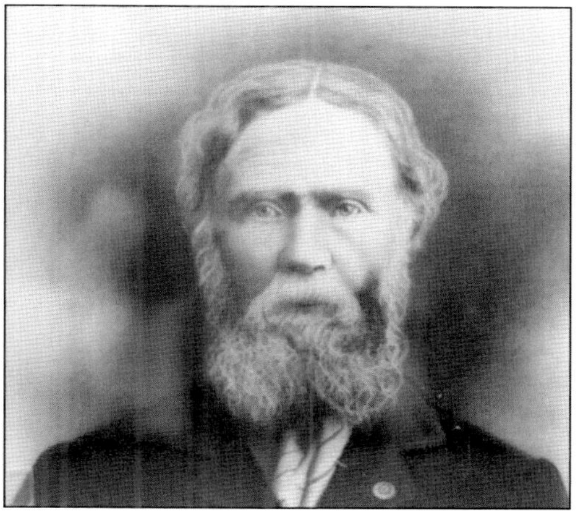

Arriving in 1882, John Betz and his three oldest boys worked the Cheney homestead while Sibilla, his wife, and the four younger children held a quarter-section homestead in Lincoln County to meet the one-year residency requirement. This was a common way to acquire additional land. Descendants of John and Sibilla Betz still farm and work in the Cheney area.

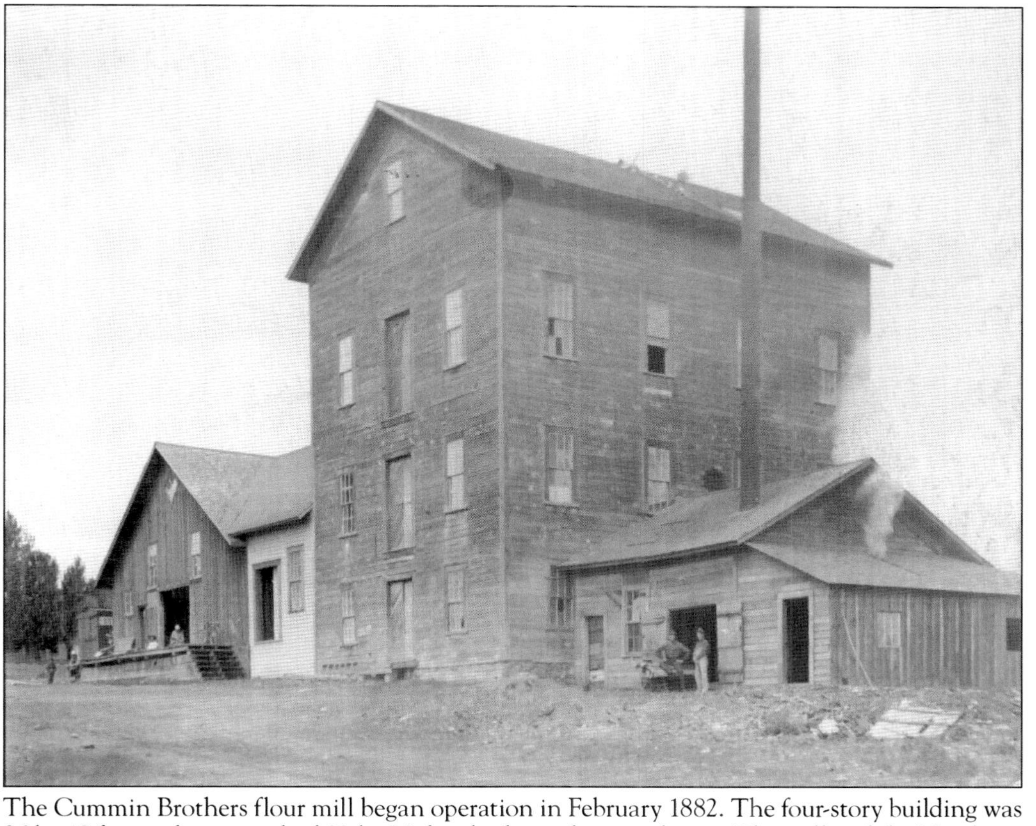

The Cummin Brothers flour mill began operation in February 1882. The four-story building was 36 by 48 feet with an attached 22-by-28-foot boiler and engine house. The mill and the Northern Pacific Elevator Company operated along the railroad tracks near the Cheney Spangle Road. Cummin Brothers moved to Paha in 1900, leaving Cheney without a flour mill. The building burned down in April 1905.

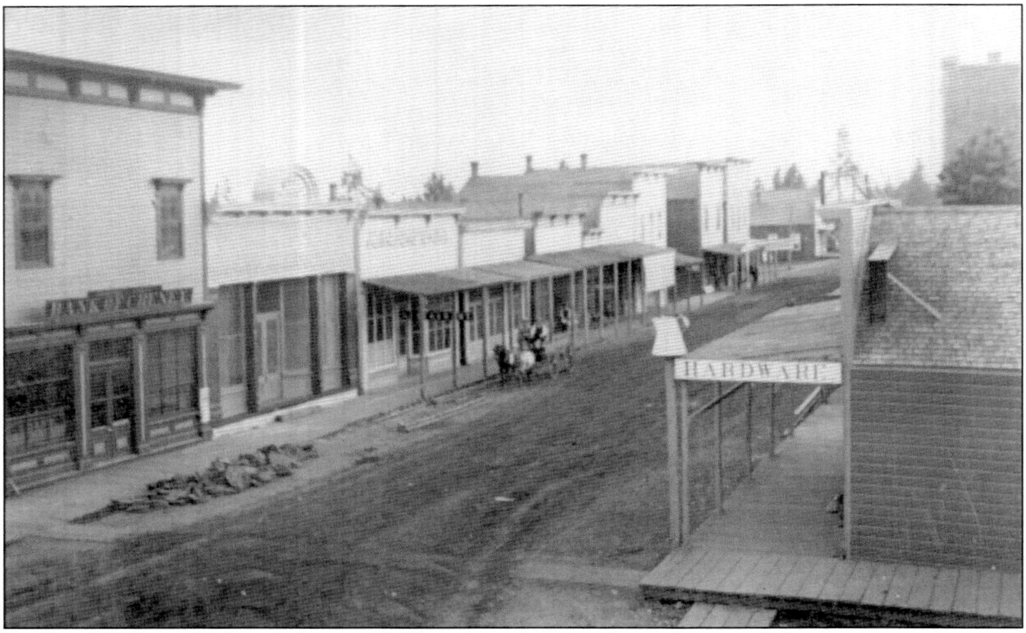

This 1887 photograph shows the view west along First Street. Daniel Percival's Bank of Cheney is on the corner, followed by Louis Walter's harness shop and P.F. Cedarholm's furniture and undertaking business. On the right is Joseph Hughes's hardware store. Walter and Percival replaced their buildings with brick structures, saving their businesses from the devastating fire on April 18, 1889, which destroyed much of downtown.

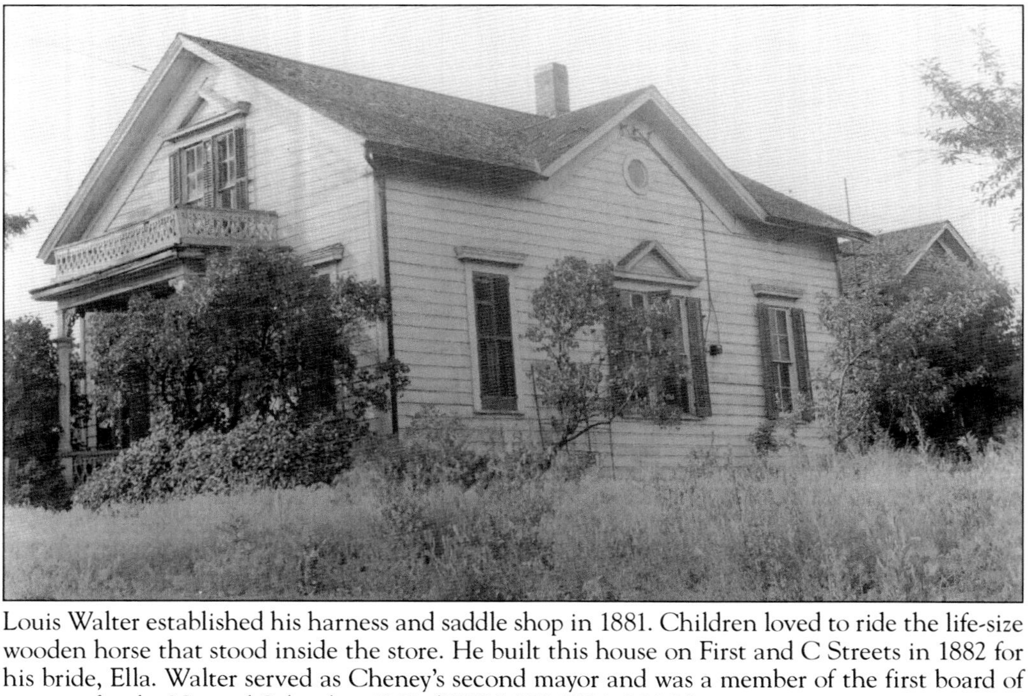

Louis Walter established his harness and saddle shop in 1881. Children loved to ride the life-size wooden horse that stood inside the store. He built this house on First and C Streets in 1882 for his bride, Ella. Walter served as Cheney's second mayor and was a member of the first board of trustees for the Normal School in 1891. (EWU-007-0584_236-2.)

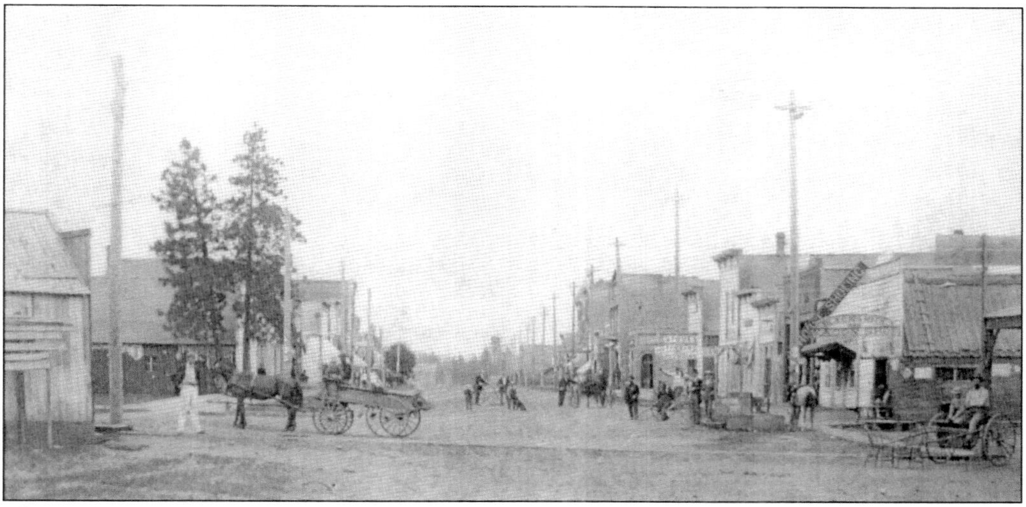

This is the view east on First Street in 1894. People gathered horses, wagons, and even a pair of bicycles for the photograph. To the right, several businesses can be seen, including Steven Harris's blacksmith and wagon shop, in operation since 1878; John Garner's secondhand store; a hardware store; a bakery; and a store advertising stoves, tinning, and plumbing.

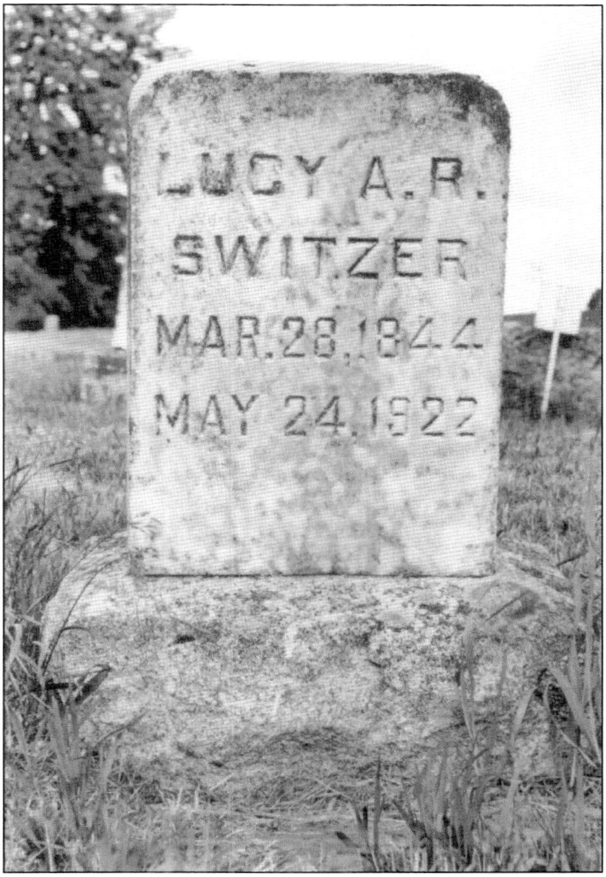

Lucy Robbins Switzer was a leader in the Women's Christian Temperance Union. Arriving in Cheney in 1880, she established temperance unions throughout Washington Territory and wrote regular features in local newspapers, as well as in temperance journals. Switzer saw the fruits of her life's work when in November 1909, Cheney voted for a local prohibition, and in 1910, when Washington women permanently gained the right to vote.

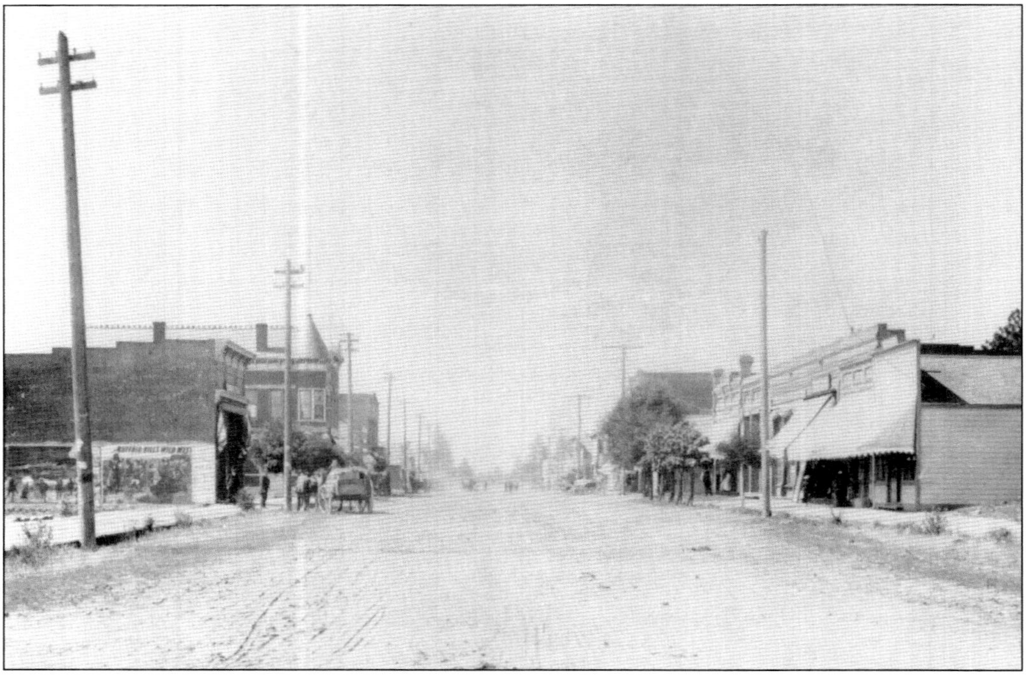

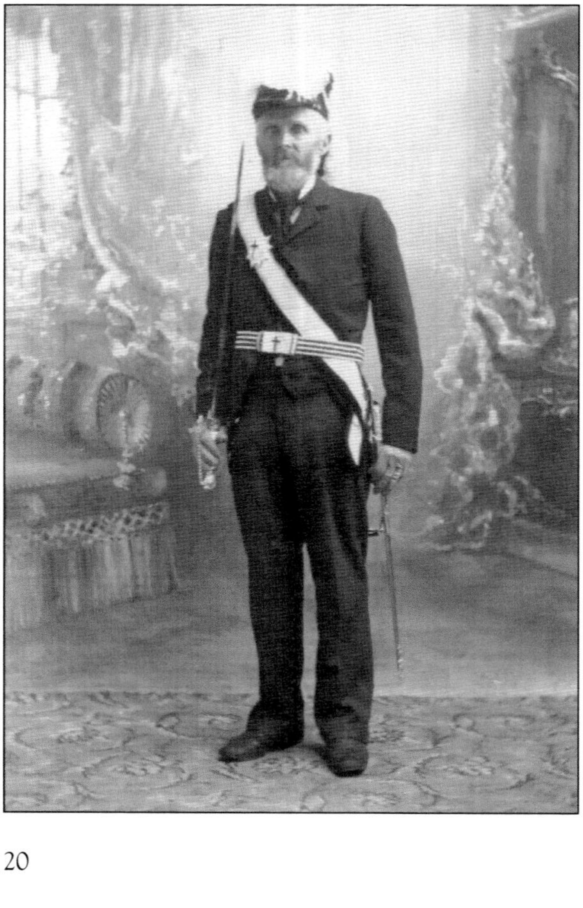

This view of First Street, taken from D Street about 1898, shows the turret of the National Bank of Cheney on the left. Brick buildings replaced many of the wooden structures after major fires destroyed much of the business district in the 1880s. Businesses in the downtown district had electricity and telephones by this time. (EWU 007-0584_2-9-1.)

Lodges, clubs, and debating and literary societies sprang up with the increase in population. The International Order of Odd Fellows Lodge No. 21 organized in Cheney with eight charter members in 1881. It was the second lodge in Spokane County. The Masonic Temple Lodge No. 42 F&AM was chartered in June 1882 and is still active today. This photograph shows Thomas McFeron in his Knights Templar Masonic regalia.

Two

Academy to University

The new community recognized the need for a proper school. A meeting of representative citizens was called in 1881, held in the offices of the *Northwest Tribune* newspaper. Daniel Percival was appointed chairman, and newspaper editor Lucien Kellogg acted as secretary. They discussed raising money, but soon realized that the new town would not be able to raise sufficient funds to build a school adequate to the needs of a county seat.

Alex Abernathy, of the Northern Pacific Railway land department, suggested that Benjamin Cheney might "humor his pride" by furnishing the means to build a school that would stand as a monument to his memory. Secretary Kellogg wrote the letter, and the town's hopes were fulfilled when Cheney sent $10,000 as well as two teachers from Boston. The Benjamin P. Cheney Academy opened on April 3, 1882.

At first, the school met the needs of the community, but discord over the dominance of the Congregational church in the academy led to a split in 1887. The Cheney School District hired the newly arrived William J. Sutton as principal, and he proved such a popular teacher that the academy was headed for closure for lack of students.

As Washington became a state, it needed an institution for the training of teachers. Cheney offered its academy and land to the state, and it became the state's first Normal School on March 22, 1890.

The early years were a struggle; twice the school burned to the ground, and three times the governor vetoed funding for the school. Yet the determined citizens of Cheney found ways through the adversity to keep the school going and overcome the political hurdles.

Throughout the 20th century, the Normal School expanded its programs, including offering bachelor's degrees in 1933, and becoming Eastern Washington College of Education in 1937. A shift to offering more liberal arts programming instigated a name change to Eastern Washington State College in 1961. In 1977, EWSC became Eastern Washington University. The university, with its over 10,000 students, is the central economic engine of the community.

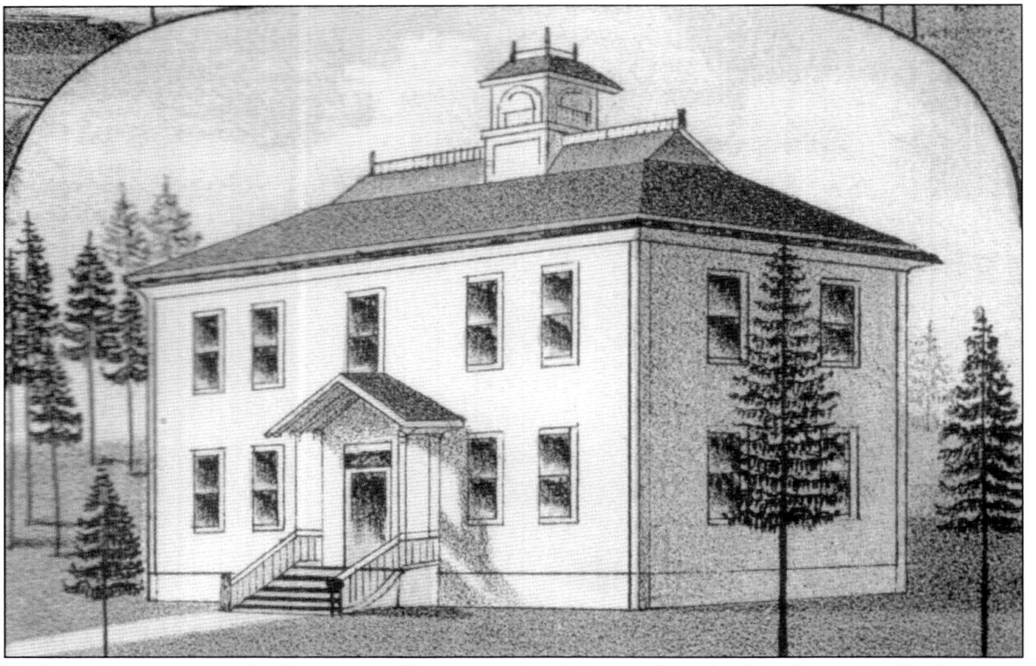

Built with money sent by Benjamin Cheney on land donated by the Northern Pacific Railway, the Benjamin P. Cheney Academy opened April 3, 1882. The two–story wooden structure was 36 by 66 feet. Each floor was divided into two classrooms with a hallway the length of the building running between them. It served as the town's only school until 1887, when the Cheney School District established a separate facility.

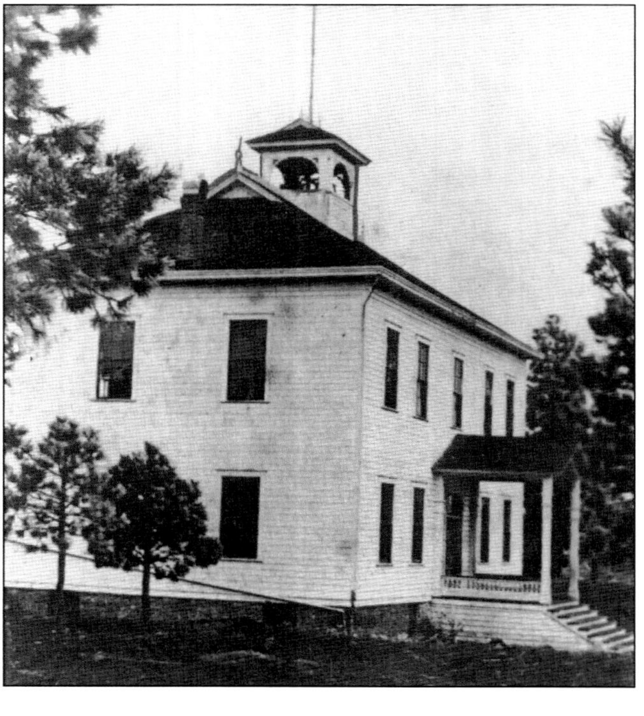

As a requirement of statehood, Washington needed a school for training teachers. Cheney offered its academy and land. Through political maneuvering, it became the state's first Normal School on March 22, 1890. On August 27, 1891, it was destroyed by fire during construction of new classrooms and a gymnasium. Not deterred by the loss, the first class of three graduated on June 17, 1892. (EWU 007-0583_1-1-1.)

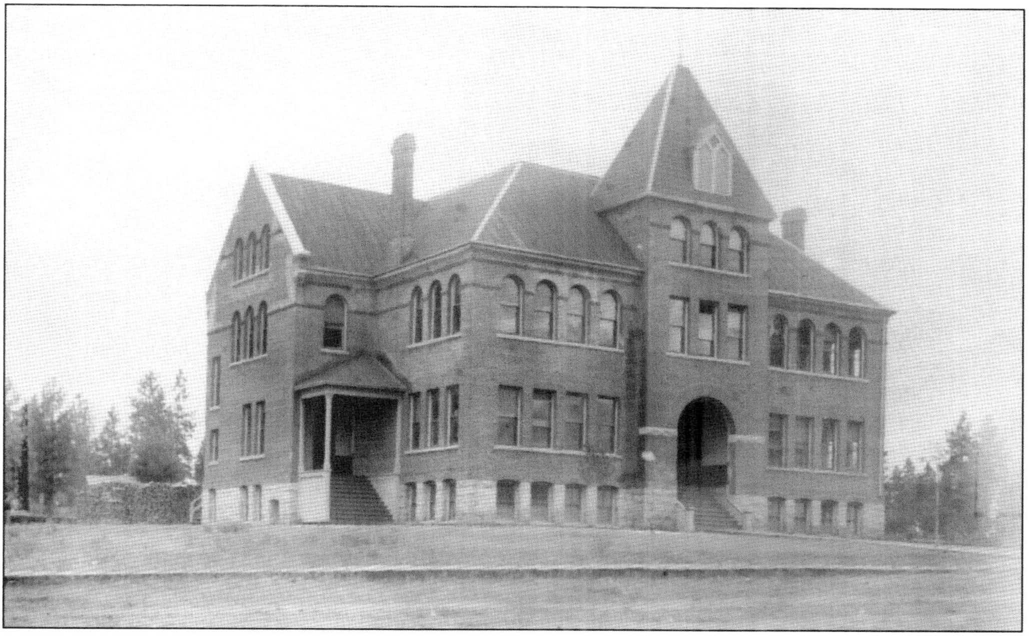

In 1893, Governor McGraw vetoed the funding to rebuild the Normal School. The citizens of Cheney then voted for a bond to build a new public school, designating that the building would be shared with the Normal School until funding for their new school could be secured. The shared arrangement was in place from 1893 to 1896.

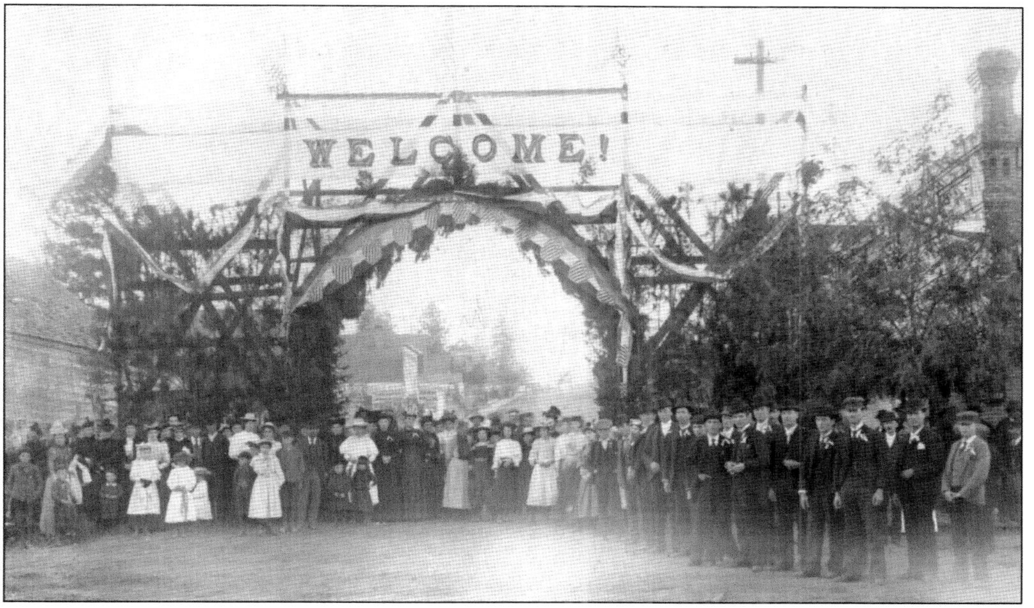

On October 15, 1895, students and citizens gathered under the welcome arch on Normal Avenue to await the arrival of the train from Spokane. The out-of-town dignitaries were coming for the ceremony to lay the cornerstone for the new Normal School building. It had taken two years of political action to secure the legislation and overcome the governor's veto for funding of the replacement school building.

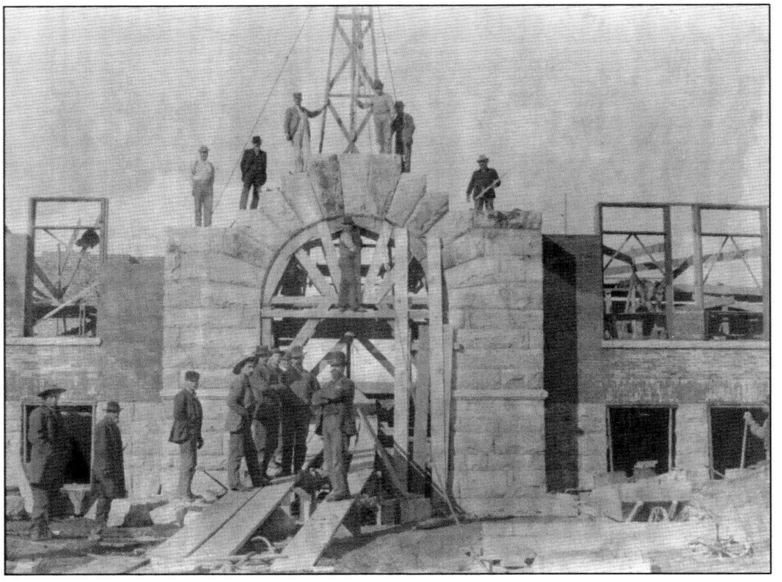

The Normal School construction crew posed for this photograph in spring 1896. The new Normal School opened for classes that October. The wood-frame brick building had a granite foundation and front entry arch and was erected by a crew of local men. The granite was hauled from a quarry outside the town of Medical Lake.

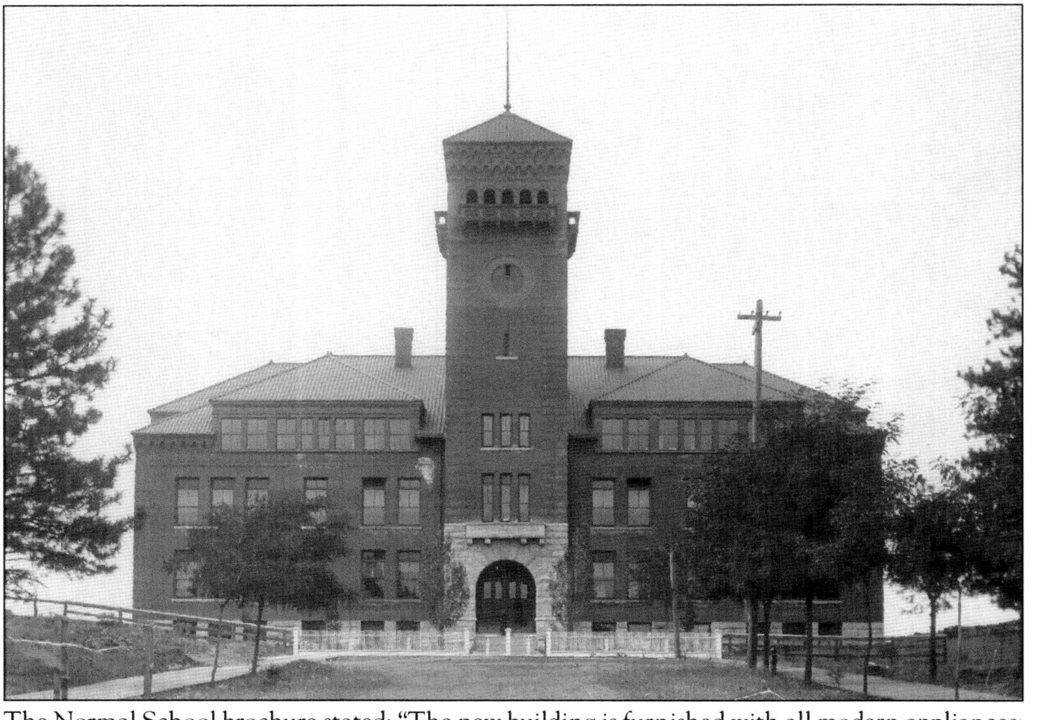

The Normal School brochure stated: "The new building is furnished with all modern appliances; and, in addition to the usual class rooms and laboratories, contains a large, well-lighted library on the first floor." The men's and women's restrooms were also located on the first floor. The third-floor attic had rooms for the literary societies to meet, while the tower held living quarters for a few teachers.

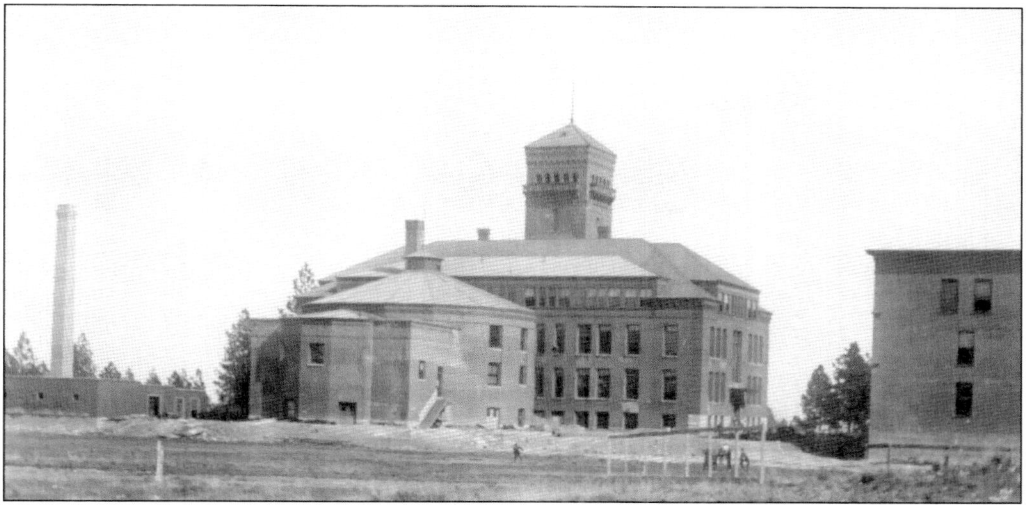

Attached by a corridor to the back of the Normal School was the circular gymnasium on the ground floor, while the second story contained an auditorium that could seat 750 people. To the right is the Training School building erected in 1908, and to the left is the heating plant.

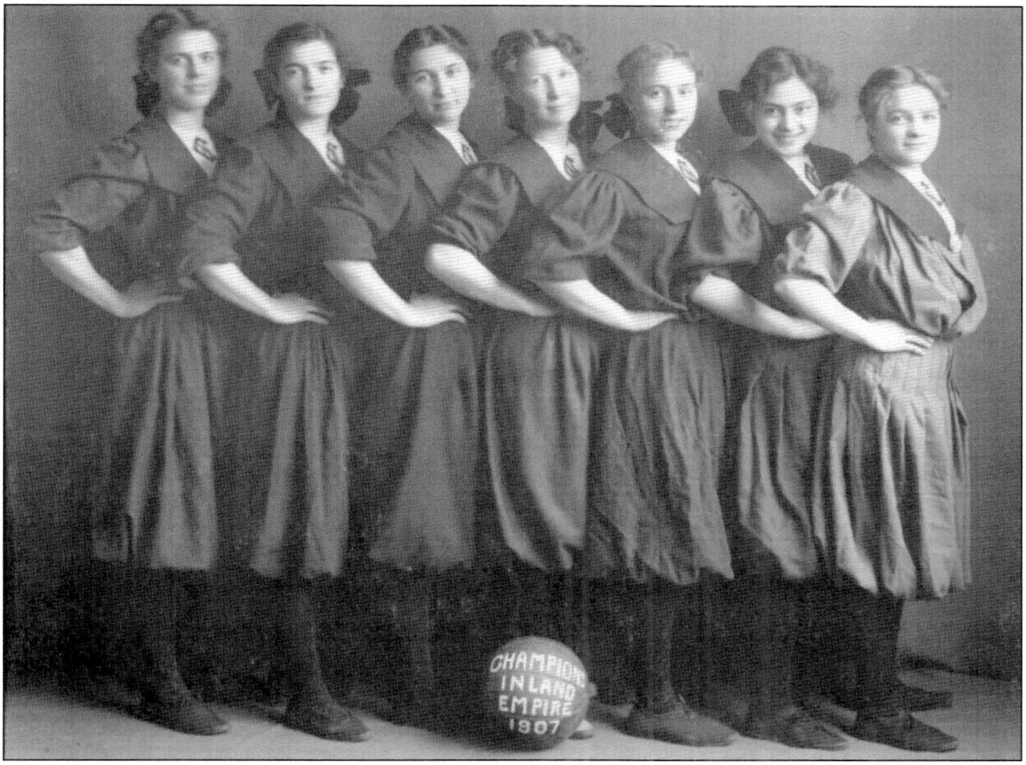

The Normal School women won the 1907 Inland Empire basketball tournament. Men were a minority at the school in the early years, with too few to make football or basketball squads in some years. The champions pictured here are, from left to right, Mabel Williams, Agnes Dempsey, Charstie Williams, Bess Hostettler, Mabel Tennison, Edith Taylor, and Clara Everson.

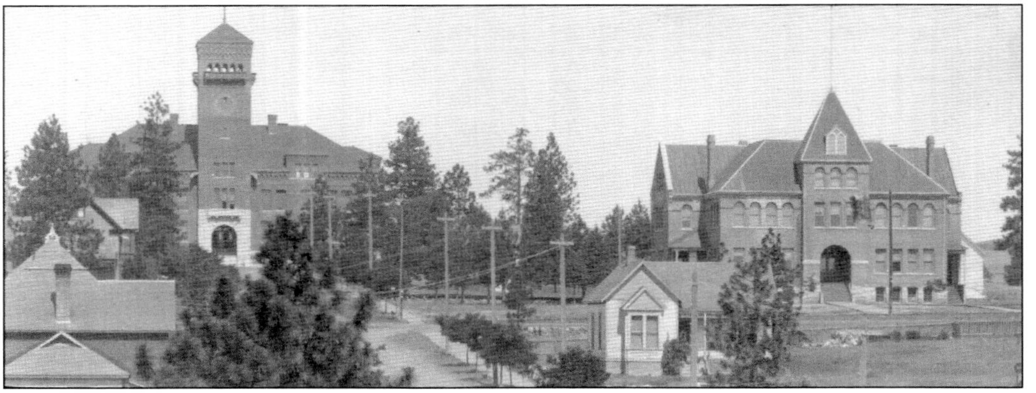

This was the view up Normal (now College) Avenue around 1903, with the state Normal School at the top of the hill and the Cheney Public School on Fourth Street to the right. There was a tennis court next to the public school bordering on Normal Avenue. Both buildings were later replaced with the new school buildings that stand today.

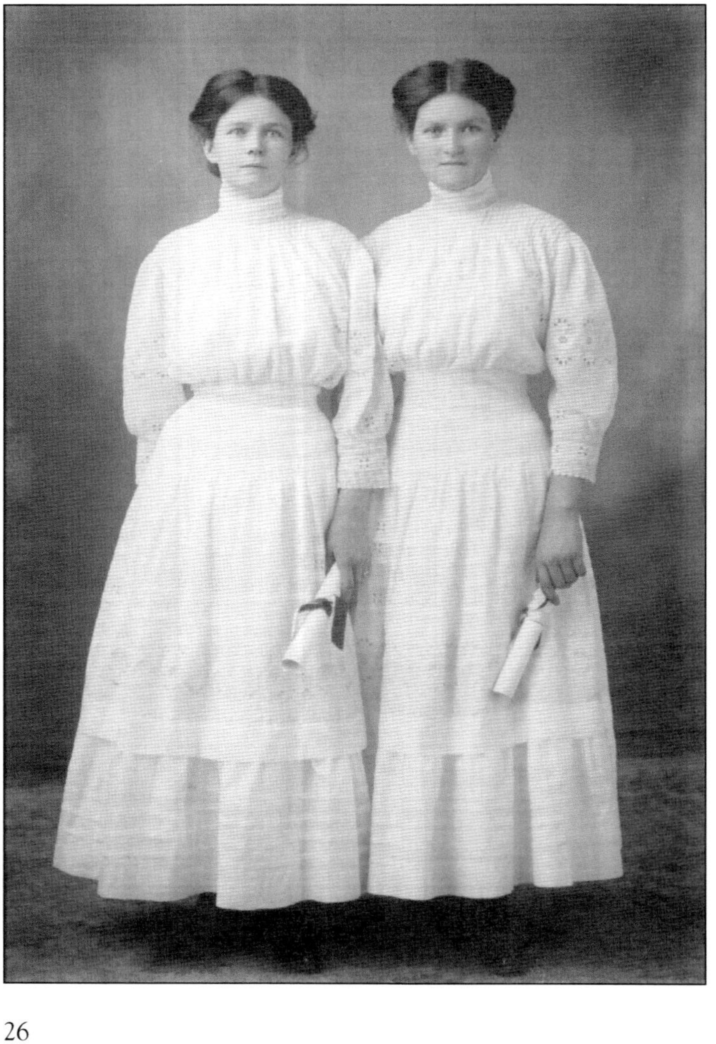

Students could take course work to receive one, two, or three-year teaching certificates from the Normal School, which authorized them to teach in the state of Washington. In this photograph, sisters Mamie (left) and Maud Krous hold three-year certificates from their graduation in May 1910.

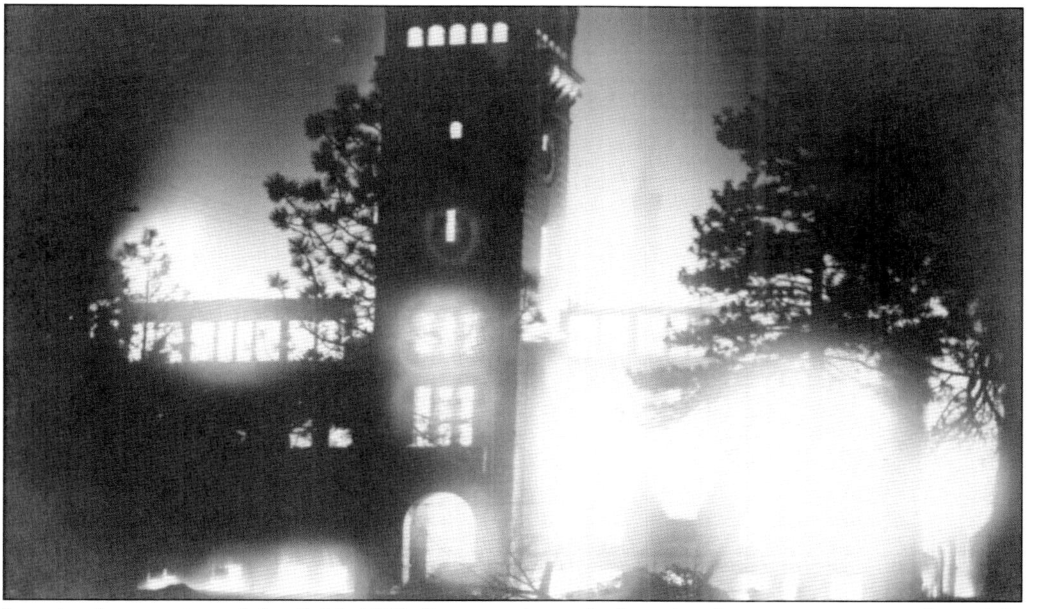

Late in the evening of April 24, 1912, fire tore through the school, trapping two teachers, Mr. Wert and Mr. Miranda, in their third-floor tower room. Firemen pulled a carpet from a nearby home and yelled for the men to jump. Wert was safely caught. Billowing smoke obscured Miranda, and he was badly injured, as the firemen were not properly set for the catch. (EWU-SPC-BFSC 996-0418_1-24.)

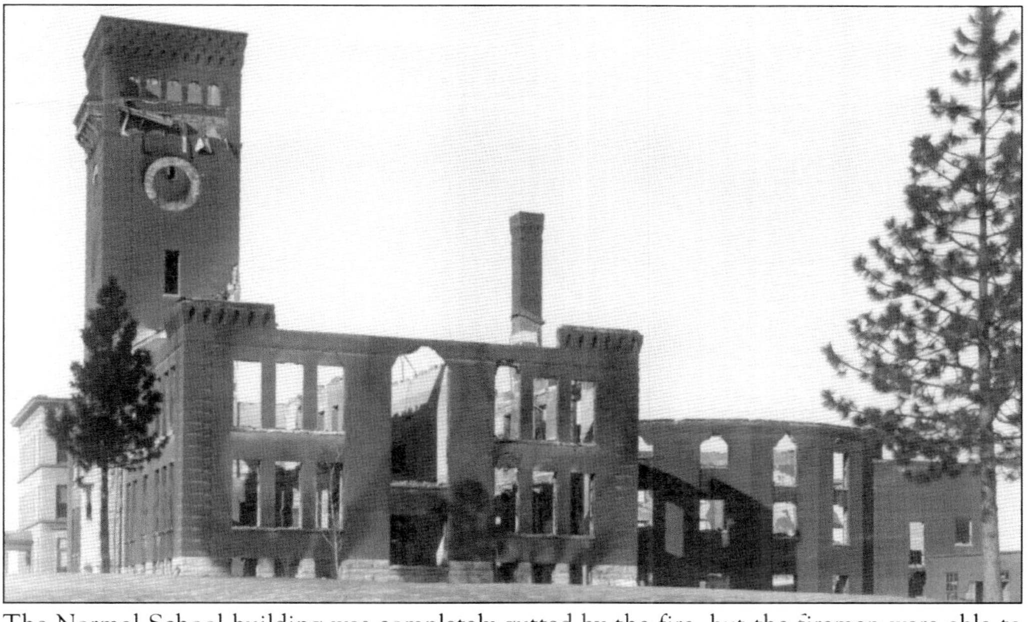

The Normal School building was completely gutted by the fire, but the firemen were able to save the Training School and the nearby heating plant. The next day, classes resumed at the Congregational church, the Training School, and the upstairs lodge rooms of businesses downtown. The tower was later brought down with explosives, and the bricks and granite foundation stones were reused in other buildings.

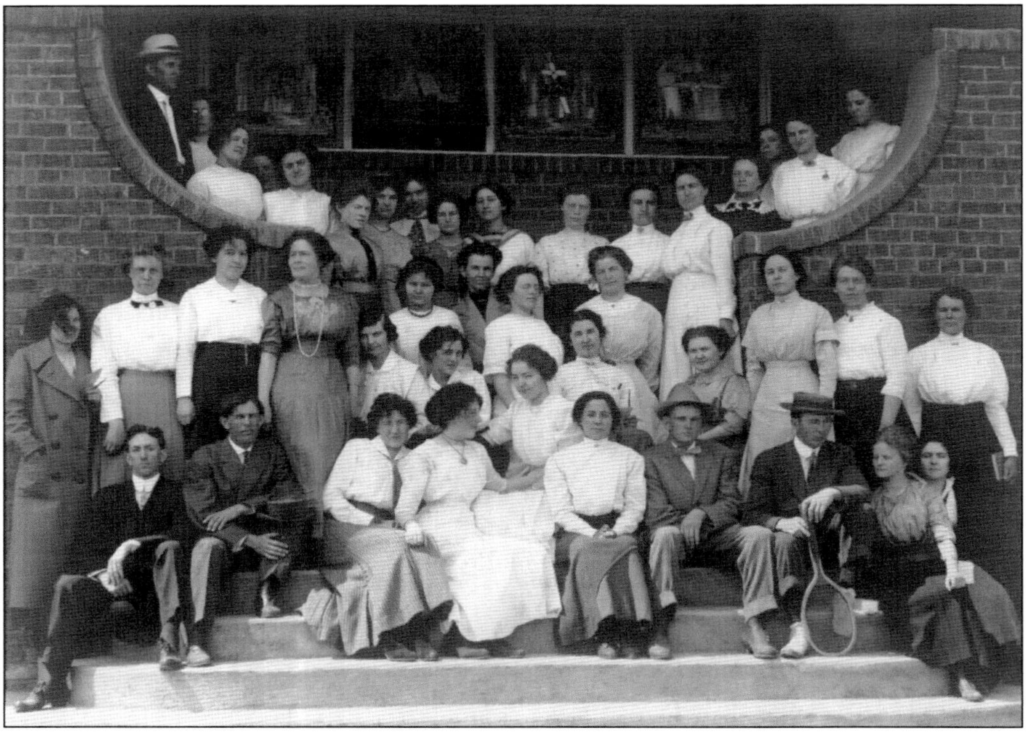

Normal School students pose on the steps of the Congregational church at Fourth and F Streets, where they had temporary classroom space after the 1912 fire. Most classes were moved into the Training School building, while some of the Training School classes moved into the public school after the new Cheney High School opened in 1913.

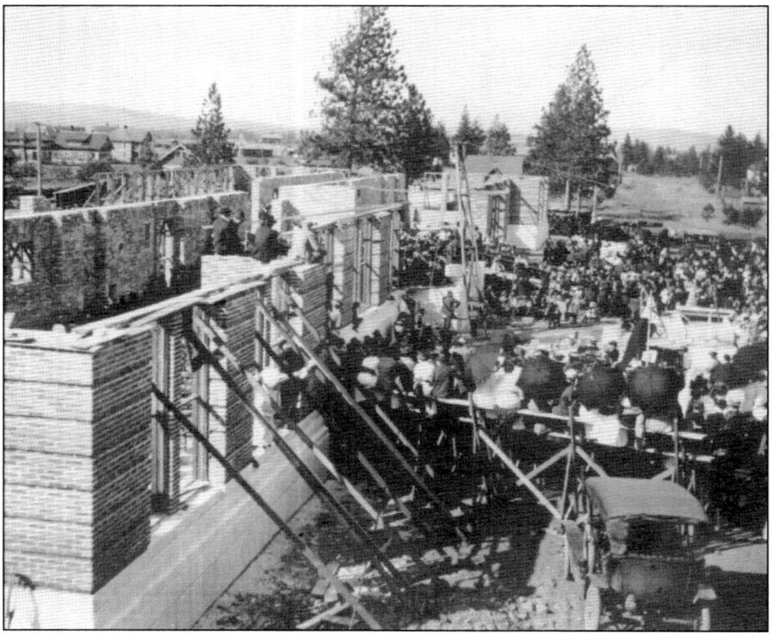

On June 27, 1914, an estimated 2,000 people watched as the cornerstone of the new Normal School building was laid in a ceremony led by Sen. William J. Sutton, grand master of Masons of Washington State. The school also acquired the land in front of the building and closed Sixth Street, thereby extending the campus to Fifth Street.

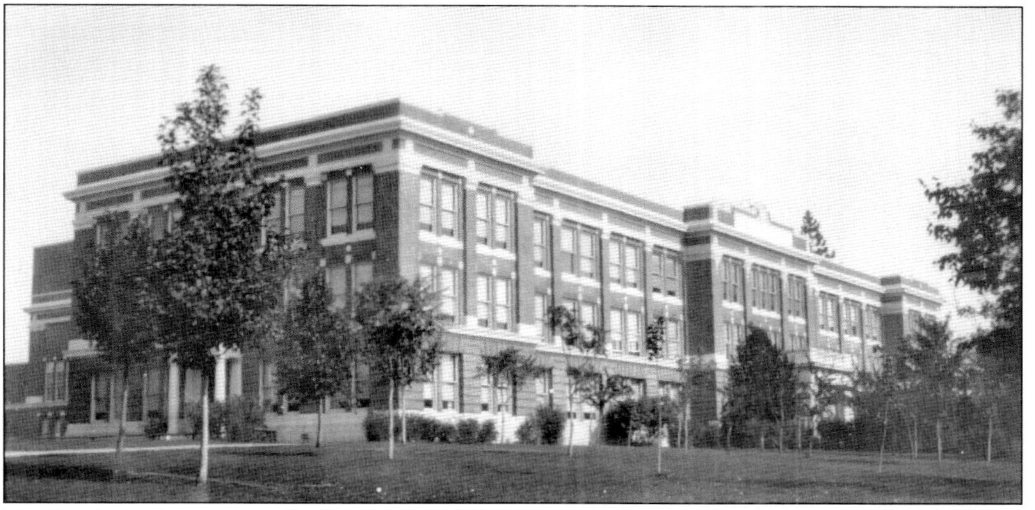

The brick was from Mica, Washington, and the terra-cotta used in the decoration of the building came from Renton, Washington. The interior was finished in oak with marble floors. The right wing of the first floor held the domestic sciences, with a kitchen, dining room, sewing, and fitting rooms. The left wing was devoted to agriculture and the biology laboratories. The second floor held administration offices and classrooms.

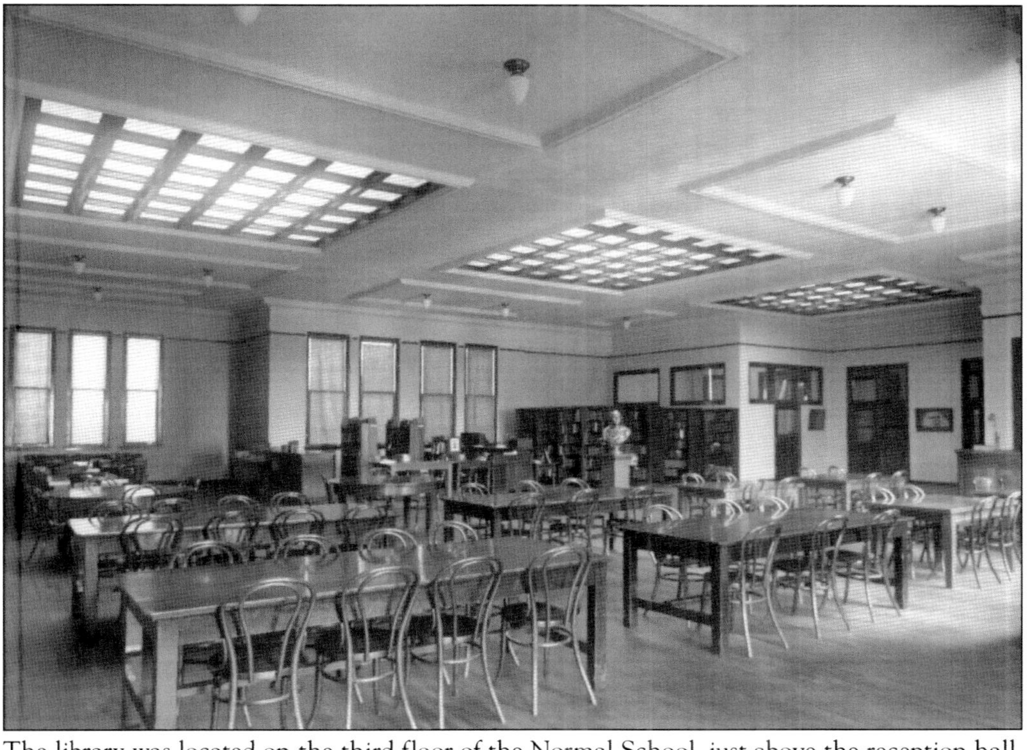

The library was located on the third floor of the Normal School, just above the reception hall. This library served the campus from 1915 until 1940, when Hargreaves Library opened. There was also an entrance to the balcony from the third floor. The main portion of this floor was divided into chemical and physical laboratories. (EWU 007-0583_10-11-2.)

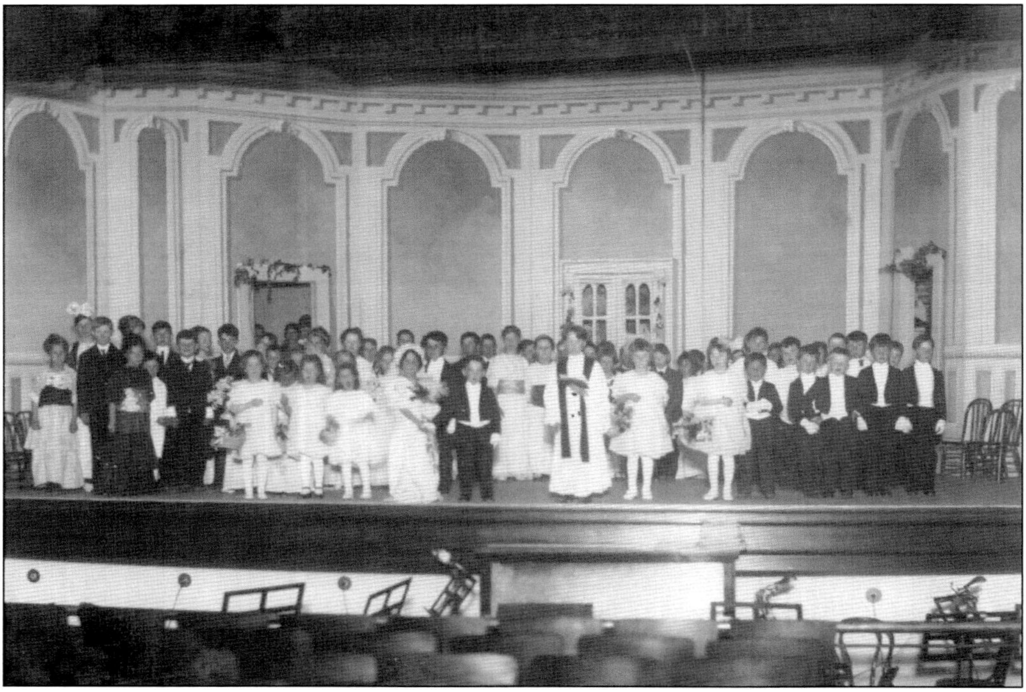

Students of the Training School prepare for a performance during a dress rehearsal on stage in the Normal School auditorium in 1916. Student plays, speeches, and pageants were regular features of the school year, as well as community celebrations such as May Day, Flag Day, Independence Day, and Christmas.

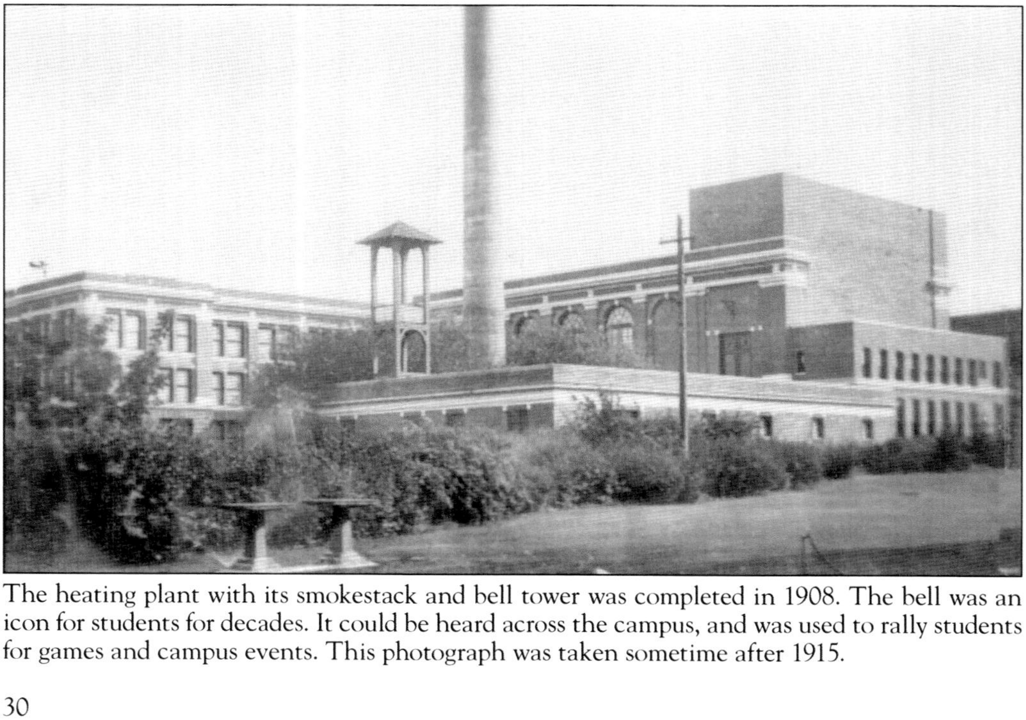

The heating plant with its smokestack and bell tower was completed in 1908. The bell was an icon for students for decades. It could be heard across the campus, and was used to rally students for games and campus events. This photograph was taken sometime after 1915.

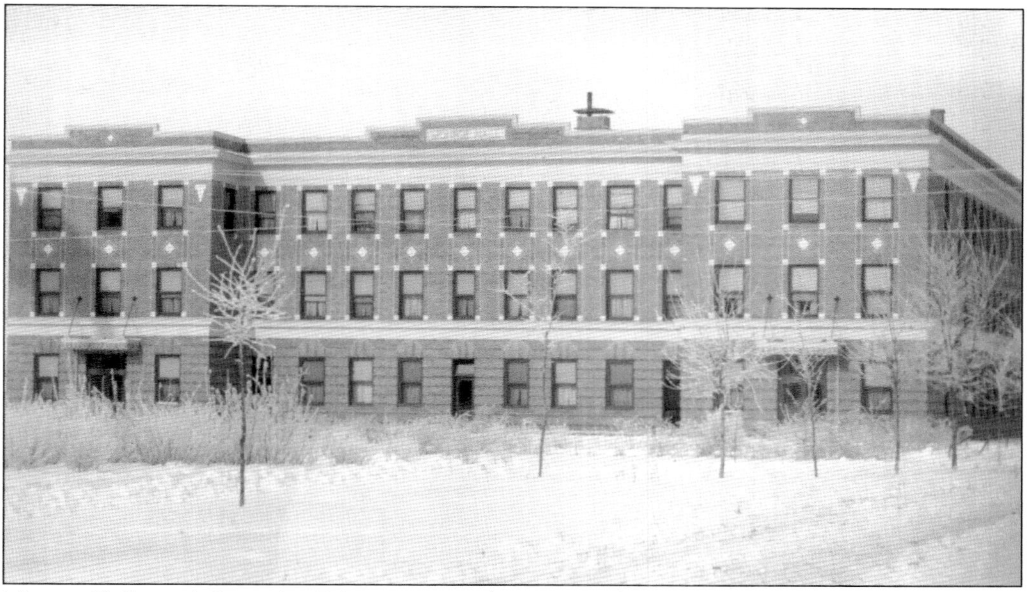

Monroe Hall was dedicated in February 1916. The women's dormitory was named for Mary Monroe, chairman of the Normal School Board of Trustees. Prior to this, all students boarded in private homes, boarding houses, clubs, and light housekeeping rooms. Those who made a living from providing room and board saw this as killing private enterprise. This began the town and gown schism, as students had more of their needs met on campus.

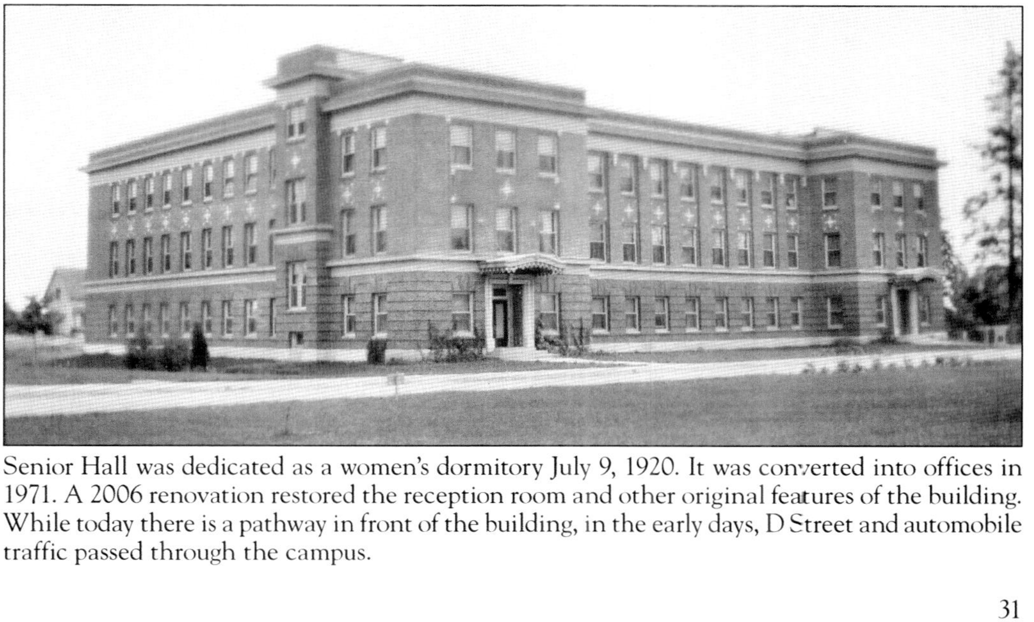

Senior Hall was dedicated as a women's dormitory July 9, 1920. It was converted into offices in 1971. A 2006 renovation restored the reception room and other original features of the building. While today there is a pathway in front of the building, in the early days, D Street and automobile traffic passed through the campus.

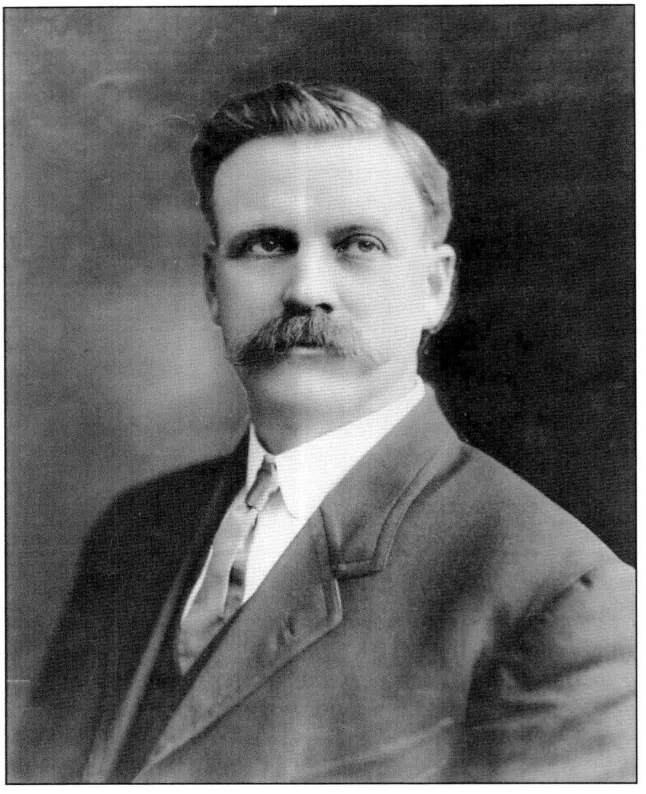

In 1887, twenty-two-year-old William Sutton was hired as the principal teacher of the public school. He was a popular and charismatic teacher, and was principal of the Normal School from 1892 to 1897. Both as principal, and later as a state senator, Sutton successfully fought for funding in the legislature. He was also a successful farmer and took pride in the quality of his horses. (EWU 007-0581_7-53-1.)

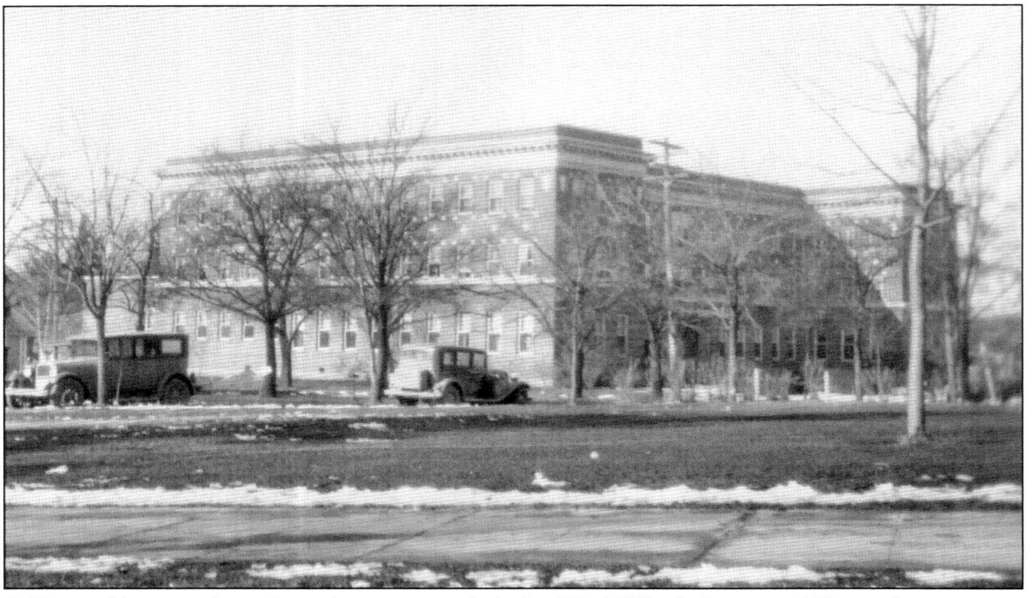

Additional housing for male students was needed after World War I. A group of Cheney businessmen used private bond funding to erect a new men's dormitory. In honor of the service William J. Sutton had given to the community, they dedicated the new hall in his name on September 21, 1923. It was changed to an office building in 1978.

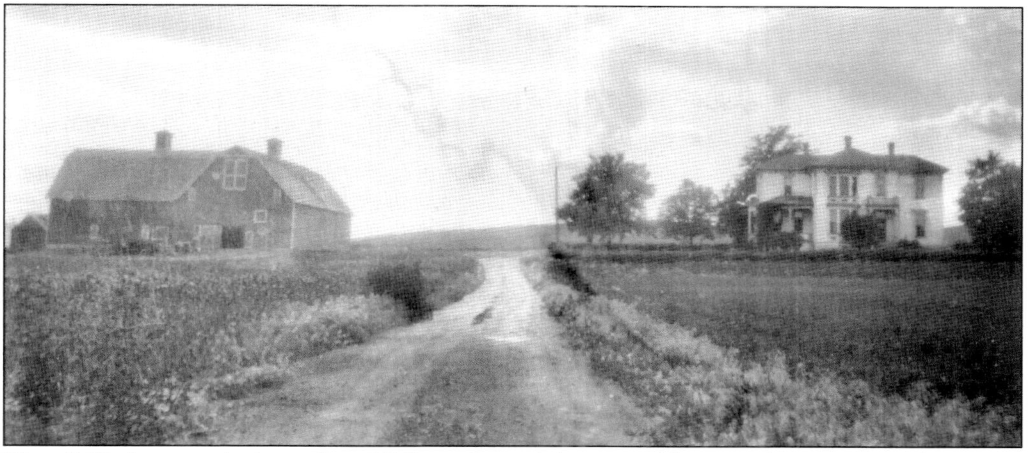

This 1935 photograph shows Sen. William Sutton's home and barn at the western end of town. The Suttons owned extensive wheat land in the area. The barn was built in 1884 by William Bigham. The house was demolished in the 1960s, but the barn was rescued for use by the university in the 1970s.

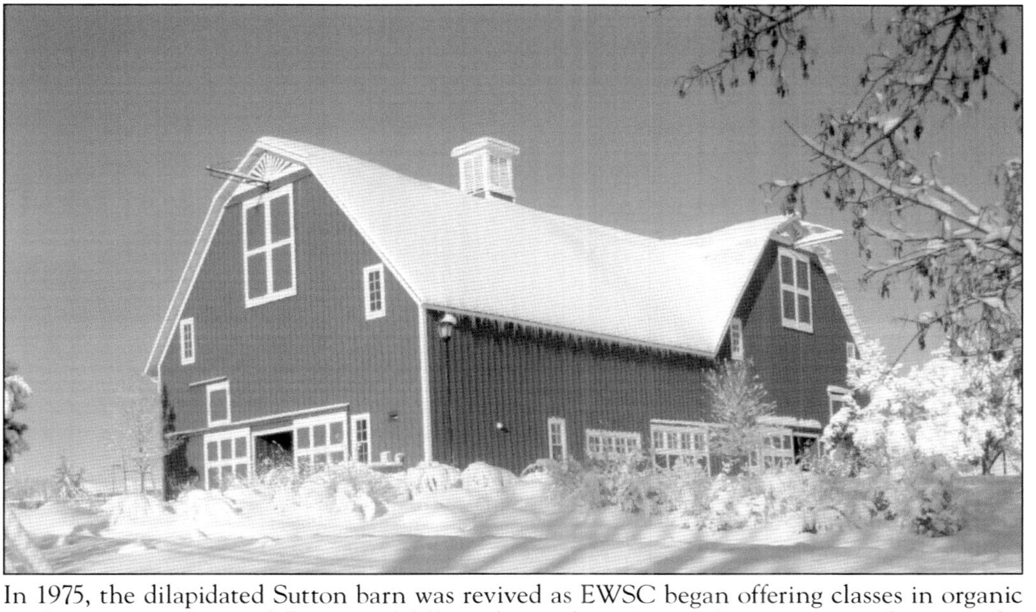

In 1975, the dilapidated Sutton barn was revived as EWSC began offering classes in organic gardening, composting, folk art, and folk medicine there. It was this renovation that gave the barn its red color. Cheney's recycling center began its life as a kiosk at the barn. In 1979, the barn was remodeled to house the campus police and parking facilities offices. This photograph was taken in 2010 by Joan Mamanakis.

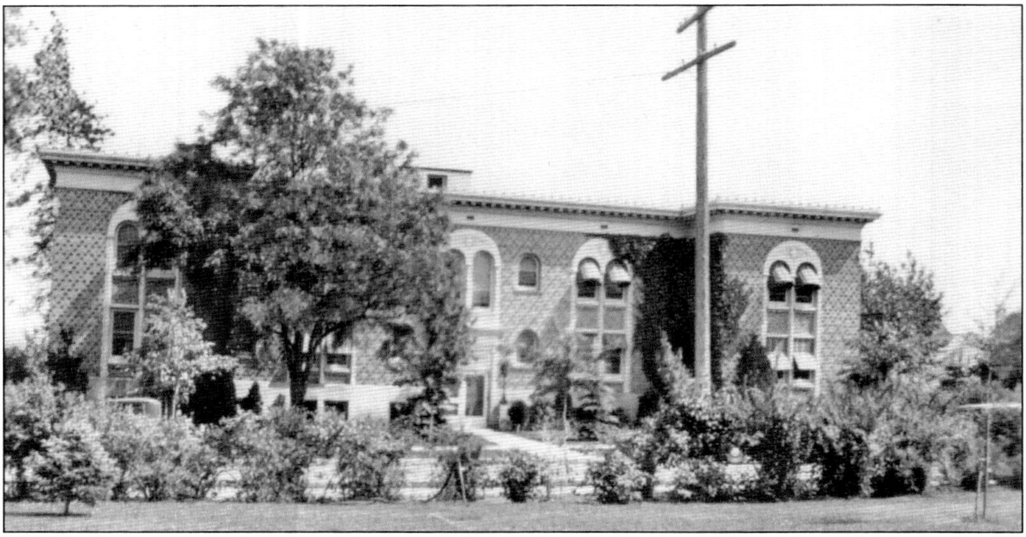

Named for his mother, the Philena apartments were built in 1930 by Clarence D. Martin as housing for Normal School faculty. The building was later used as student housing. The business space on the ground floor along College Avenue once housed an ice cream parlor and a beauty salon. In recent years, the Sigma Phi Epsilon fraternity has occupied this grand old building.

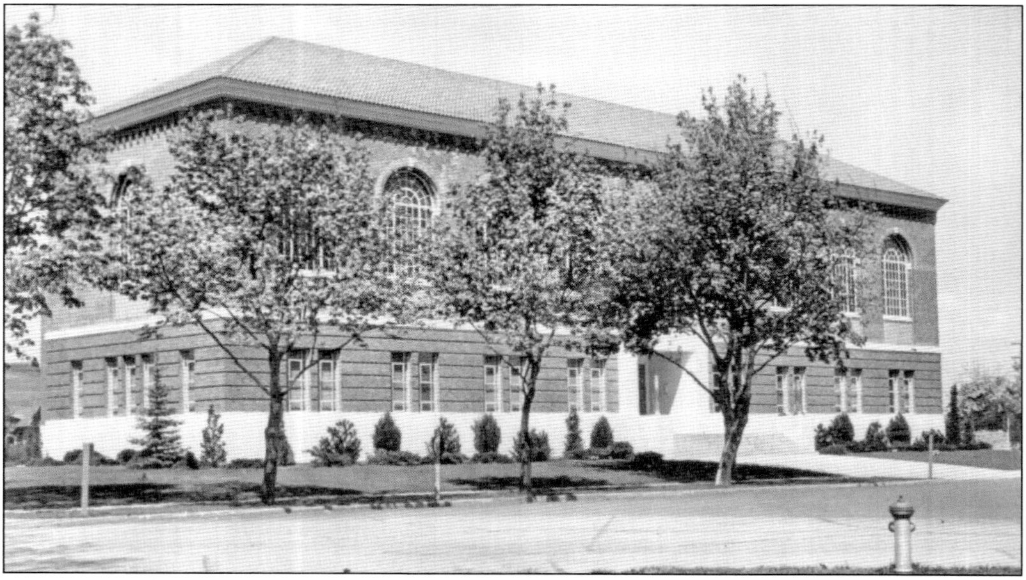

Hargreaves Library was dedicated June 4, 1940. It was named to honor college president Richard T. Hargreaves, who died in office in 1939. When the Kennedy Library was completed in 1967, the building was renamed Hargreaves Hall and was used for classrooms and offices, including the college newspaper office.

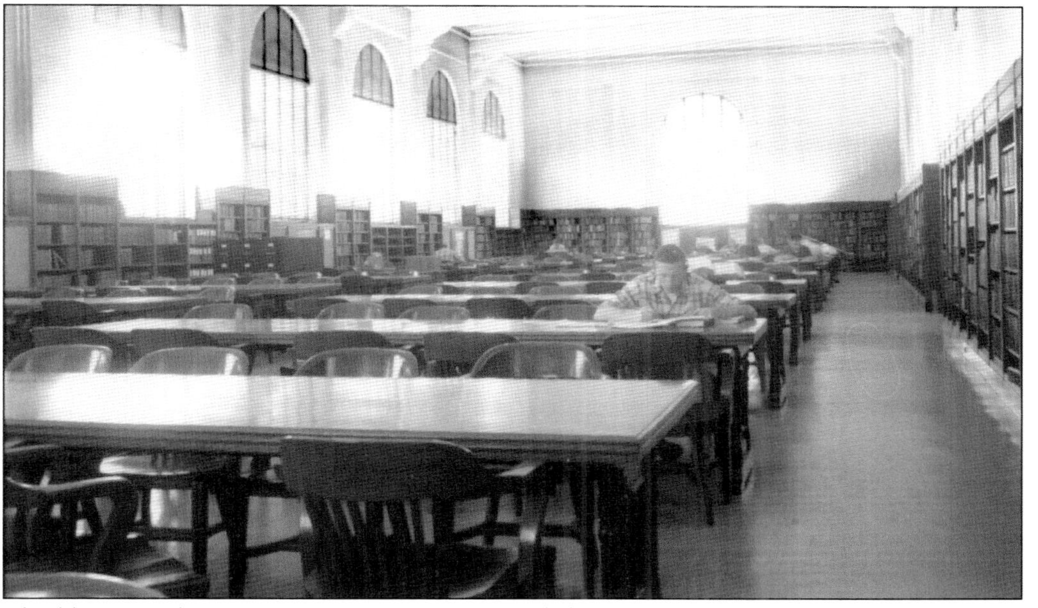

The library reading room of Hargreaves occupied the entire front of the second floor of the building. It featured large arched, blue glass windows to filter ultraviolet rays while offering students plenty of natural light for reading and studying. In 2009, the university completed a project to update the classrooms and offices, as well as bring back the historic character of the reading room. (EWU 007-0583_4-18-7)

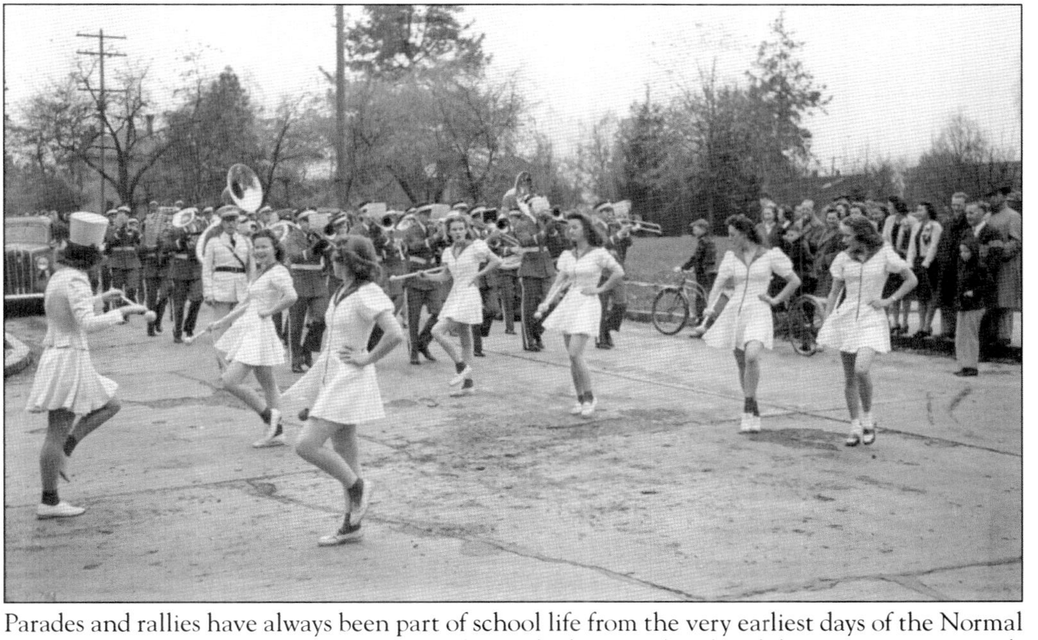

Parades and rallies have always been part of school life from the very earliest days of the Normal School. Here, the Eastern Washington College of Education band and drum majorettes march through town during the homecoming parade in 1940. Two years later, students were actively participating in the many wartime bond rallies. This photograph was taken by Bruce Penny. (EWU 007-0582_1-23-1.)

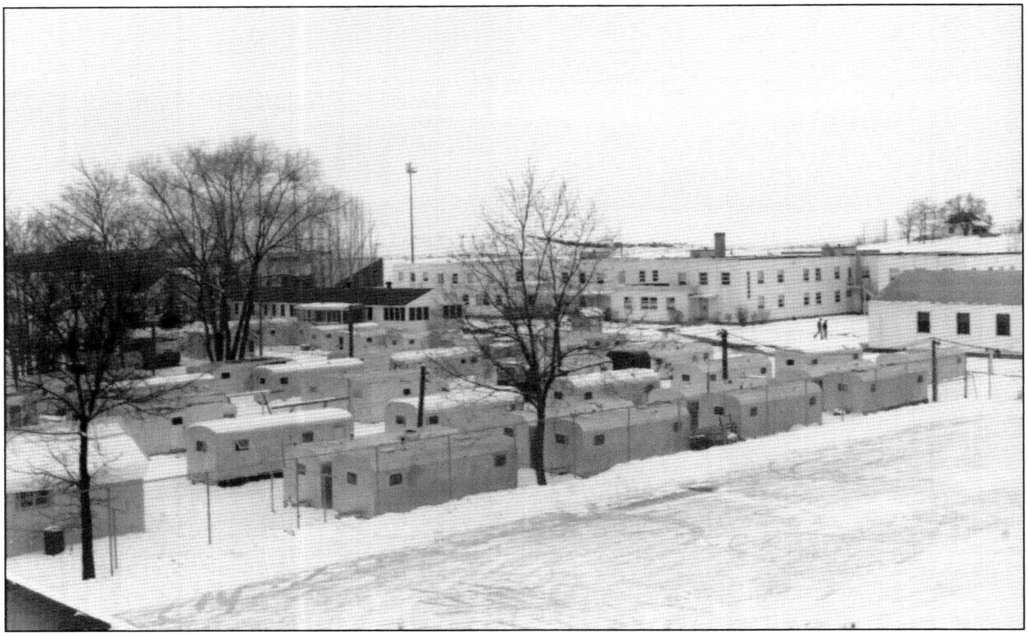

There was a shortage of housing for married ex-servicemen entering Eastern Washington College of Education after World War II. Trailers were placed behind Monroe Hall in 1946 to accommodate the students and their families. Affectionately known as Trailerville, the camp housed 70 families at $15 per month, with heat and lights furnished by the college. (EWU 007-0583_11-14-1.)

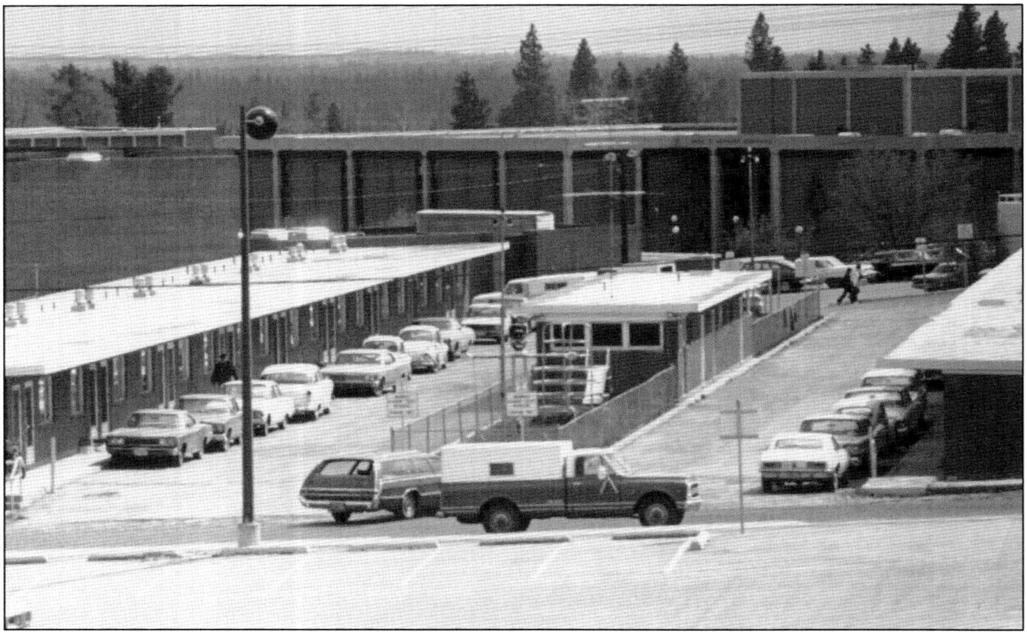

Married Student Court, located at Tenth and Elm Streets, opened in 1957, replacing the postwar Trailerville. This view from around 1970 is looking to the south and west, with Patterson Hall visible in the background. The apartment complex was demolished to make way for the EWU Recreation Center, which opened in 2008. (EWU 007-0583_6-9-1.)

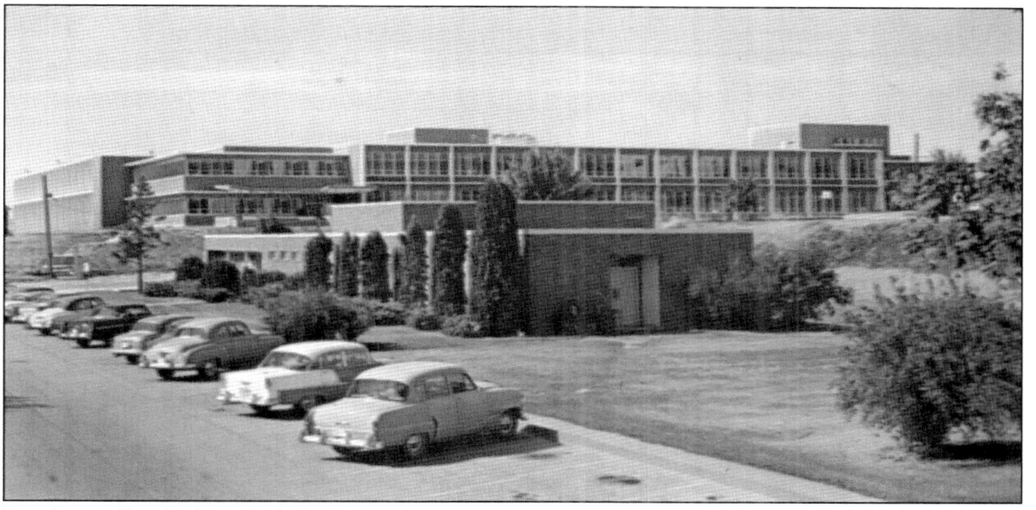

Rowles Hall, which included the music department, was completed in 1949 and served students until a new fine arts complex opened in 1970. In the background is the Hallet science building, which was dedicated in October 1962 and continues to serve students today. Streets through the center of the campus were closed around 1980 to create a campus mall.

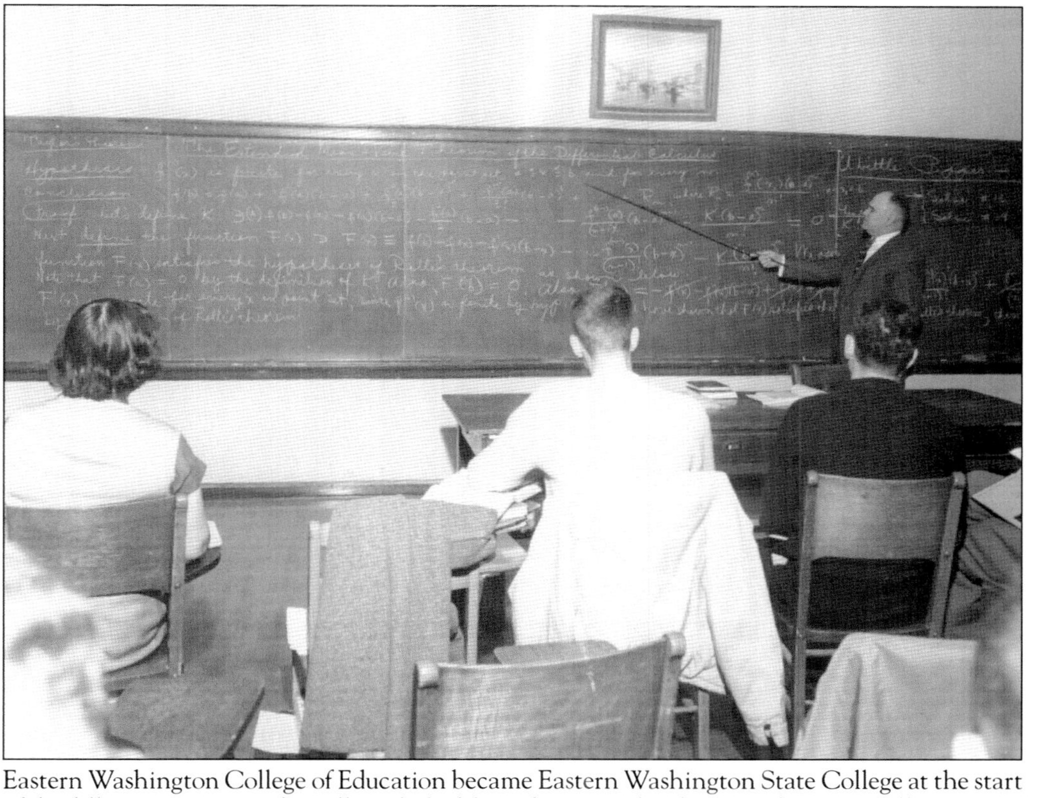

Eastern Washington College of Education became Eastern Washington State College at the start of the fall term in 1961 as the college shifted focus from strictly education degrees to offering more liberal arts options. The department of mathematics was organized in 1907. Students are shown here studying differential calculus around 1960. (EWU 007-0582_6-9-11)

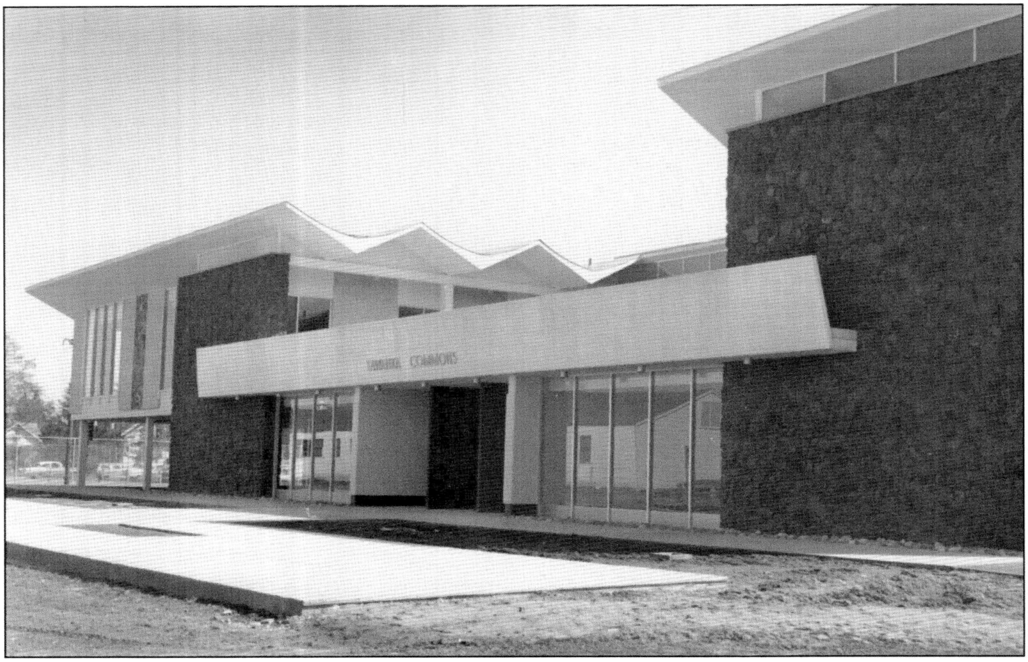

The first centralized dining hall on campus opened in 1964. Tawanka Commons was named for the women's service club, which operated on the campus from 1926 to 1960. The name Tawanka was said to be derived from an Indian word for friendship. The facility was completely remodeled, as shown here in 2003, erasing its original Century 21 architectural style. (EWU 007-0583_11-12-1.)

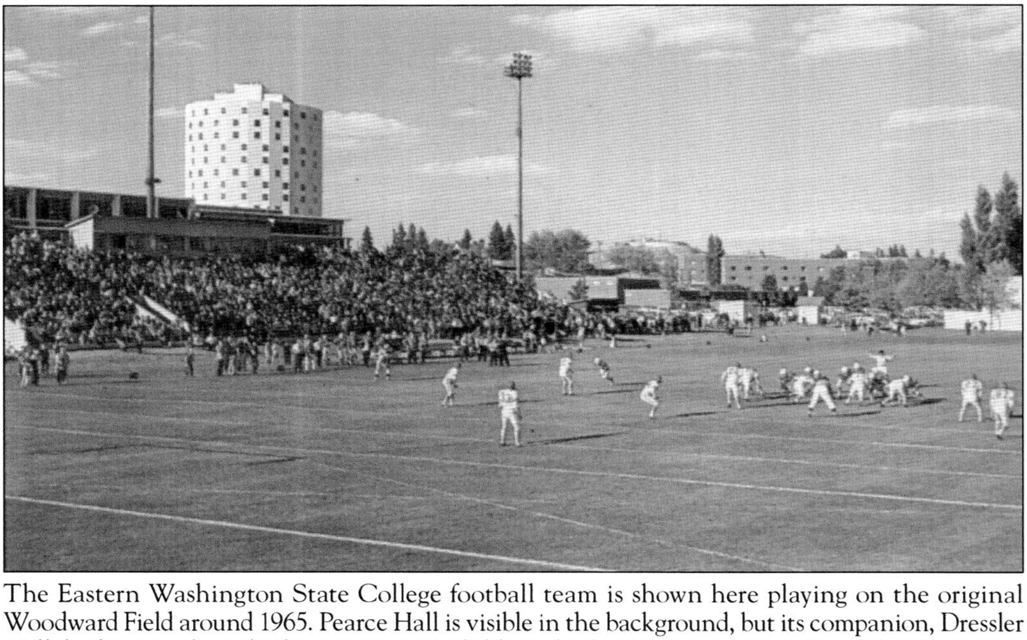

The Eastern Washington State College football team is shown here playing on the original Woodward Field around 1965. Pearce Hall is visible in the background, but its companion, Dressler Hall, had not yet been built. A new sports field was built to the west when Kennedy Library was constructed in 1967.

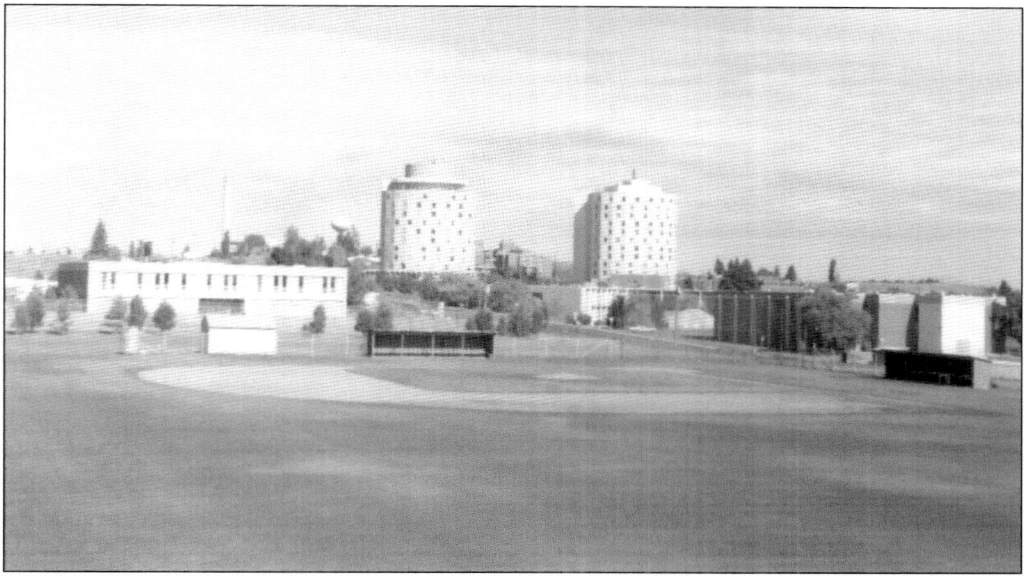

Eastern Washington State College became Eastern Washington University in 1977. In this 1978 photograph, the athletic complex is on the left with intramural sports fields in the foreground. The silo dormitories Dressler and Pearce Halls, the science building, and Cheney Hall appear to the right on the east side of Washington Street.

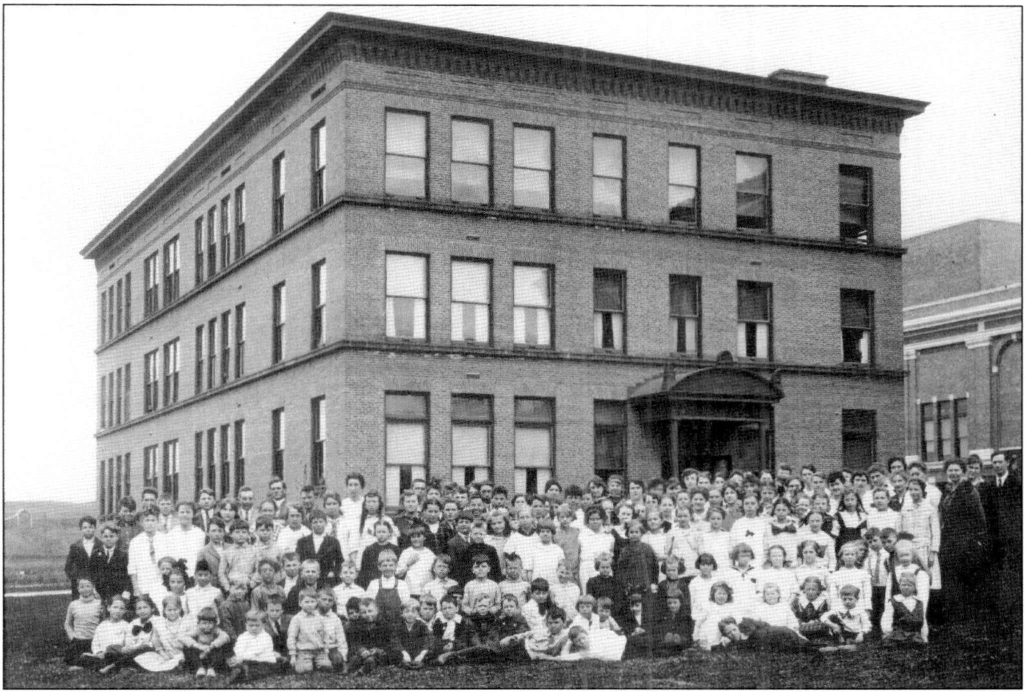

The three-story Training School was built adjacent to the Normal School in 1908. It served as both a public school for the common school grades, first through sixth, and as the training facility for student teachers of the Normal School. This photograph of the faculty and students was taken around 1918.

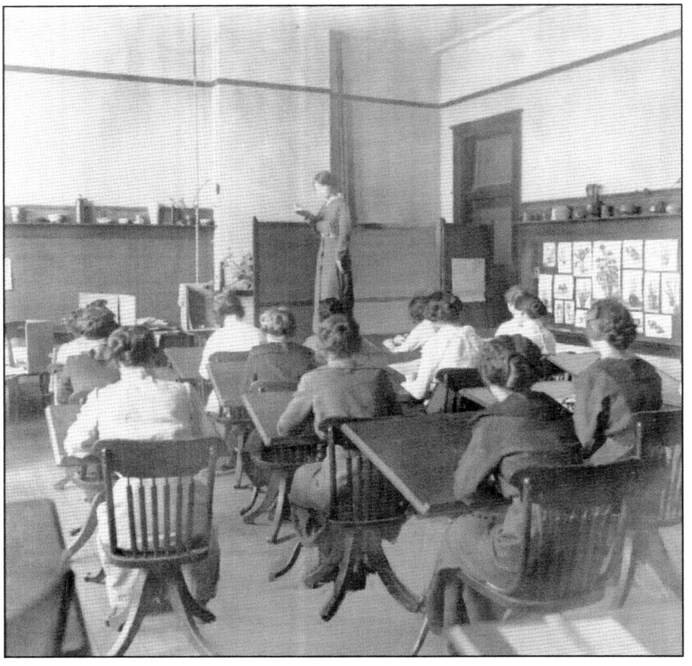

After fire destroyed the Normal School in 1912, some classes shared space in the Training School. This photograph, showing a model at the front of the room from about 1914, is of Normal School students using the art classroom for their life drawing class. (EWU 007-0582_1-10-1.)

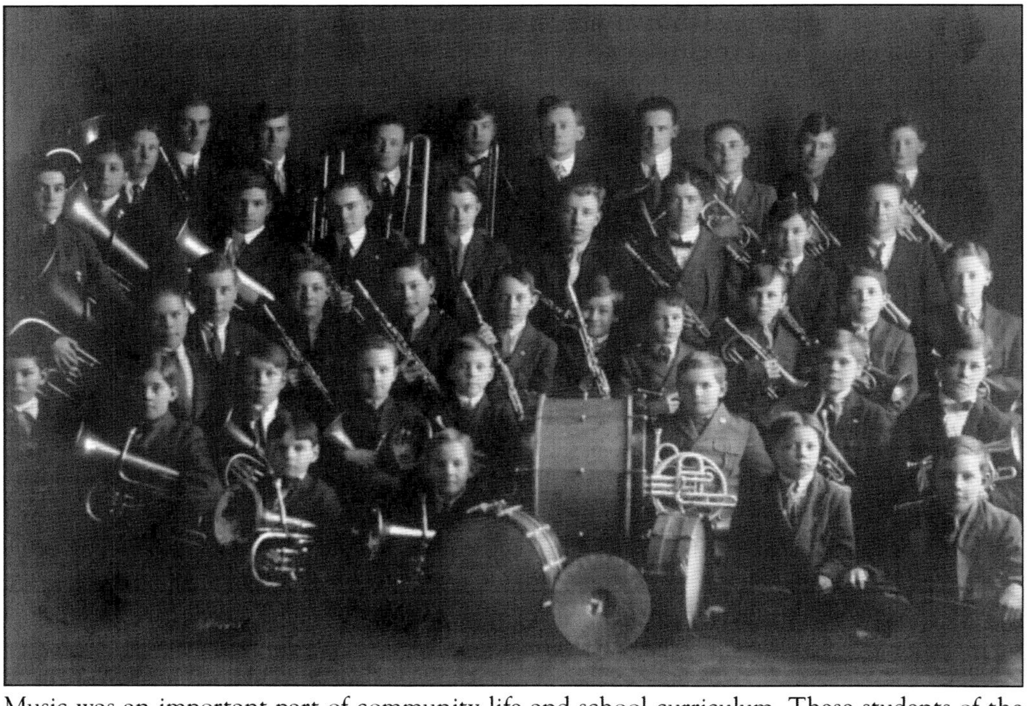

Music was an important part of community life and school curriculum. These students of the Training School band, from around 1916, would have performed not only in school concerts, but also for community pageants such as the May Day Festival and Fourth of July celebration. The Tilicum Club, a women's organization, often invited students from the band class to perform during their meetings.

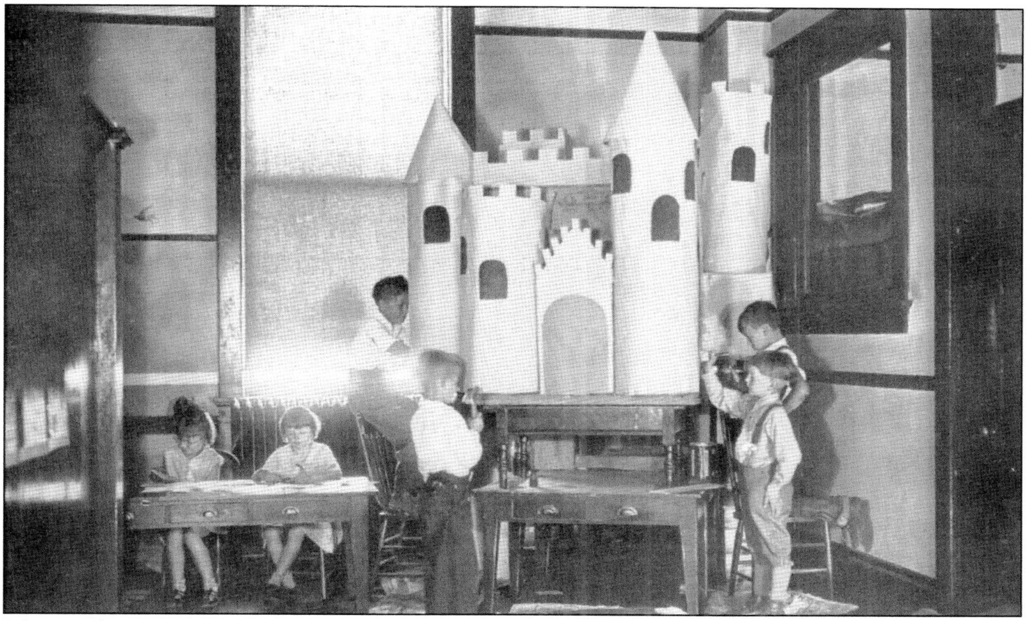

The teachers in training of the Normal School learned by observation, as well as through actual classroom teaching in the Training School, such as in this 1931 class. Their training also included instruction in finances, organization, and administration needed to run an isolated rural school, where a single teacher might be in charge of students in multiple grades.

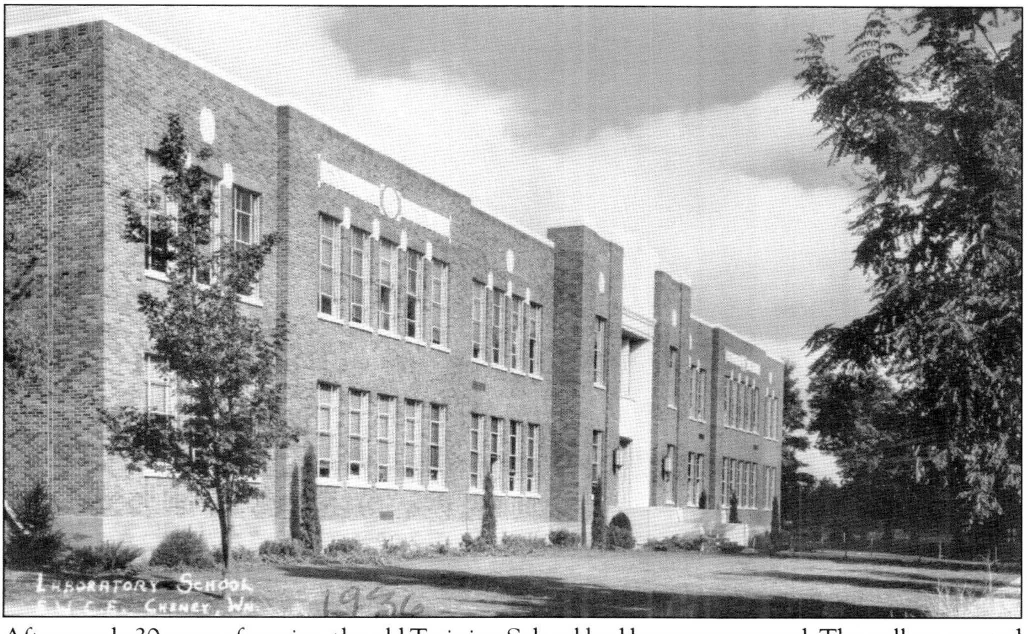

After nearly 30 years of service, the old Training School had become unsound. The college erected a new facility with all the modern appliances for both its students and student teachers. Named for governor and Cheney native Clarence D. Martin, the hall was dedicated in April 1937. The Training School within the hall was renamed the Laboratory School. The old Training School building was demolished in 1940.

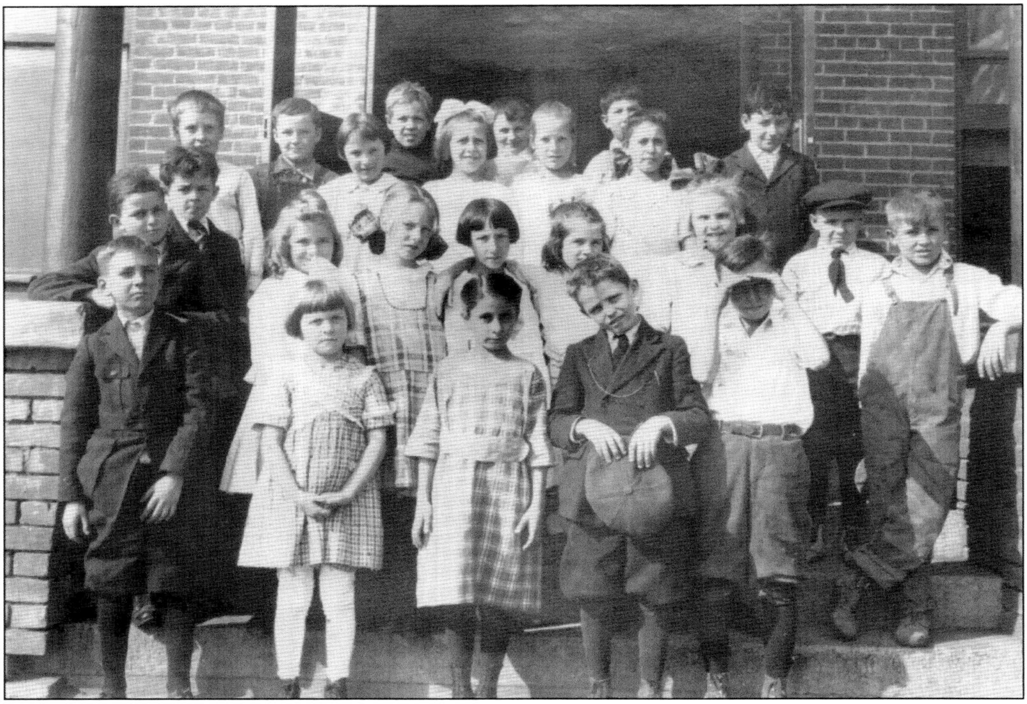

The sixth-grade class of 1919 poses for their class picture outside the Training School. Throughout the community's history, the college often provided the only elementary grade school for Cheney students, though there were times when a large student population, or philosophical disagreements, caused the Cheney School District to provide for elementary students within the public schools.

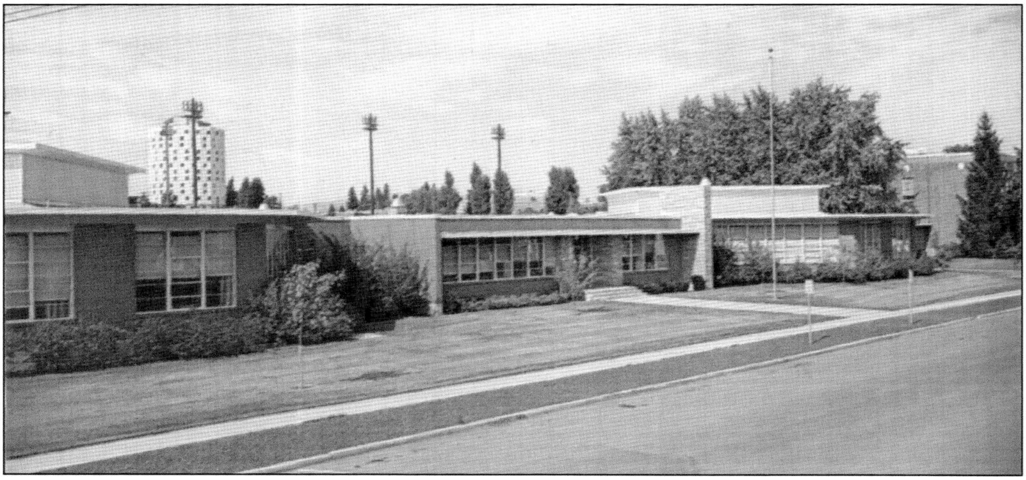

New philosophies for teacher training required new facilities, and Campus School opened in 1959 to meet them. The school served students through the sixth grade. It was later renamed in honor of educator Robert Reid. In the 1980s, the university and school district began joint operations of the school, with the university responsible for the facility. Citing issues with the building, the university closed the school in 2009.

Three

PUBLIC EDUCATION

Rural schools sprang up as pioneers settled onto homesteads. In 1878, it was unrest among the Native Americans that was foremost in pioneers' minds. Rumors of attacks in the region prompted the men to erect a defensible log building on a small hill with narrow slit windows and surrounded by an earthen trench and wall. Located on George Crunk's homestead, it was dubbed Fort Crunk. The attack never came and the unrest faded, so the pioneers used the building for their first schoolhouse and church.

Seventeen-year-old Mary Cook had recently arrived with her mother to join her father on his nearby farm. She was hired at a salary of $60 to teach a three-month term commencing on December 2, 1878, with 15 pupils of various ages. When her school money arrived, she turned it over to her father to help buy a yoke of unbroken oxen. Mary later reported how proud she was to be able to help, as her father needed those oxen badly to haul the family's provisions up from Walla Walla, Washington.

The log building blew down in a windstorm the following year, and a new school opened in the Methodist church in 1880. The Cheney School District organized that same year with 150 students. The B.P. Cheney Academy served the district's needs until dissatisfaction over salary expenses and domination by the Congregationalists caused the district to break away and open its own school in the old county courthouse in 1887.

Cheney built its first public school in 1893. High school courses were first officially offered in 1896, and the first graduation of five students took place in May 1909. With school district consolidation and population growth, the district built new high schools in 1913, 1930, and 1966. With each new high school, the old one became a junior high. A new middle school was built in 1977, and was recently replaced. Betz was the first stand-alone elementary school in Cheney, opening in 1957, but others such as Amber, Sunset, Garden Springs, Windsor, and Anderson have served students through the years.

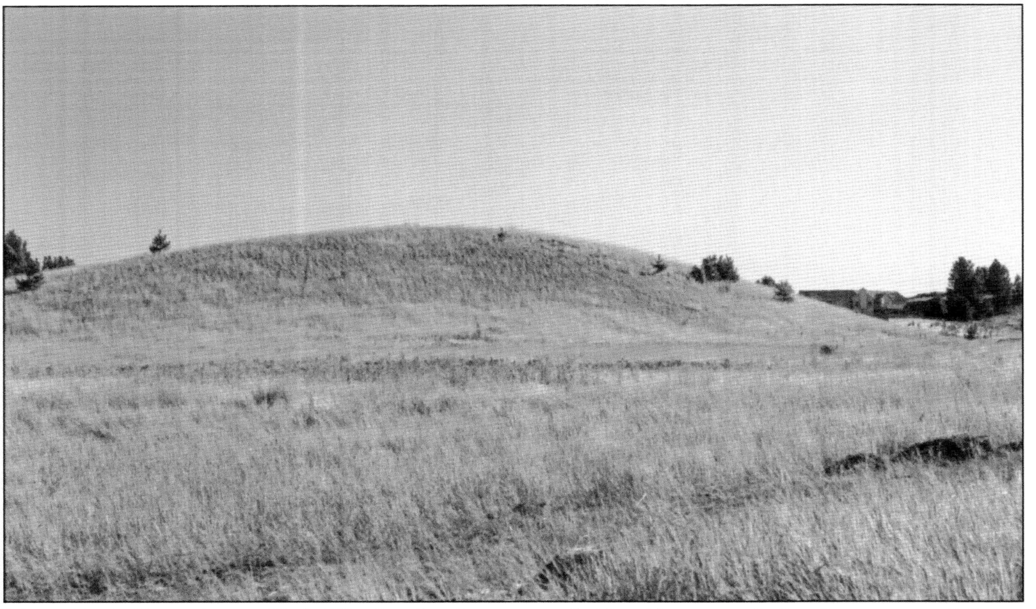

Mary Cook Spangle recalled: "Under the direction of old soldiers, my father being one of them, breastworks were thrown up and a log structure erected on a small hill, known by the early settlers as Fort Crunk. Fortunately, there were no more Indian scares, so the building was used for school and church purposes." Crunk's Hill, in north Cheney, was leveled in 2013. This photograph was taken by Carlene Shilliam Hardt.

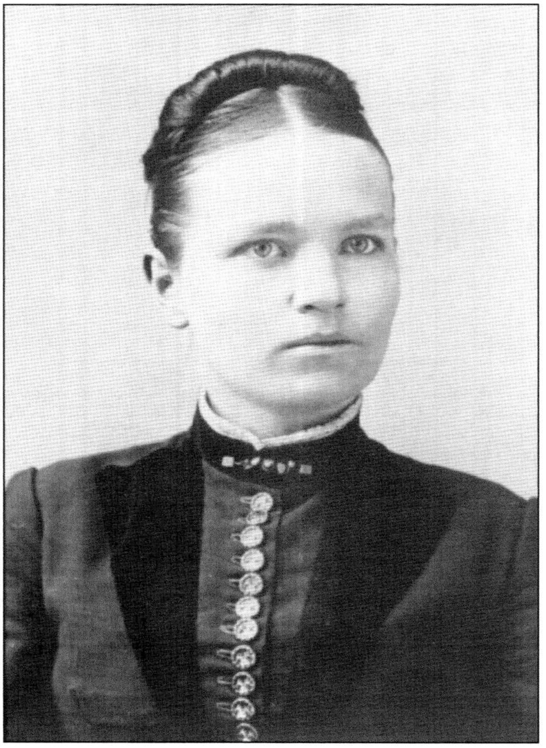

"On December 2, 1878 at age seventeen, I began teaching. My pupils numbered about fifteen. The building was a log structure, lighted by two small windows. In one end was a fireplace, made of rough stones, opposite it, the door. The floorboards were not nailed; consequently it was not a very quiet room. Perhaps you can imagine the clatter, clatter as one walked across it," Mary Cook Spangle recalled.

In 1893, the governor vetoed funding to rebuild the Normal School. The citizens of Cheney voted to tax themselves to erect this building, which they shared with the Normal School. Once state funding was restored and the new Normal School opened in 1896, the building served as Cheney's high school, junior high, and then elementary school until 1929. This photograph is dated May 16, 1908.

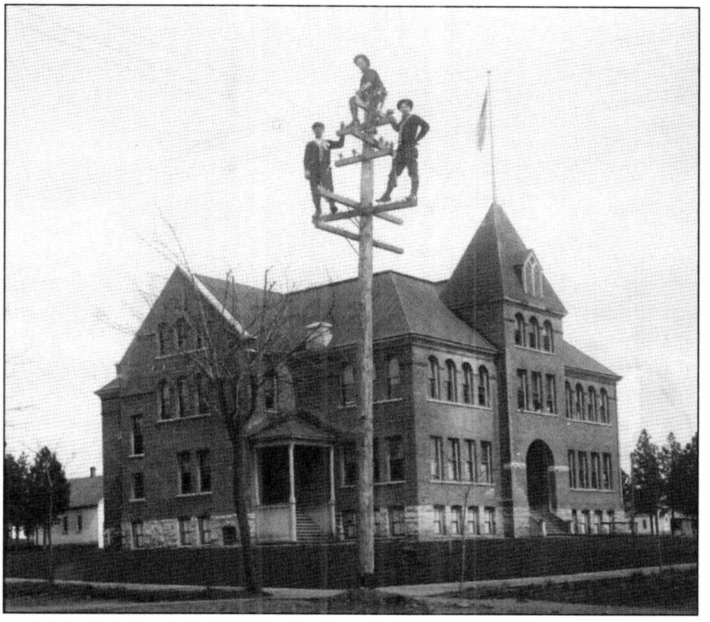

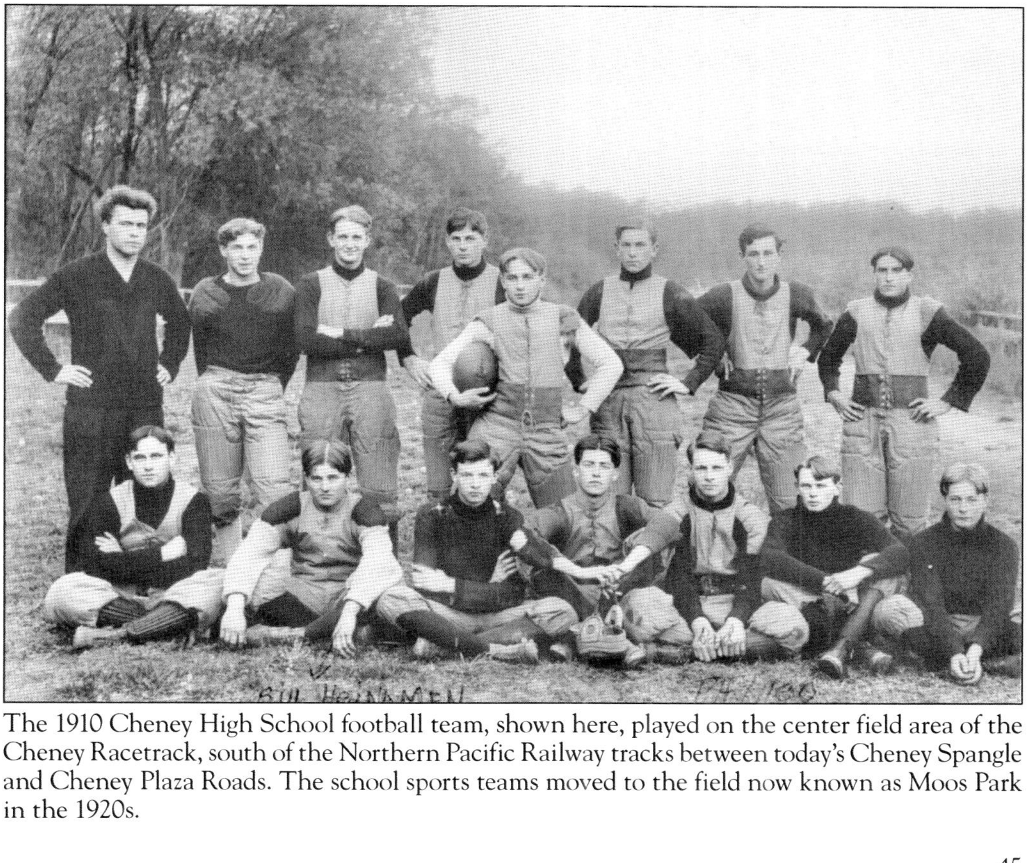

The 1910 Cheney High School football team, shown here, played on the center field area of the Cheney Racetrack, south of the Northern Pacific Railway tracks between today's Cheney Spangle and Cheney Plaza Roads. The school sports teams moved to the field now known as Moos Park in the 1920s.

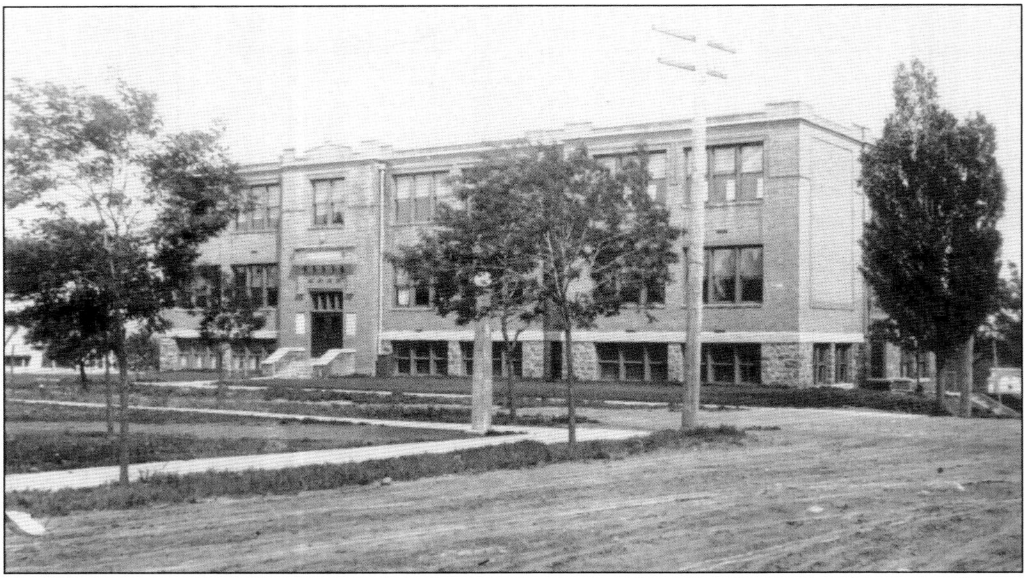

Cheney's first high school opened April 25, 1913, at Fourth and D Streets. It became Cheney Junior High in 1930 when the new high school opened, though it sometimes included elementary grade students when the Normal Training School was overcrowded. In 1966, it became the administration building. The building was demolished in 1972, and the Cheney Fire Station was built on the site.

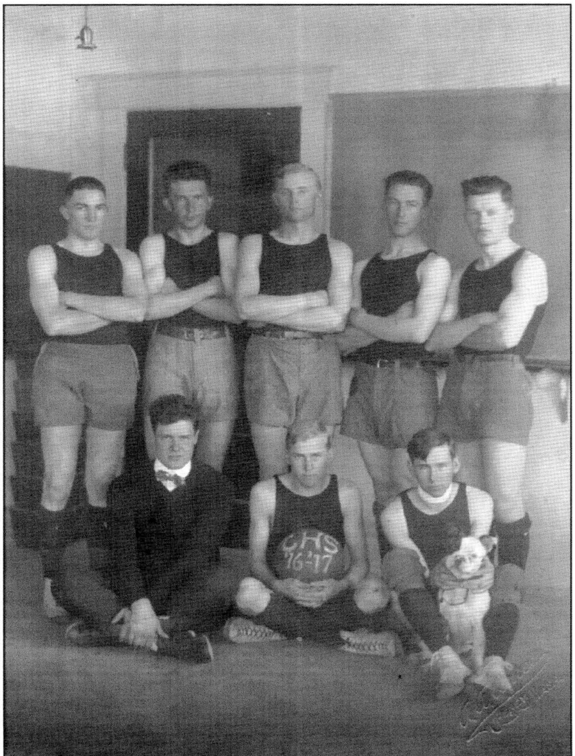

The 1917 Cheney High School basketball team posed for this photograph with their mascot in a classroom. From left to right are (seated) Coach Harris C. Christopher, Henry Wynstra, and Noble Leach; (standing) Harry Montague, Walter Mason, Walter Wynstra, Roy Mashburn, and Dewey Riggs. The following year, most of these young men joined the military to serve in World War I.

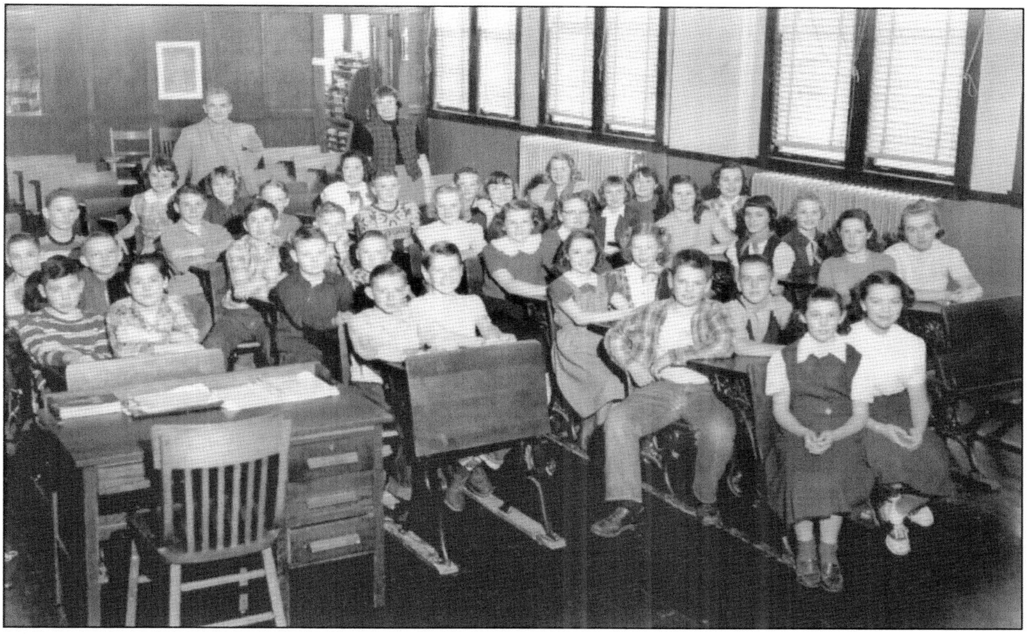

This photograph of the eighth-grade class of 1953–1954 was taken in their classroom in Cheney Junior High School. Note the rows of desks, which date back to the school's opening in 1913. Radiators provided heat for the room, though students seated near them sometimes sweltered while those on the other side of the room fidgeted to keep warm.

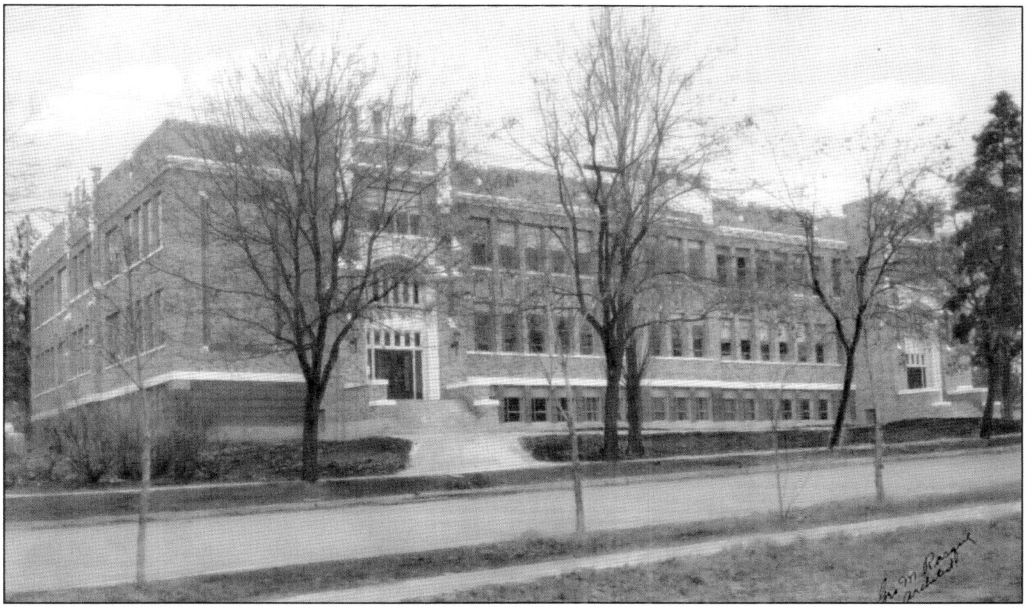

Approved by voters in 1929, the new Cheney High School opened on January 22, 1930. Bricks from the old public school were reused in its construction. After it was replaced with a new high school, the building was renamed Fisher Junior High after longtime coach, principal, and Cheney mayor George A. Fisher. When a new middle school opened in 1977, the district administration used the Fisher Building until 2014.

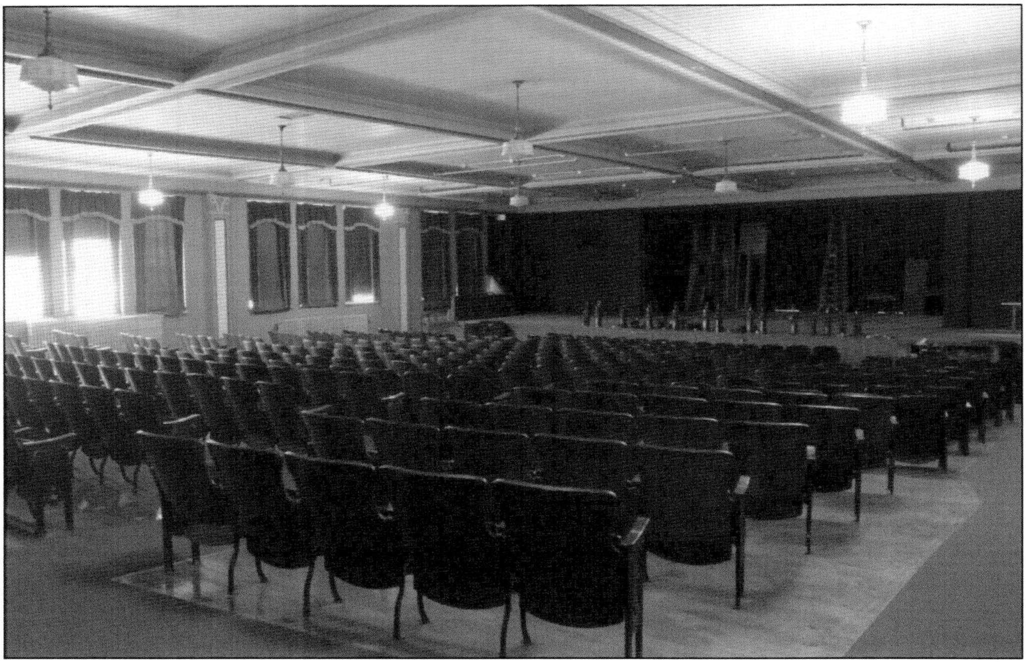

In 1930, students provided $300 from their class bank account to purchase window curtains to beautify their new high school's auditorium. Made of red velvet, the curtains matched the stage curtains. Those original curtains still hang in the auditorium today. This photograph was taken by Scott Wilbanks in 2013.

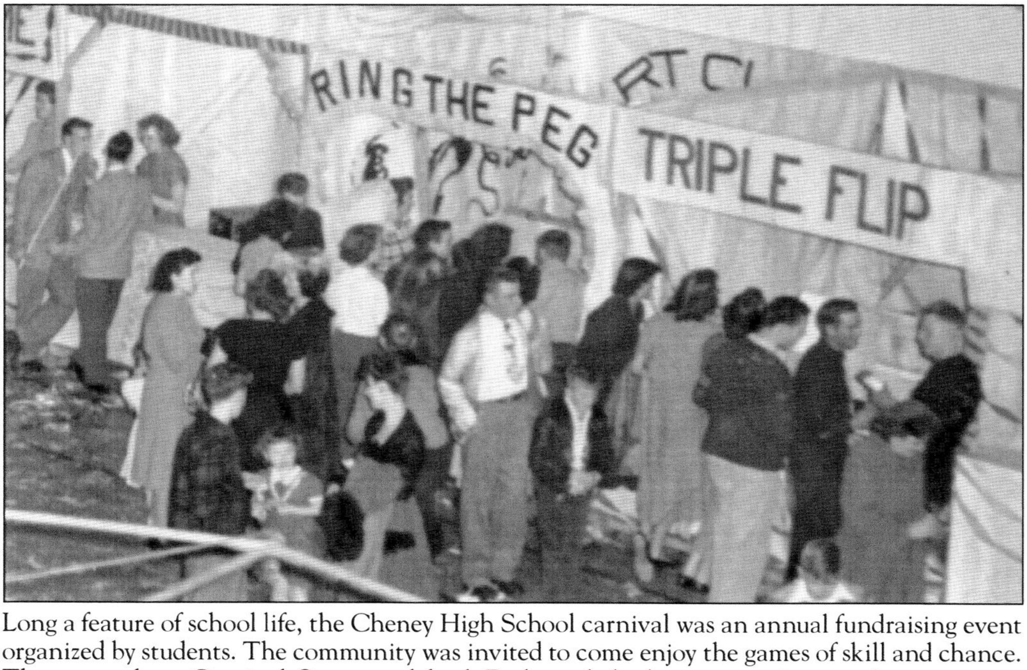

Long a feature of school life, the Cheney High School carnival was an annual fundraising event organized by students. The community was invited to come enjoy the games of skill and chance. There was also a Carnival Queen and food. Each grade had representatives on the committee and duties assigned to organize and transform the school gymnasium for the event.

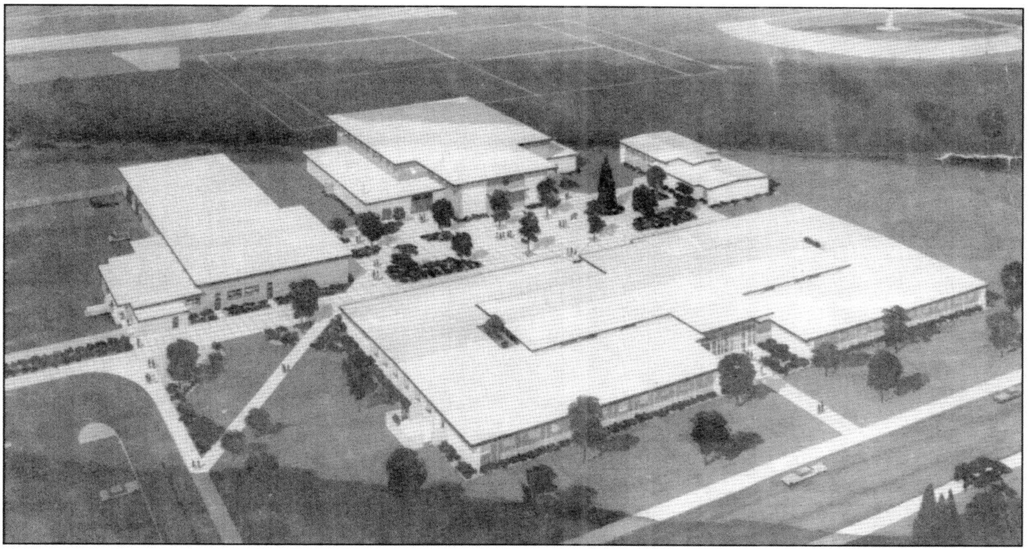

The baby boom generation was answered with a new high school complex that opened in September 1966 while it was still under construction. Situated on a large piece of land on North Sixth Street, there was room for onsite football, track, and baseball fields. The school has been extensively remodeled and expanded as the student population has continued to grow.

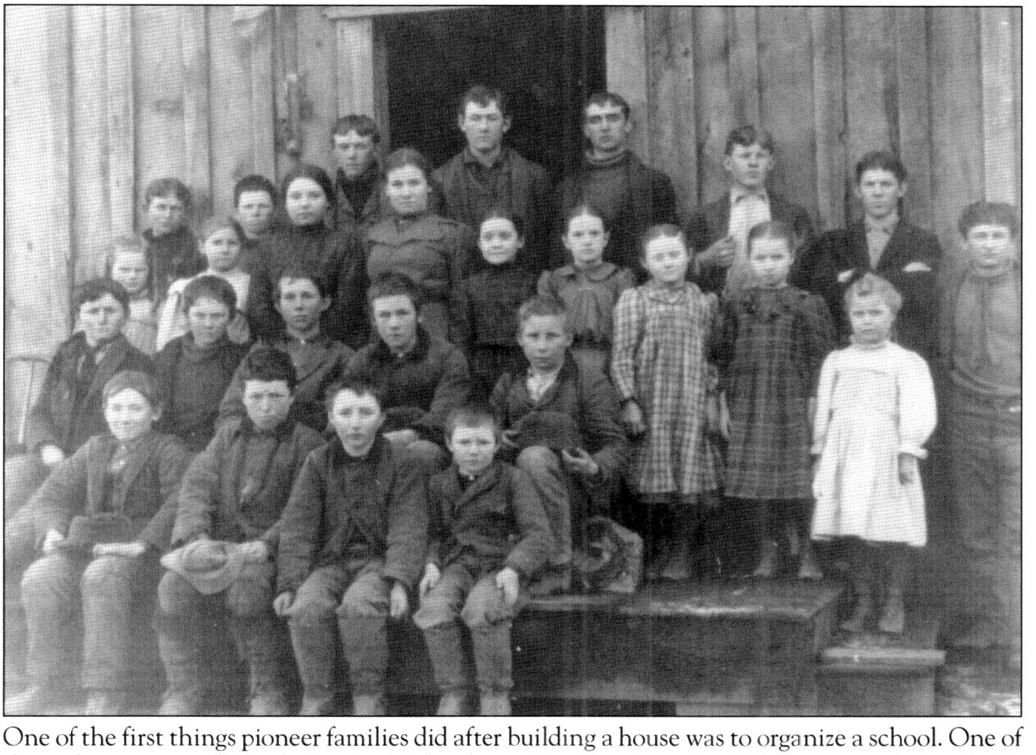

One of the first things pioneer families did after building a house was to organize a school. One of the earliest on record was the Percival School near Pine Creek south of Cheney, organized in 1872. This photograph from about 1895 shows the students of the Wright School at the intersection of Pine Grove and Wells Roads.

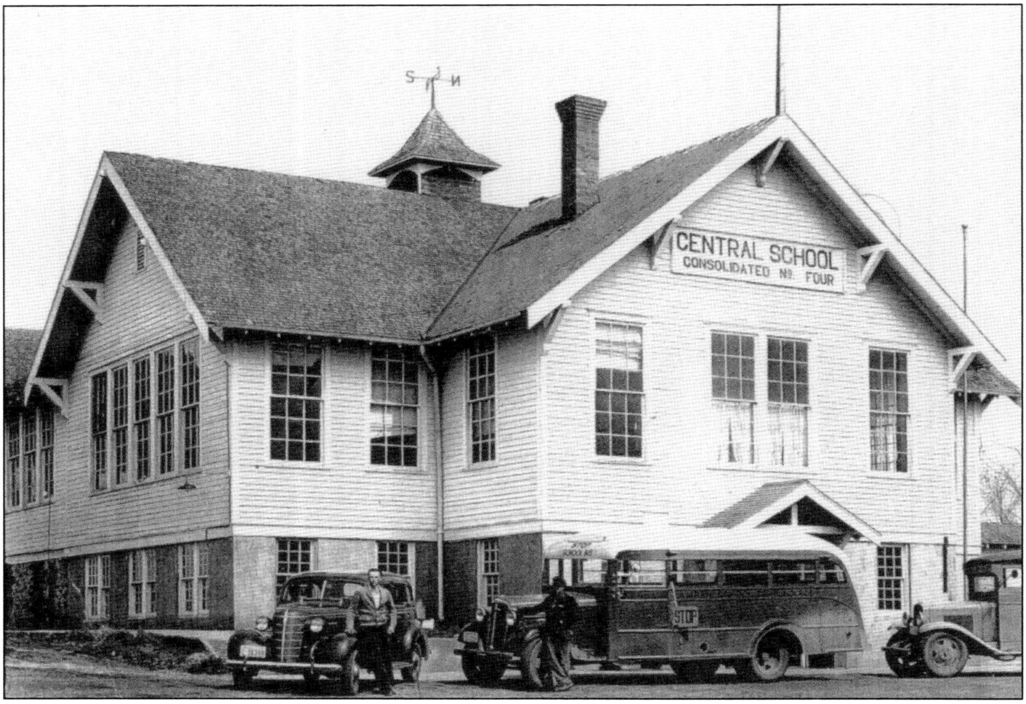

The Amber School, shown here in 1938, was the first consolidated district in the region in 1910. It served students in first through twelfth grades. The first students graduated in 1915, and the last in 1945. The school continued serving grades one through six until Amber merged into the Cheney School District in 1969. Afterward, all students were bussed into Cheney.

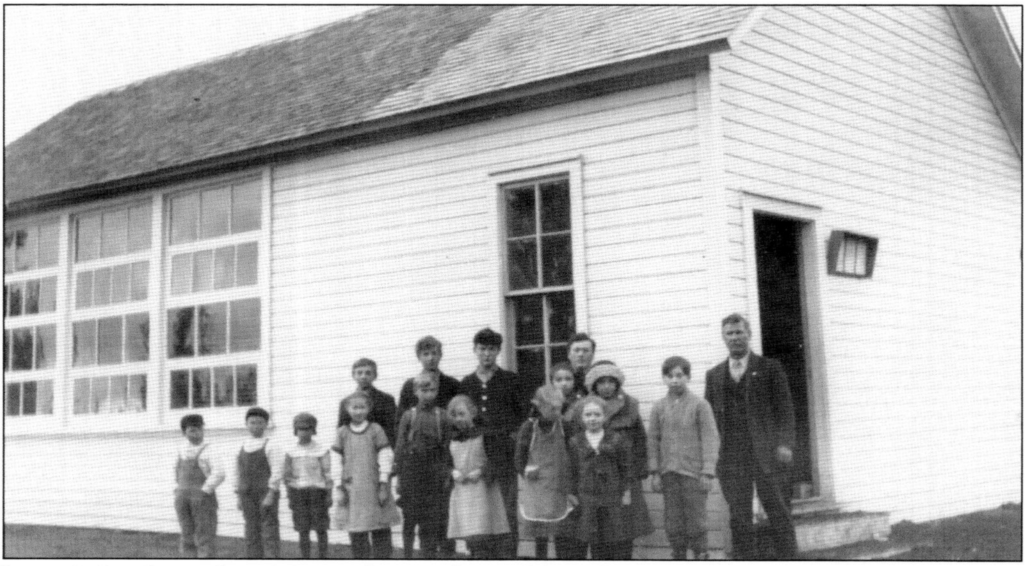

James S. Smith stands with his students in front of the Lakeview School, south of Cheney, around 1917. Schools were built around clusters of families, with a goal that no student had to walk more than five miles to reach it. Some students rode, or shared a ride, on a horse. The student was responsible for bringing feed and making sure the animal had water while at school.

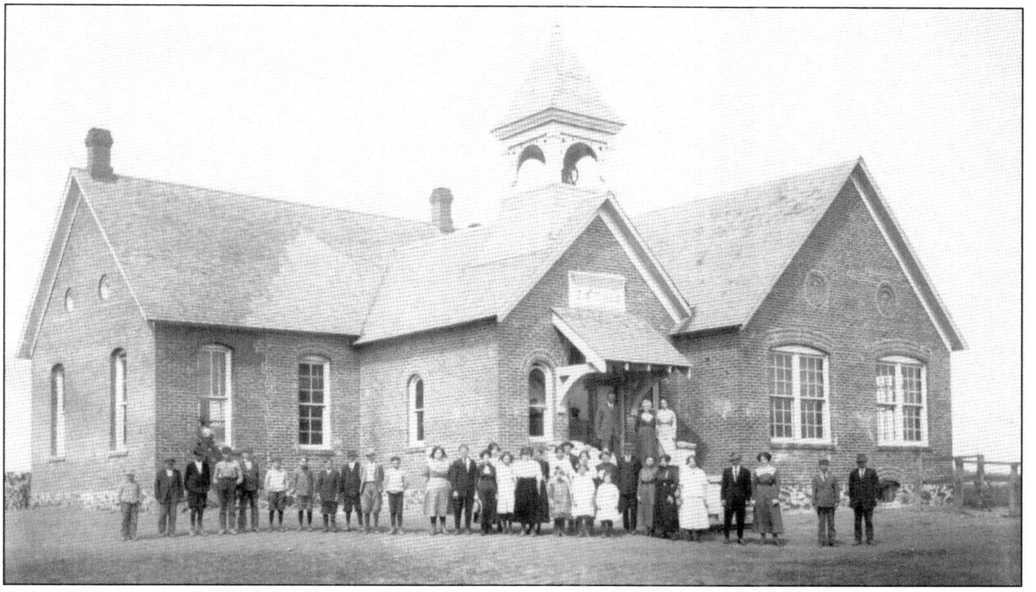

Schoolhouses, such as the Grier School west of Cheney, shown here about 1900, also served as a community center and township hall. Families held basket socials, spelling bees, choral events, literary societies, and debate contests in the schoolhouse. Each rural school was its own district with a board of directors. As many as 57 rural schools were located in what would eventually grow into the consolidated Cheney School District.

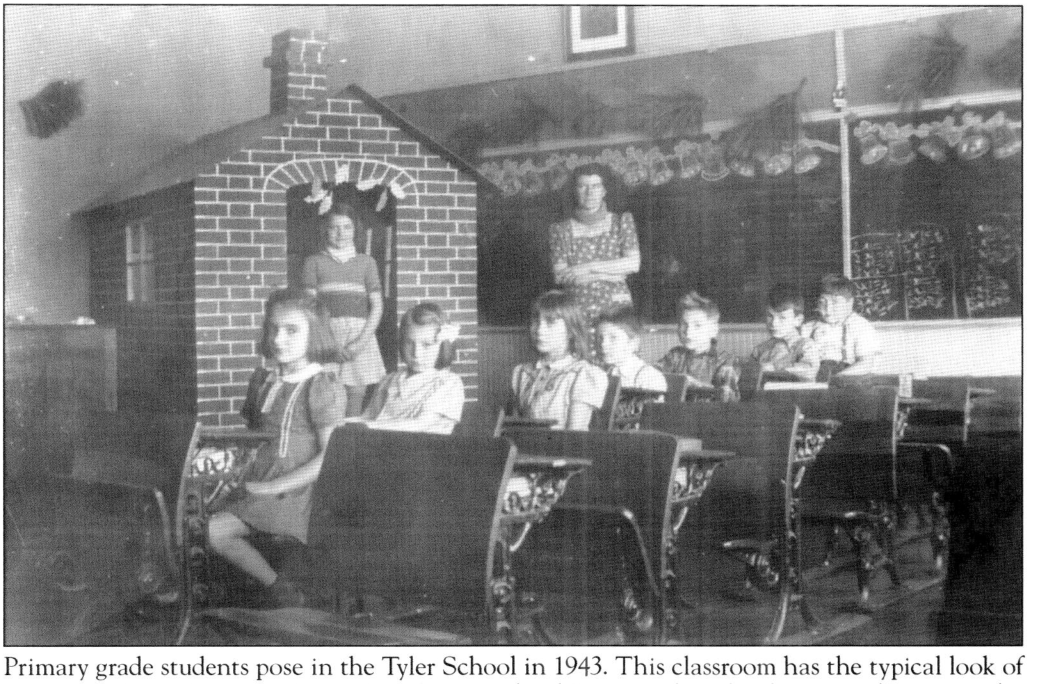

Primary grade students pose in the Tyler School in 1943. This classroom has the typical look of its time. After Tyler merged into the Cheney School District, the school remained active as the Tyler Grange Hall and a community center. The building was destroyed during the firestorm of 1960, which came close to wiping Tyler off the map.

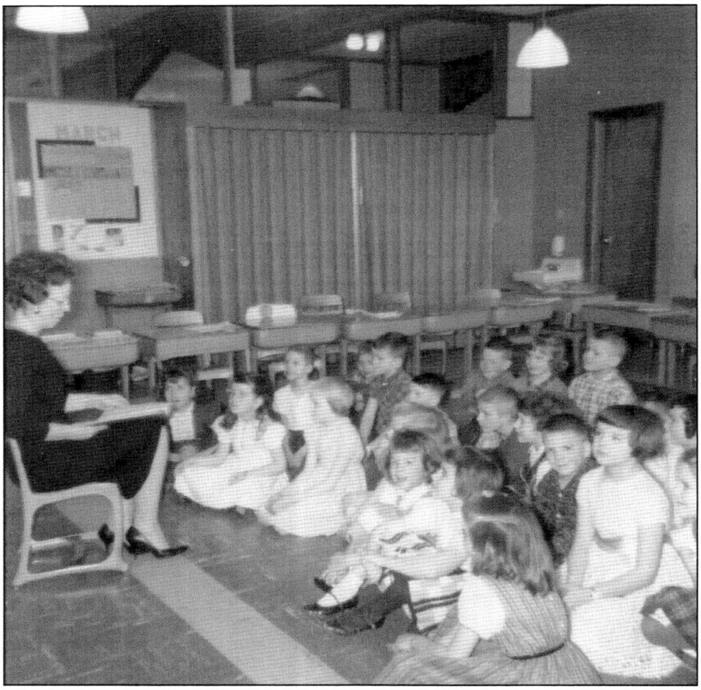

Ruth Jackson's second-grade students listen as she tells a story in 1962. The Edward F. Betz Elementary School was dedicated on March 31, 1957. It was the first standalone elementary school in Cheney and included all the modern features of the time. As the population continued to grow, Salnave Elementary school was added in 1971. Both schools have been substantially remodeled and enlarged since their opening.

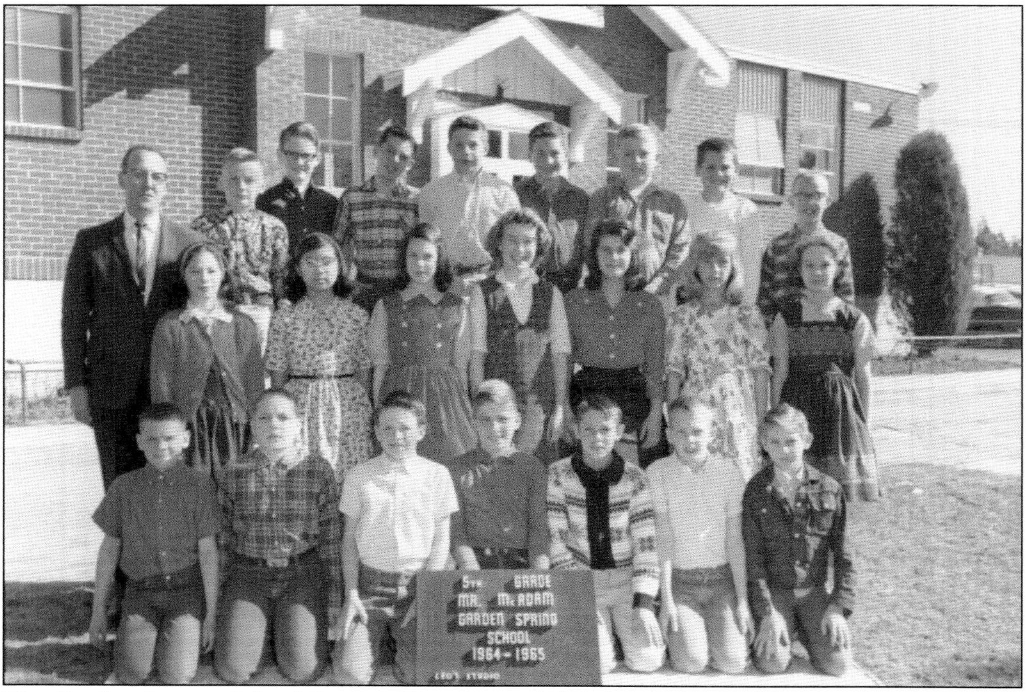

The Garden Springs School District No. 42 consolidated with the Cheney district in 1951. The elementary grades continued to use the Garden Springs School until it closed in 1997. In this photograph, the fifth-grade class of 1964–1965 poses in front of their school. With all of the school consolidation, Cheney was the largest geographic district in the state for many years.

Four

FOUNDATIONS OF FAITH

From the earliest days, pioneers gathered into communities of faith. In 1881, as the population boomed in Cheney, congregations organized Methodist, Congregational, Baptist, and Catholic churches. All but the Baptist church continued an unbroken history in the community. Those churches were soon joined by the Disciples of Christ Christian Church in 1886.

Two missionary priests built the little brown, shake-covered chapel to establish St. Paul's Episcopal Church. The names of the men and the date are unknown, but records show services being held in the chapel in 1915. The Church of the Nazarene was established in 1918.

Each church created a community of support, cooperation, spiritual growth, and a place for social gatherings. Particularly in the early days, there could be rivalry and suspicion between the various denominations. But ministers and churches also worked together on the community service council during times of need.

On Pentecost Sunday in 1949, forty-seven worshipers met in the American Legion Hall to form the Lutheran church. Five families organized the Cheney Community Church in 1955. Claude and Marilyn Nichols are recognized as organizing members of the first ward of the Church of Jesus Christ of Latter Day Saints in 1962. The Seventh-day Adventists organized in 1964.

The pioneer Baptist church, which stood at Third and D Streets, dissolved in the 1930s. New Baptist orders returned to Cheney in later years.

Over the last 25 years, new Christian fellowships, as well as Islamic centers, have joined the pioneer churches to serve the spiritual needs of the community.

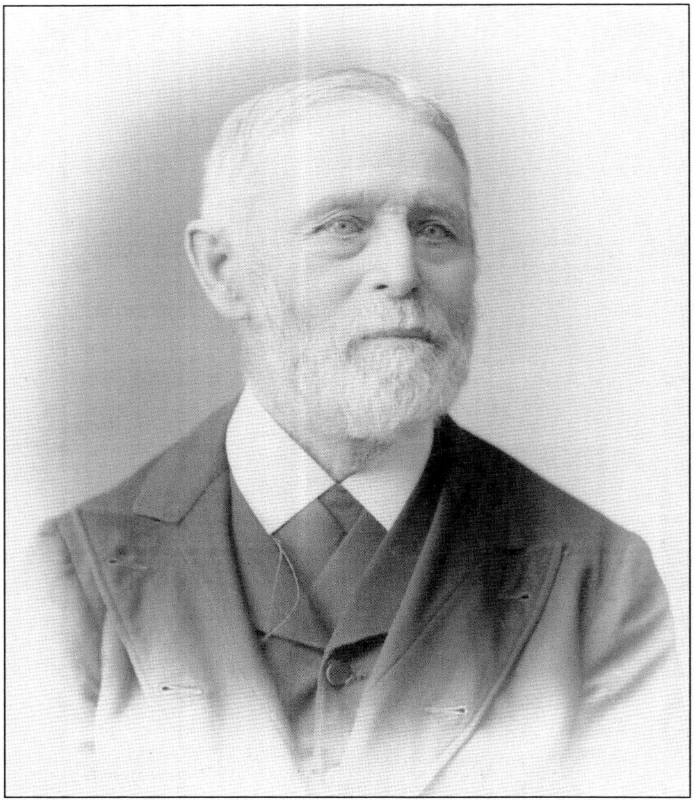

Rev. Cushing Eells was the first missionary preacher in Cheney. He came to the territory from Massachusetts in 1838 with his bride, Myra. He rode a small, white pony from place to place, calling on both Native Americans and white settlers. In 1881, he established the Congregational church in Cheney and gave the congregation a bell, which hangs in front of the United Church of Christ today.

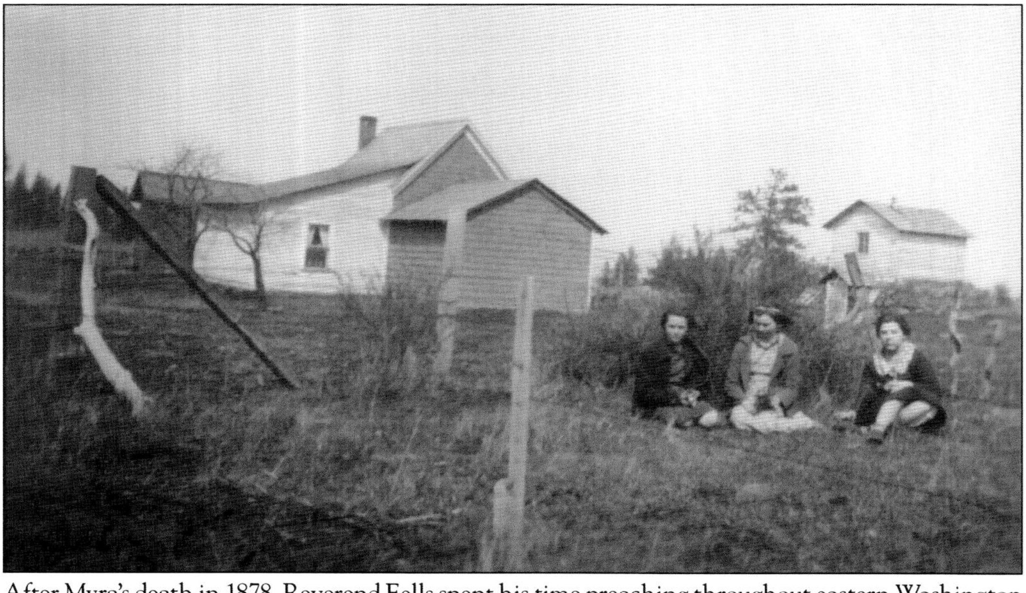

After Myra's death in 1878, Reverend Eells spent his time preaching throughout eastern Washington Territory. He was the pastor of the Cheney Congregational church in 1881, and built his home near North Sixth Street in 1882. Reverend Eells died at his son's home in Skokomish in 1893, but his house in Cheney survived into the 1960s.

The members of the Congregational church paid for, and dedicated, their first wooden church building on Fourth Street east of F Street on December 11, 1881. The 30-by-50-foot building had a 10-by-10-foot tower that was 75 feet high and held the bell donated by Reverend Eells. The church could seat 300 people and was heated by a single wood stove.

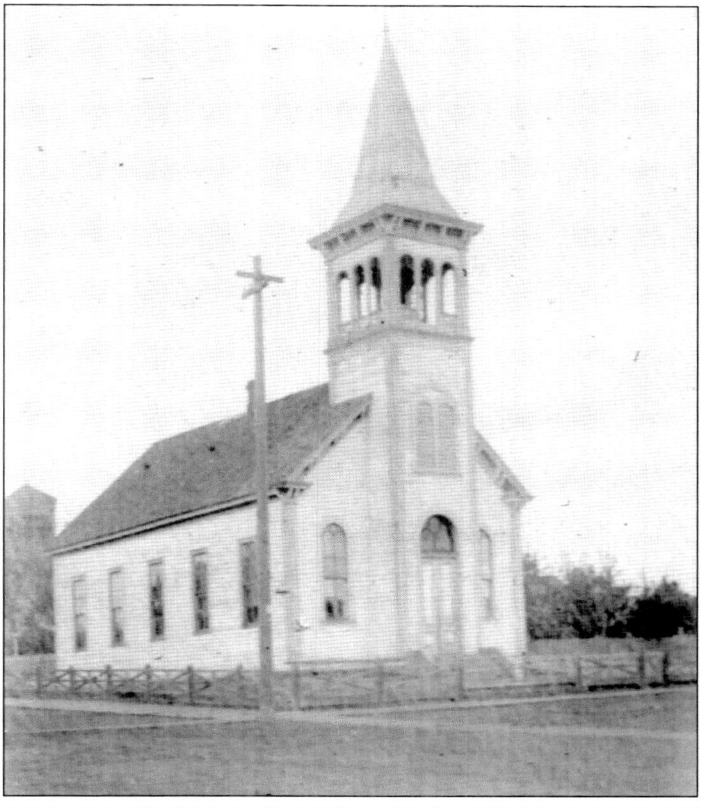

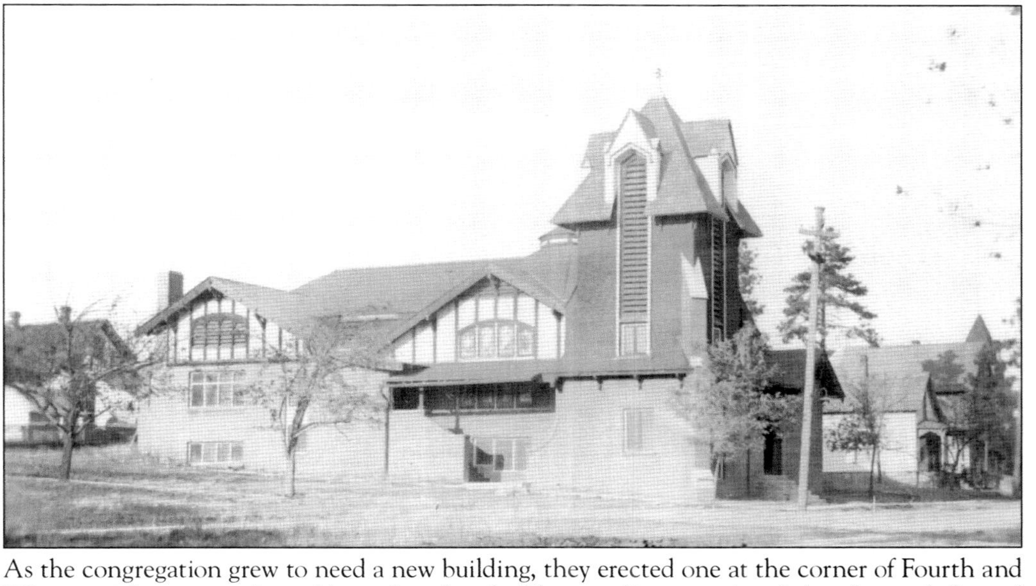

As the congregation grew to need a new building, they erected one at the corner of Fourth and F Streets right next to their old wooden church. The new Congregational church was dedicated on January 14, 1912, under Rev. Francis O. Wyatt. In 1928, the Congregational and Methodist congregations joined to become the Federated church. They continued to use both churches for various services until they separated in 1961.

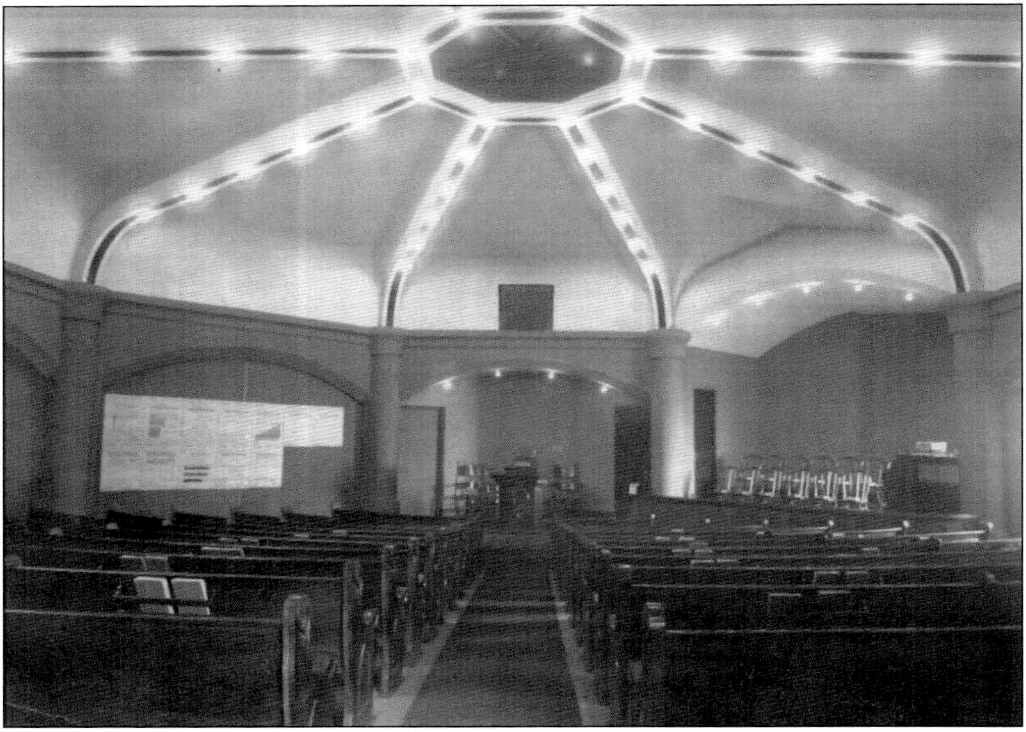

Reverend Wyatt recalled of the new church building: "My most delightful memory is the wonderful cooperation of teachers, business men, and farmers in making the new church possible and the splendid cooperation among our Cheney ministers in our united canvas of the community until every family was lined up definitely with one church or another." This photograph of the sanctuary was taken for its dedication in 1912.

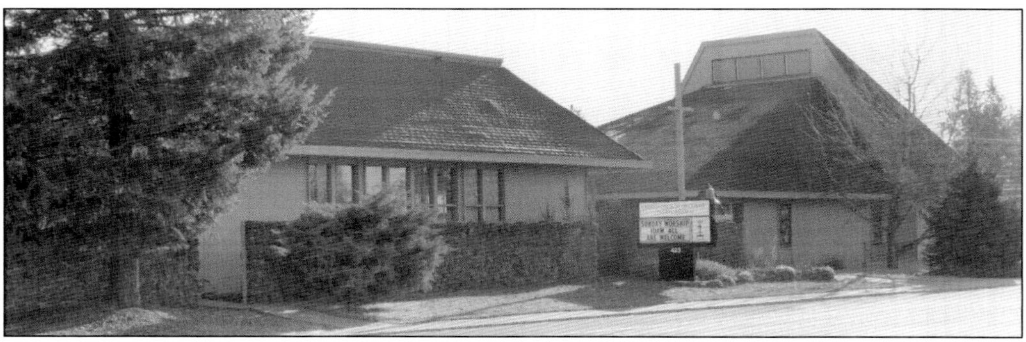

In 1961, the Congregational membership voted to join the United Church of Christ, which was a merger of the Congregational churches, a portion of the Disciples of Christ, and the German Evangelical and Reformed Church. The members began moving into their new church building on North Sixth Street in 1971 while it was still being built. Construction was completed on the new sanctuary in 1983.

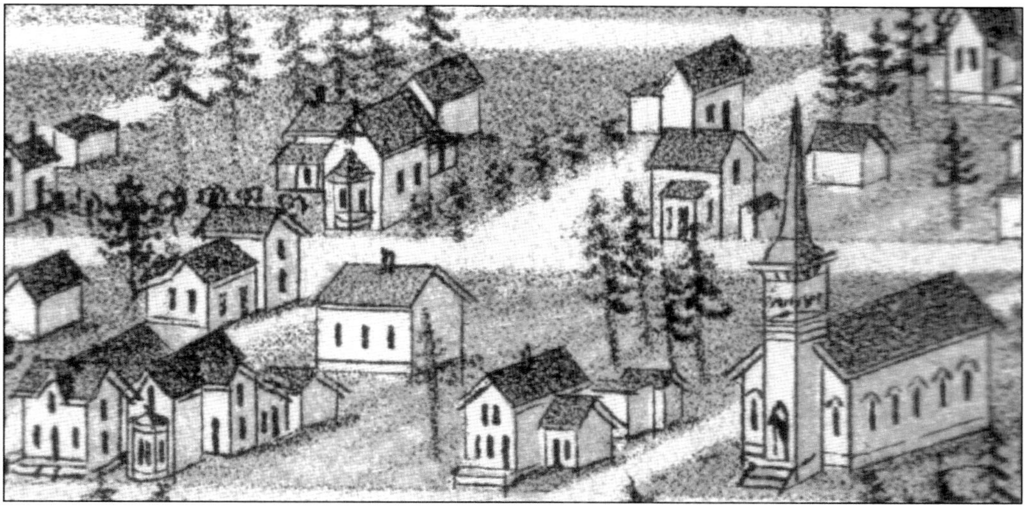

The Methodist congregation first gathered for a sermon in a butcher shop in November 1880. Their original church was a one-story building dedicated on June 3, 1881. The 20-by-36-foot building is shown here in the center of an 1884 sketch. The building was also used as a schoolhouse and a meeting place for temperance societies and suffragettes. The Congregational church is shown at lower right.

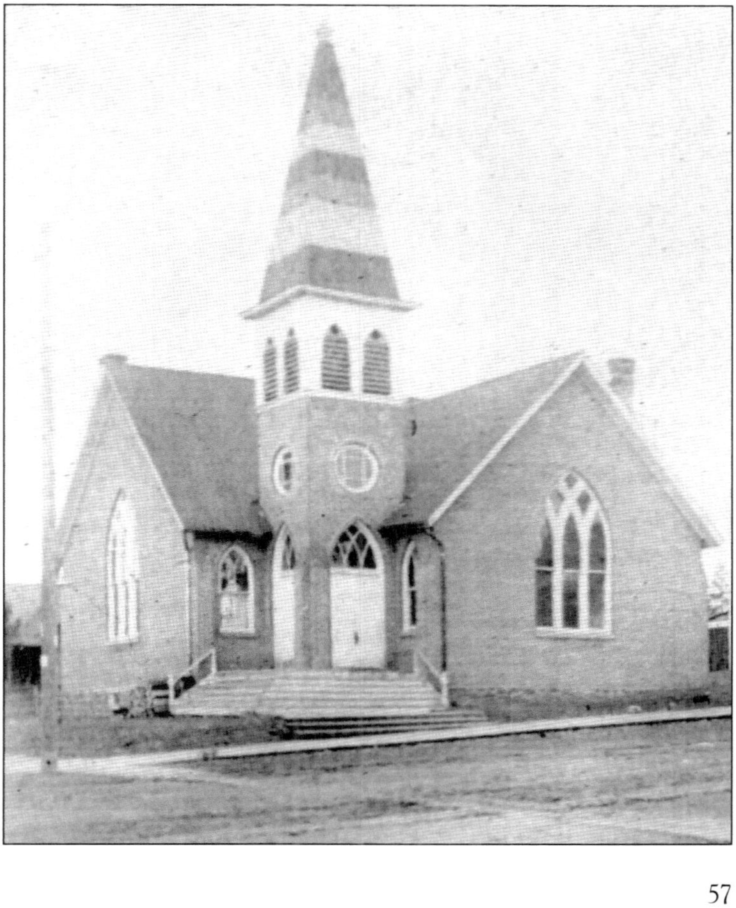

By 1889, the Methodist congregation had grown and prospered so much that a new brick church was constructed on the corner of Fourth and G Streets. The new building cost $4,000 and was dedicated November 24, 1889, under the name of First Methodist Church of Cheney. There were 70 members, with 80 enrolled in the Sunday school. A large bell was installed in the tower in 1891.

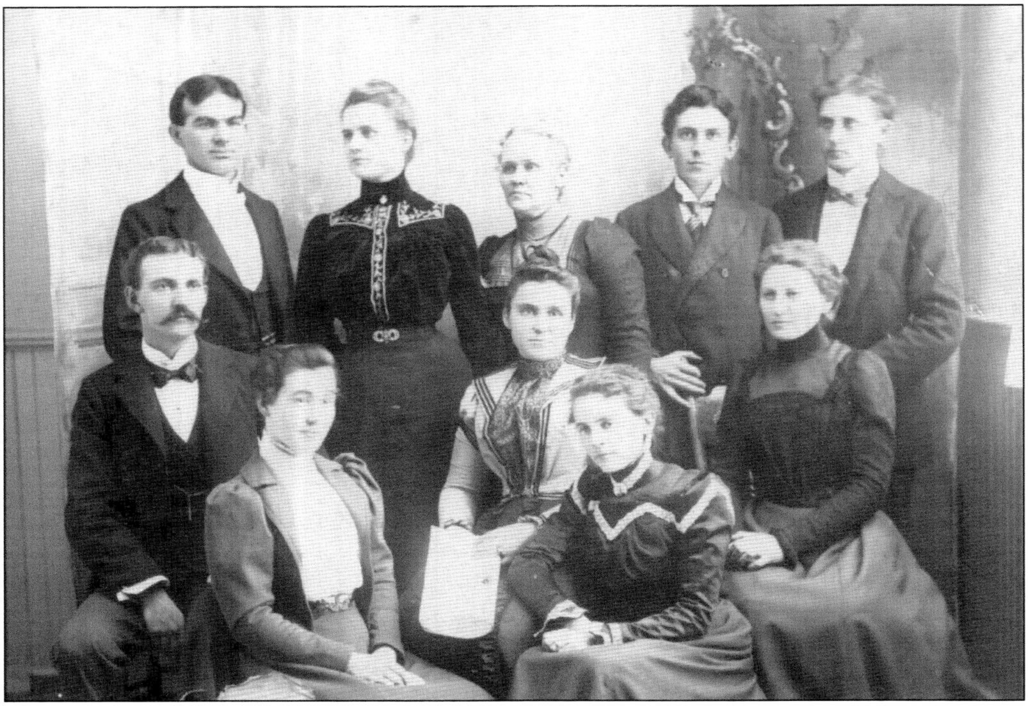

This photograph from the early 1900s is of the Methodist church choir. A story from that time relates that a lady, in a hurry to start for church, took from her closet what she thought was her dolman and threw it over her arm. On arriving at church, she threw it over the back of the pew. Only then did she discover it was her husband's trousers.

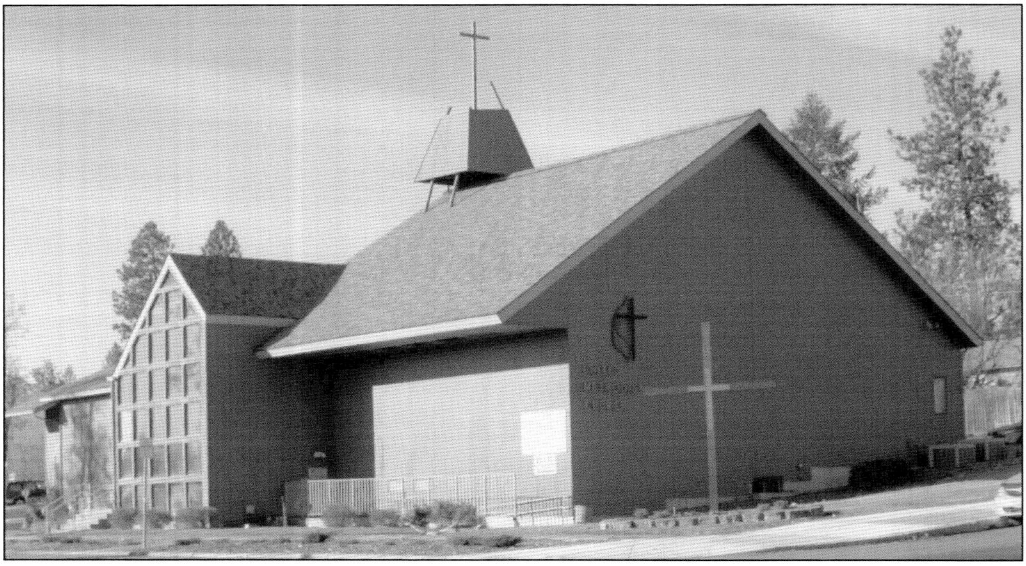

The congregation was renamed the United Methodist Church of Cheney in 1968. Soon after, they set about raising funds to remodel and enlarge their 80-year-old building. The work kept most of the original sanctuary intact, including the pipe organ. A consecration service was held for the new church on December 5, 1976.

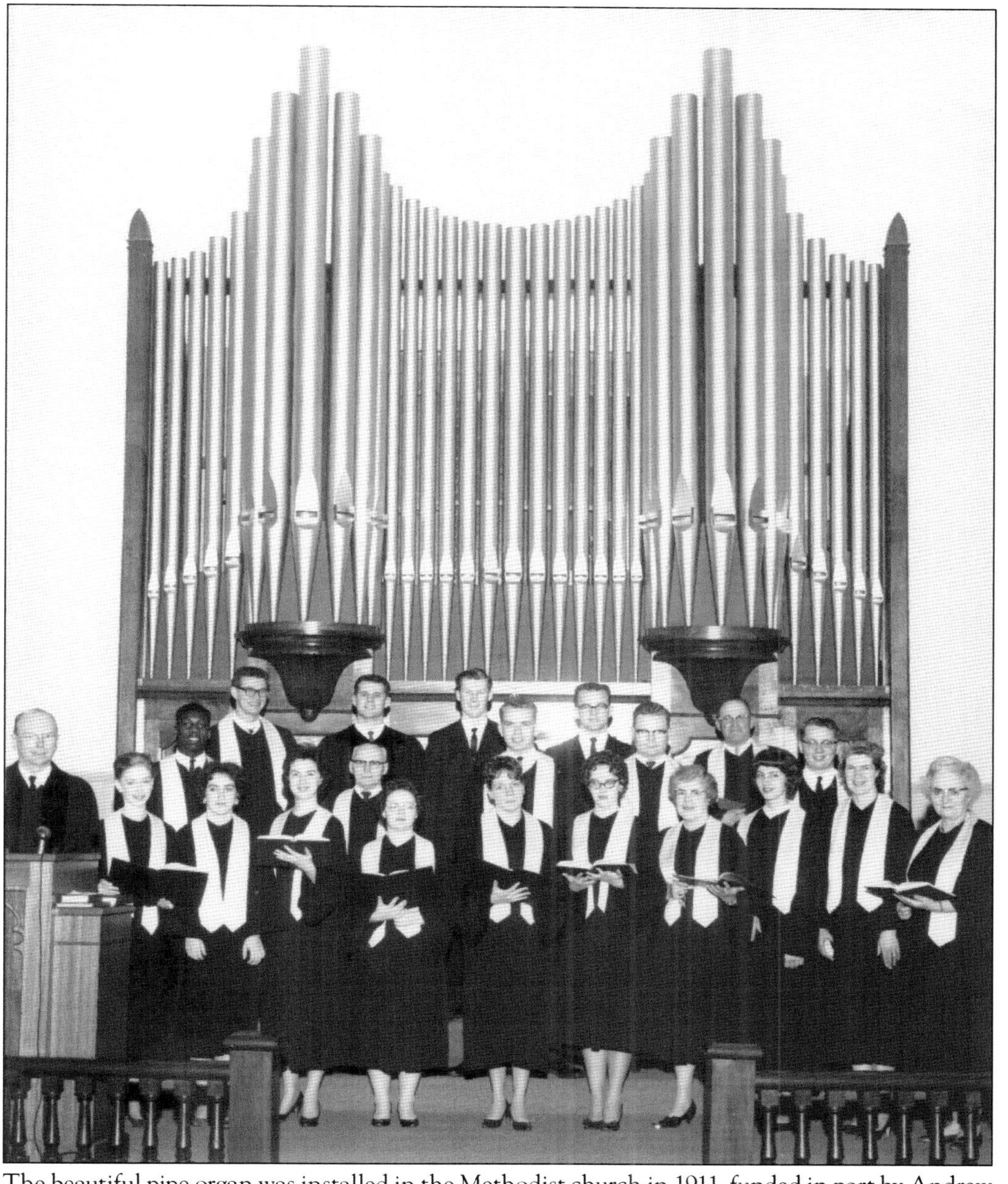

The beautiful pipe organ was installed in the Methodist church in 1911, funded in part by Andrew Carnegie following a visit to him by Normal School president Noah D. Showalter. The story related by church members is that Showalter first approached Carnegie for the building of a city library, and while talking, the subject of an organ for the church came into the conversation. Carnegie reportedly declined to fund the library, but as Showalter was preparing to leave, he offered $1,075 toward the purchase of the pipe organ. Mary Betz has been credited as being instrumental in raising the remainder of the $2,500 cost of the organ. This photograph of the choir standing in front of the organ with Rev. K.W. Larrison at far left was taken in 1963. The organ is still used during services.

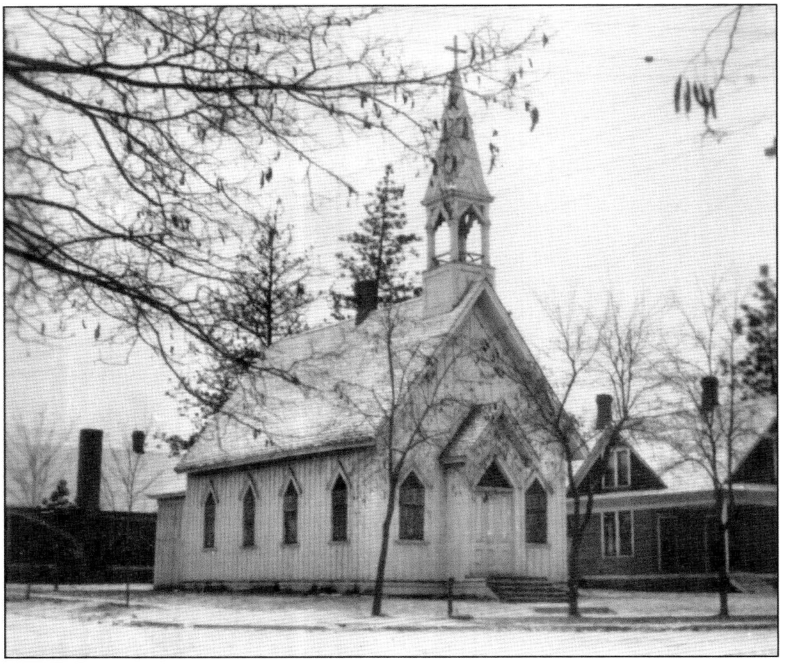

The first Catholic mass was celebrated in a hall above Abe Blefgen's furniture store on June 12, 1881. This 20-by-30-foot whitewashed church on the corner of Fifth and C Streets was completed in September 1881. A potbellied stove provided the heat, and the pews were arranged on either side of the stove. Margaret Mulligan Martin, wife of Clarence D. Martin, was the organist and soloist for many years.

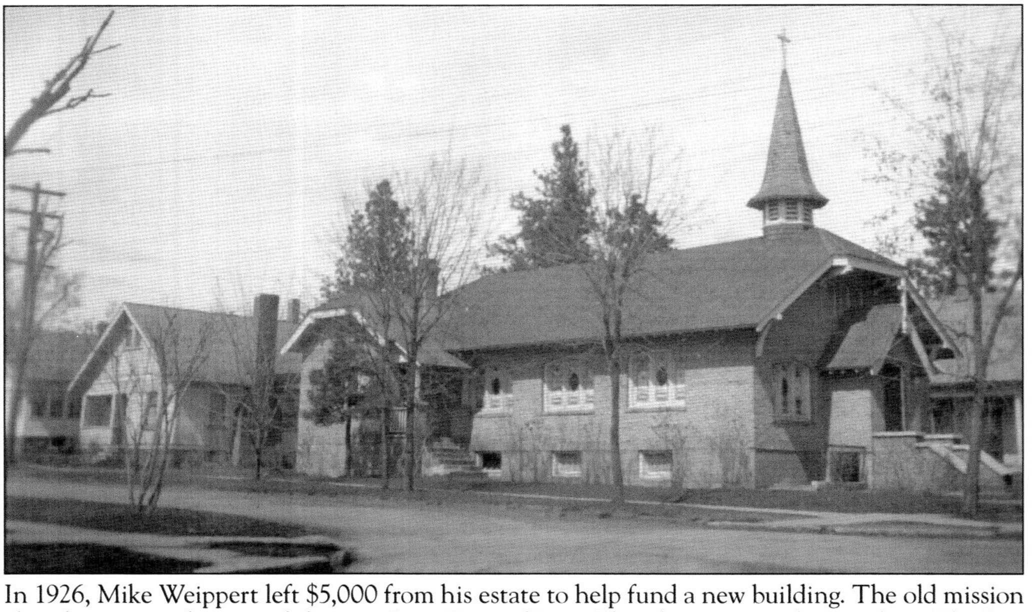

In 1926, Mike Weippert left $5,000 from his estate to help fund a new building. The old mission church was torn down, and the new Saint Rose of Lima Church was erected in its place. The first mass in the new church was offered on Christmas Eve 1928. In the 1970s, the college purchased the building for use as the Native American center.

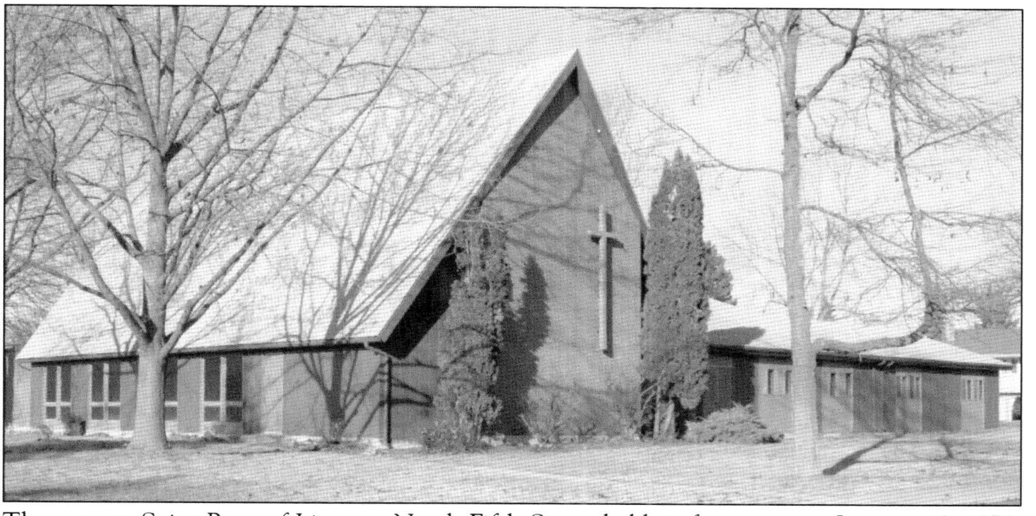

The present Saint Rose of Lima on North Fifth Street held its first mass on January 18, 1970. Marcel and Catherine Oriard recalled of the early days: "When we made our First Communion in 1909, it was a two hour trip from Marshall, a distance of six miles. The work horses could not travel very fast, so it took considerable time."

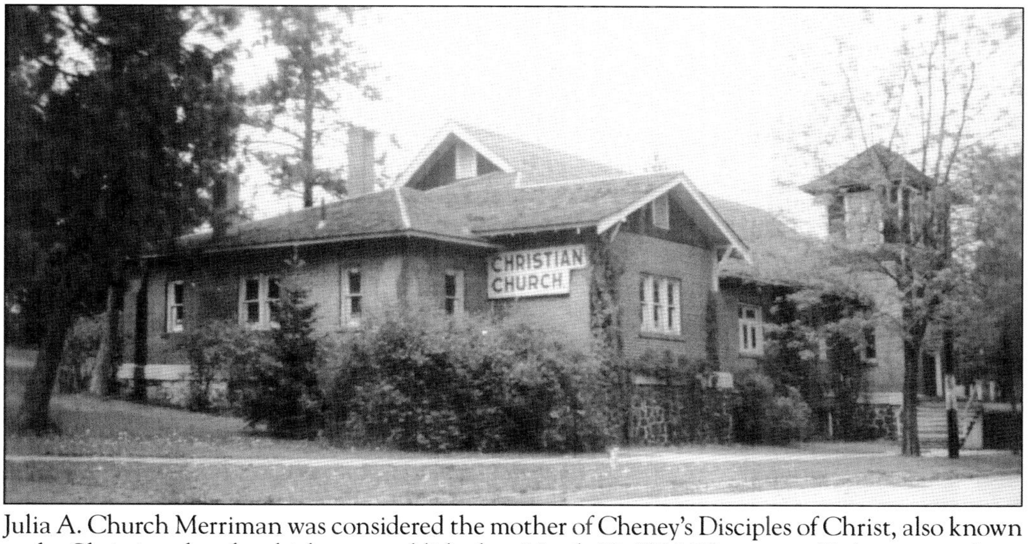

Julia A. Church Merriman was considered the mother of Cheney's Disciples of Christ, also known as the Christian church, which was established on March 28, 1886. There were 17 charter members. The original wooden church was replaced with this brick building in 1914. It still stands today on the corner of Fifth and D Streets.

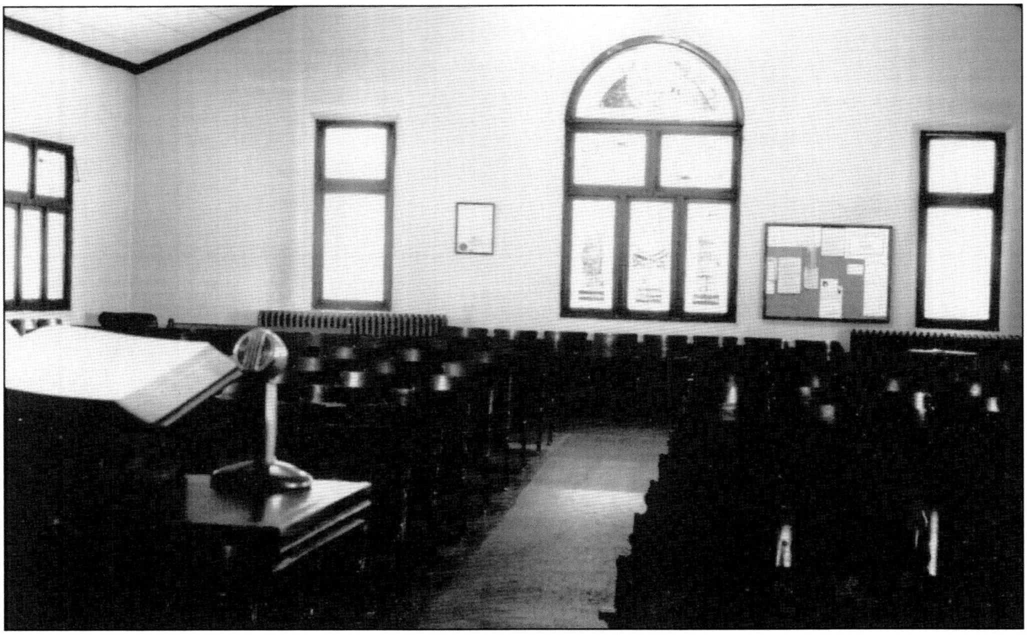

The central stained-glass window of the eastern wall of the church, at the rear of the sanctuary, was a gift from George W. and Marcella Ellison Cook, parents of pioneer teacher Mary and Sarah Jane, wife of Samuel Showalter. In 2005, the congregation dissolved and donated the church building to Eastern Washington University for preservation.

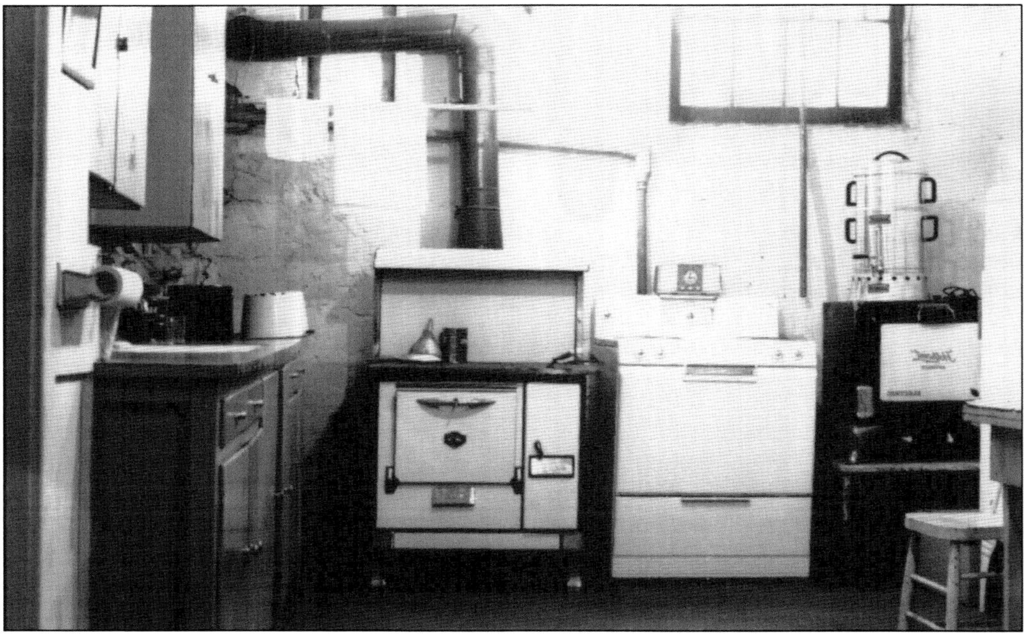

The kitchen was in the basement of the church. Generations of church ladies served lunch and supper or hot coffee for committees from here. The wood stove was still in use in 1966, when this photograph was taken, sitting next to its more modern electric counterpart. Note the large coffee maker on the right.

Five

Industry and Agriculture

Raising livestock and growing boxwood trees for timber were the earliest industries in the region. Soon after, there were sawmills to process the boxwood and native pine for the railroad and for the building of homes and businesses. The lumber also went to wagon and furniture makers who established themselves in the new city of Cheney.

Early Cheney was also known for the Bavaria Brewery, which supplied much of eastern Washington Territory and the Coeur d'Alene mining district in the 1880s.

Agriculture was by far the largest industry. Wheat was, and still is, king. The rich clay soil of the Palouse hills made dry-land wheat farming very successful. Over time, farmers added barley, oats, legumes, canola, and mustard to the mix. Early farmers drained the many scabland ponds to grow hay. Supporting industries such as flour mills, grain warehouses, implement dealers, and repairmen sprang up to serve the needs of farmers. The Cheney Weeder Company manufactured the Rotary Rod Weeder here for 43 years. Invented by Kyle Wolfe, the weeder was part of the US Soil Conservation Department's program during the Midwest's recovery from the Dust Bowl.

Early Cheney also had a burgeoning fruit orchard industry. Farmers grew apples, pears, cherries, peaches, and apricots without irrigation. However, in the early teens, drought and the emerging irrigated orchards of the Wenatchee area undercut the profitability of the industry, and it faded away. Remnants of orchards can still be found in the surrounding countryside.

Cheney was a major player in the early dairy and cheese industry in Washington. Martin and Hubbard's Creamery, with Frederick Reuter as cheese maker, was the largest producer of cheese in the state in 1897. Reuter later operated his own award-winning cheese factory for over a decade. Boone Mill's Dairy delivered milk and cream by horse-drawn wagon into the 1930s. Other local dairies in Cheney included Pine Creek, Sunrise Dairy, Meadlowland, Sumsion's Cheney Dairy Products, Ditton's Yankee Dairy, and Wilcox Farms.

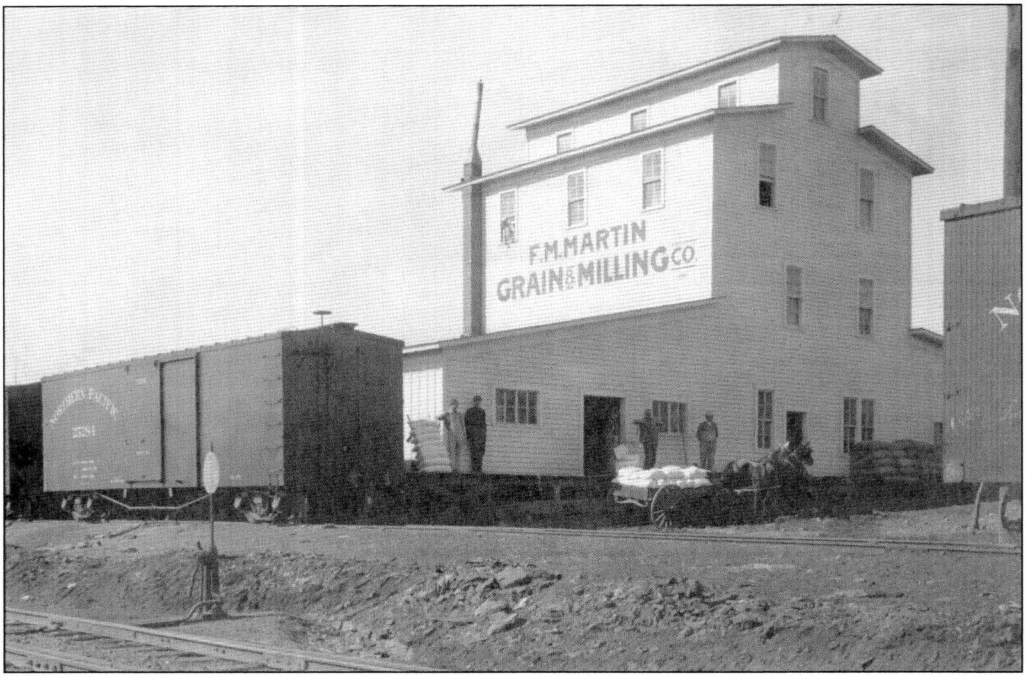

The F.M. Martin Grain and Milling Company was established by Frank M. Martin in 1907 in anticipation of the Washington Water Power Company substation, which would provide a reliable source of electricity. The substation was to be built for the interurban electric train line to Cheney. Prior to this business, Frank Martin had operated a livery stable, a creamery, and a hay and grain warehouse. (EWU 007-0584_2-3-1.)

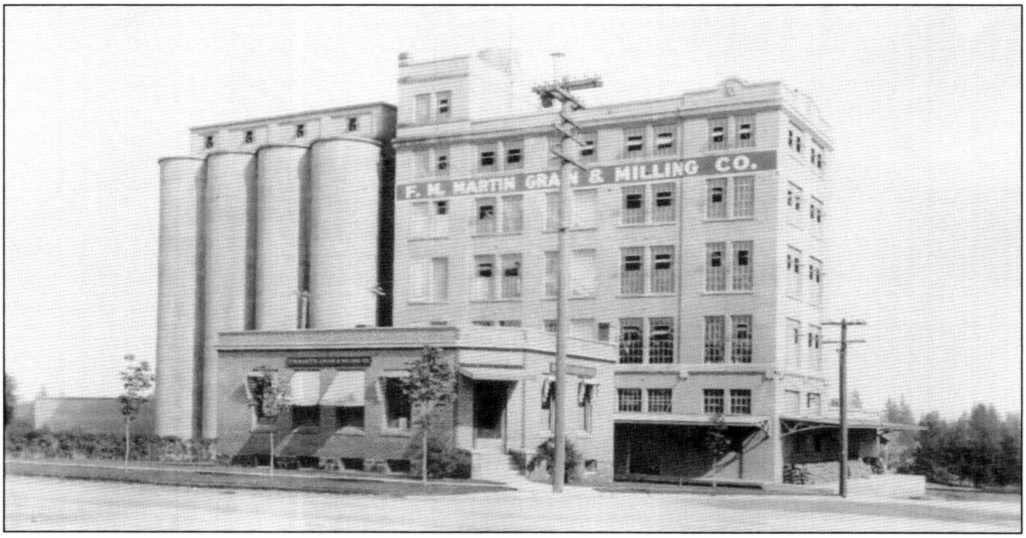

In 1917, Frank Martin rebuilt his mill with grain elevators on site, giving him the capacity to store large amounts of grain as well as mill it into flour at the same location. The nearby Northern Pacific Railway tracks facilitated this operation. Harvested grain could be brought to the storage elevators by train, milled into flour, and then shipped by train to clients. This photograph was taken around 1920.

Clarence D. Martin served as the governor of Washington from 1933 to 1941. This native of Cheney served on the city council and is the only person in the state's history to simultaneously serve as mayor and governor. While governor, he was instrumental in bringing about the Grand Coulee Dam project. Clarence took over his father's milling company in 1925 and sold the mill to the National Biscuit Company in 1946.

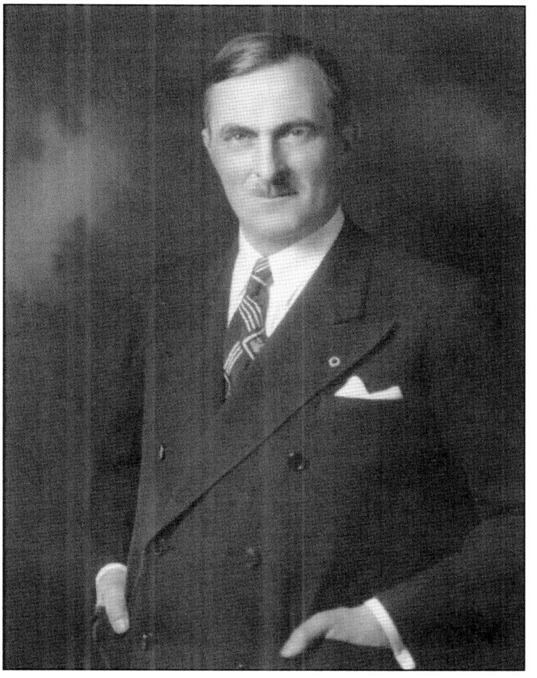

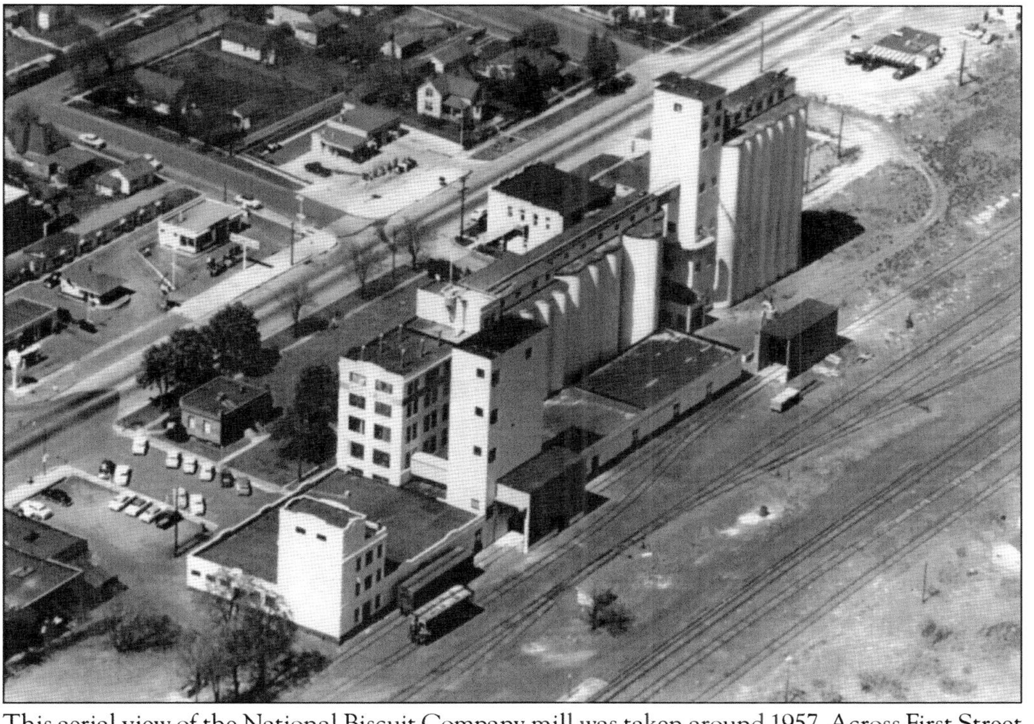

This aerial view of the National Biscuit Company mill was taken around 1957. Across First Street from the mill office building sits the Cheney Motel between two gas stations. Note the row of motel rooms behind the office with a space for a car between them. At the far right is the Fireside Restaurant, which was later remodeled and renamed the Willow Springs Station Restaurant.

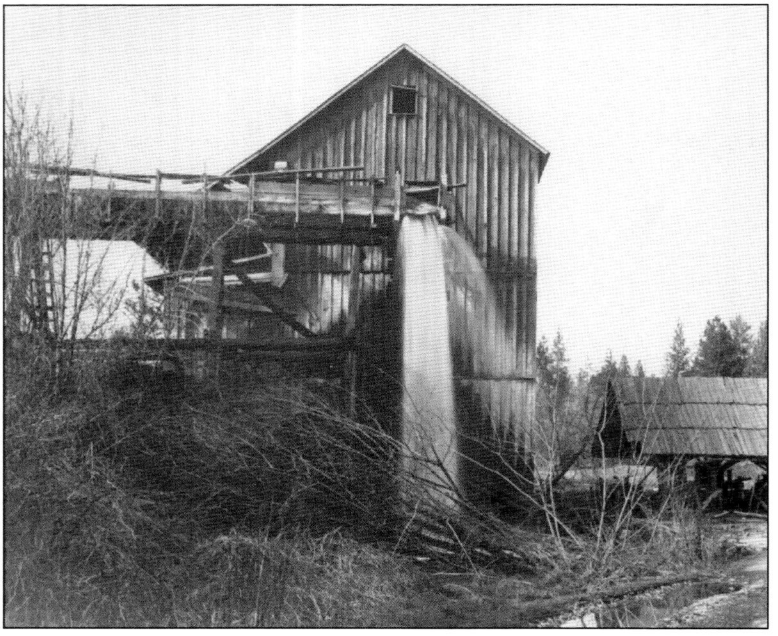

Built in 1880 by A.C. Chapman on the shore of the lake that bears his name, this mill first sawed only lumber. Flour milling equipment was added in 1897 by Wagner and Ole Dybdall Sr. The mill was still in operation for the surrounding farms on a custom basis by Ole Dybdall Jr. in the 1950s. This photograph was taken around 1910. (Washington State Digital Archives.)

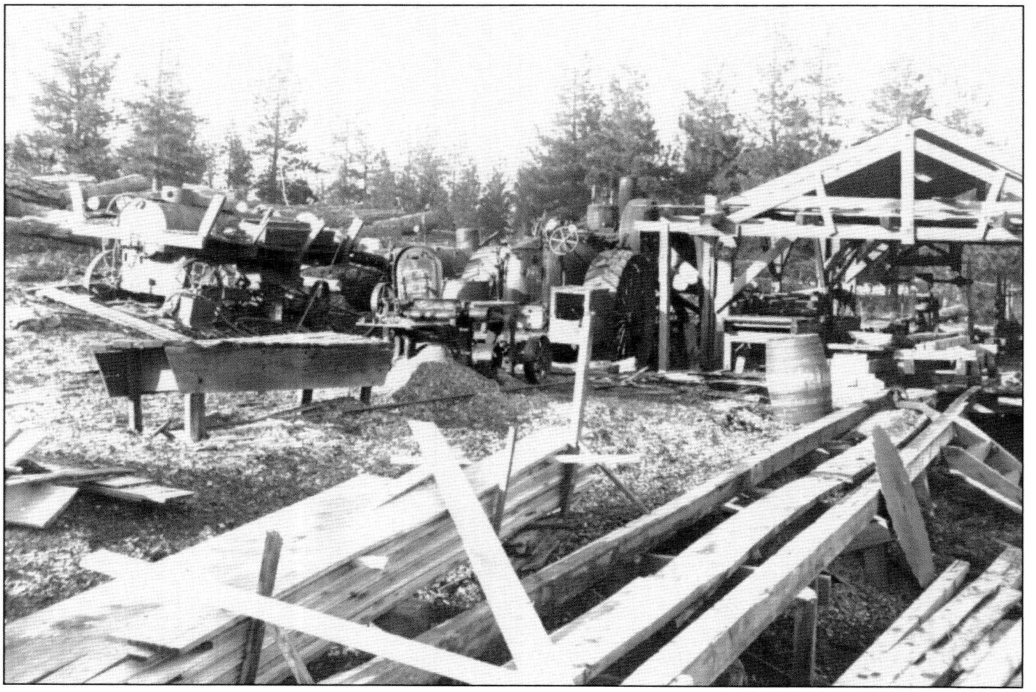

In 1906, there were eight sawmills operating within 10 miles of Cheney. This is believed to be Edgar Chambers's sawmill operation near Badger Lake, south of town. A steam engine sits next to the mill building to power the equipment. In the background on the left is a stack of logs and a wagon used for hauling them to the mill.

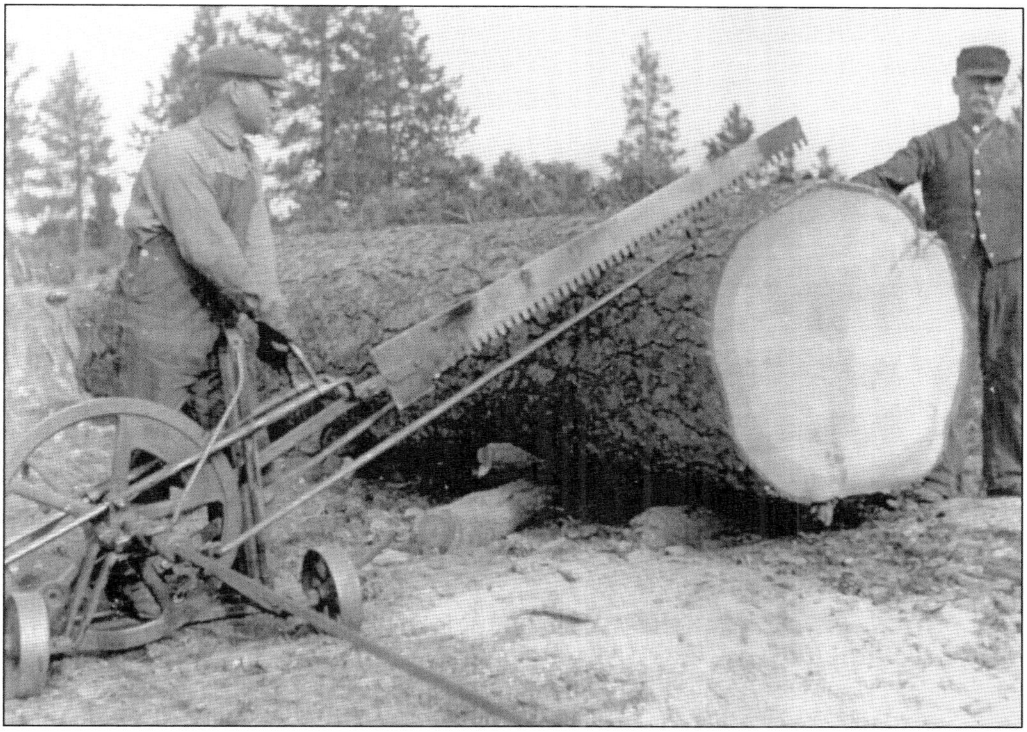

Most of the pine forest south of Cheney today is second growth, as the early settlers harvested the original trees to build homes, barns, fences, commercial buildings, wagons, and furniture. The steam-powered saw, such as this one from the early 1900s, eased the labor and cut the number of workers needed to supply the mills.

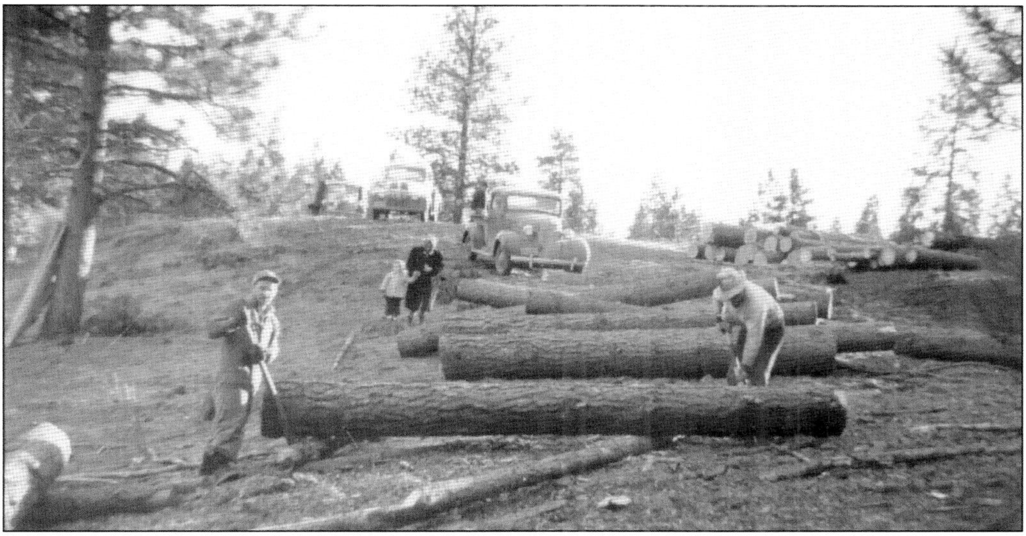

While the commercial lumber mills disappeared or converted to milling flour, individual farmers continued to harvest trees on their own land. In this photograph from around 1947, Barbara Babb and her mother, Bette, watch as Emery Babb and Roy Stevenson roll logs down a hill to the family's milling operation.

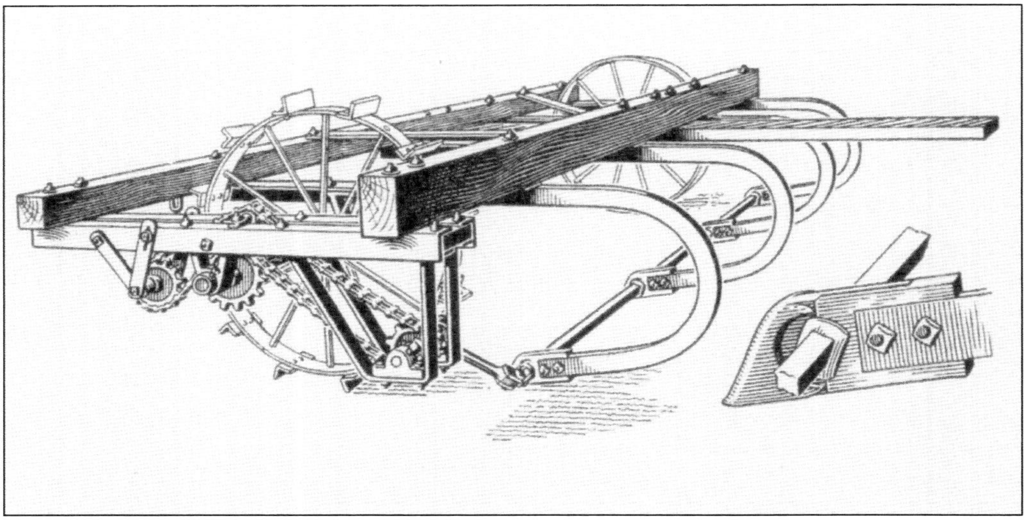

In the fall of 1907 while working his summer fallow field, 26-year-old Henry Kyle Wolfe had an inspiration. With the help of his 23-year-old brother, Cleve, he designed a rotating rod self-cleaning weeder that uprooted the weeds but left them on the ground to die while conserving the soil. A patent for the Rotary Rod Weeder was issued January 10, 1911.

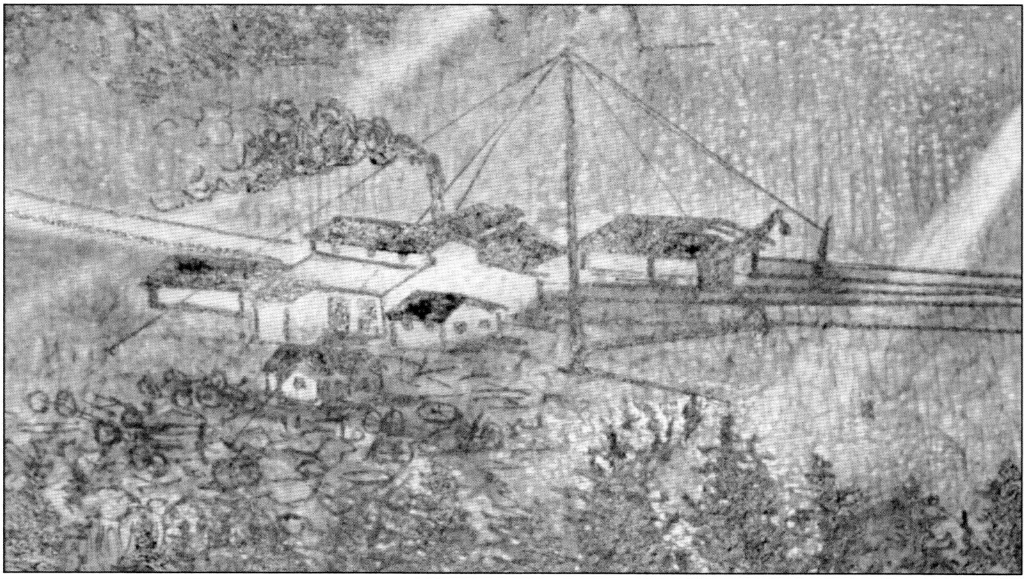

The Rotary Rod Weeder Manufacturing Company opened near Cheney Plaza Road in 1912 and was soon renamed the Cheney Weeder Company. Louis Van Patten was the general manager overseeing production of the farm implement. The building was destroyed by a fire on August 8, 1926. With a backlog of orders, workers returned to work within a few days using salvaged machinery.

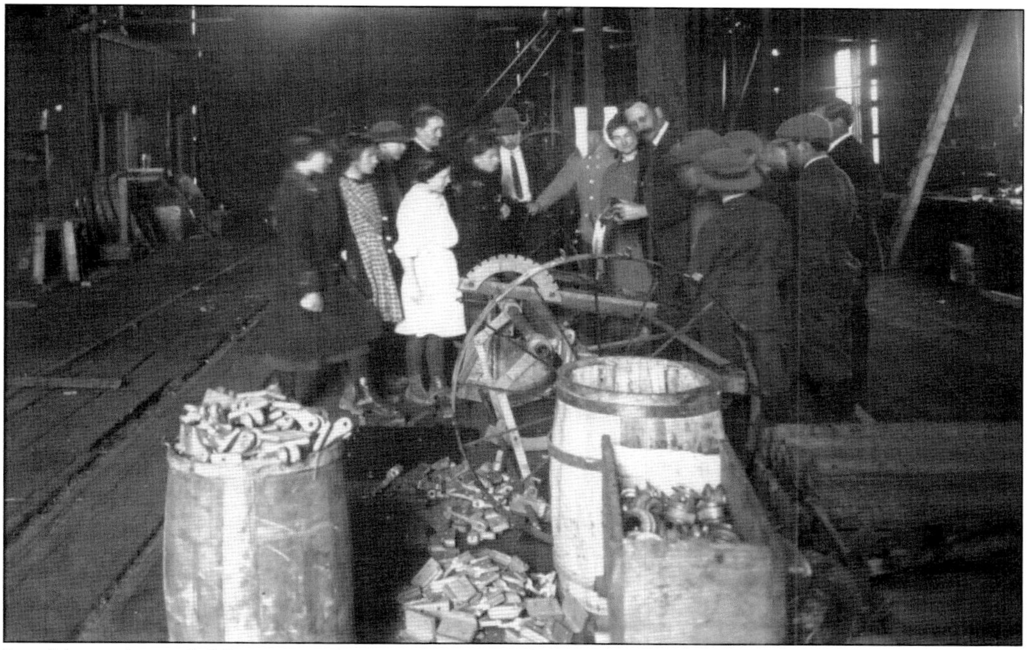

Just like today, a field trip to a factory was a popular outing for students of the Normal Training School, seen here around 1914. The making of the parts and the assembly of the weeders took place in the factory, which shipped nearly 300 Rotary Rod Weeders during 1915. General manager Louis Van Patten traveled throughout the Northwest to demonstrate the weeder to farmers.

Shown here around 1935, the second Cheney Weeder Company manufacturing plant was located south of the Northern Pacific Railway tracks between Cheney Spangle Road and G Street. The weeders were shipped all over the world. After the patent expired, the Cheney Weeder Company diversified, but the firm struggled. It was sold in 1952 and operations moved to Spokane in 1955. Today, the Cheney Weeder Company is located in Canada.

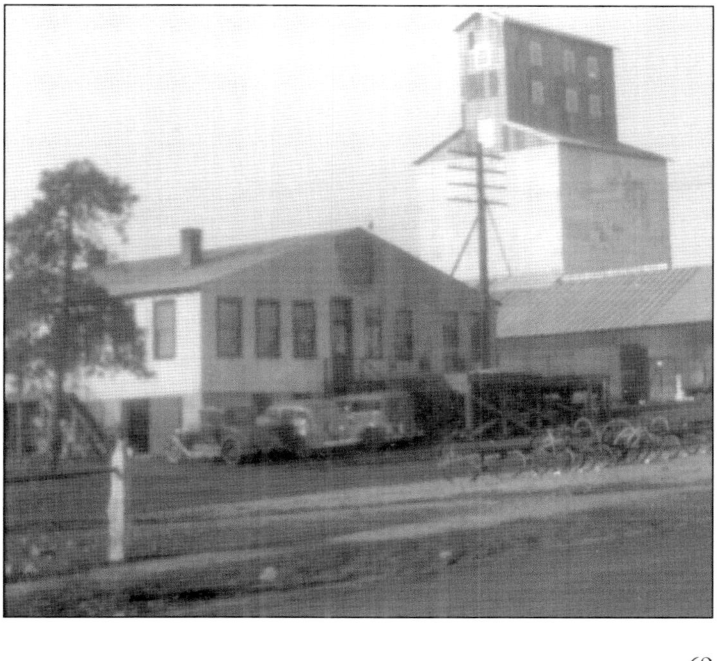

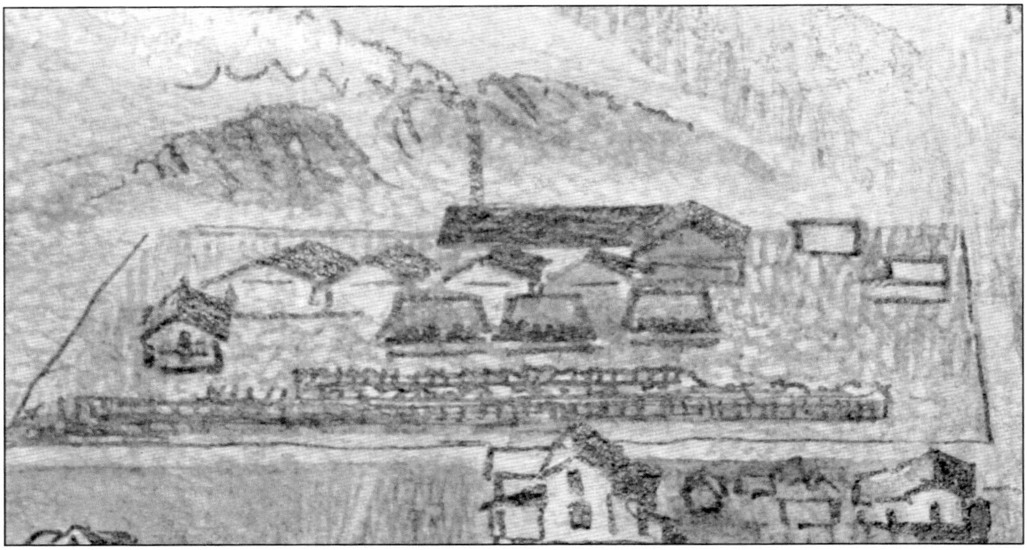

The Cheney Brick and Tile Manufacturing Company had a number of owners, starting with Charles Carreau in 1881. Most of the businesses in downtown were built with Cheney brick. The plant was located near the site of Cadet Hall on the EWU campus. In 1904, the company boasted of owning 20 acres of clay soil land. It employed 25 men and could produce 25,000 bricks per day.

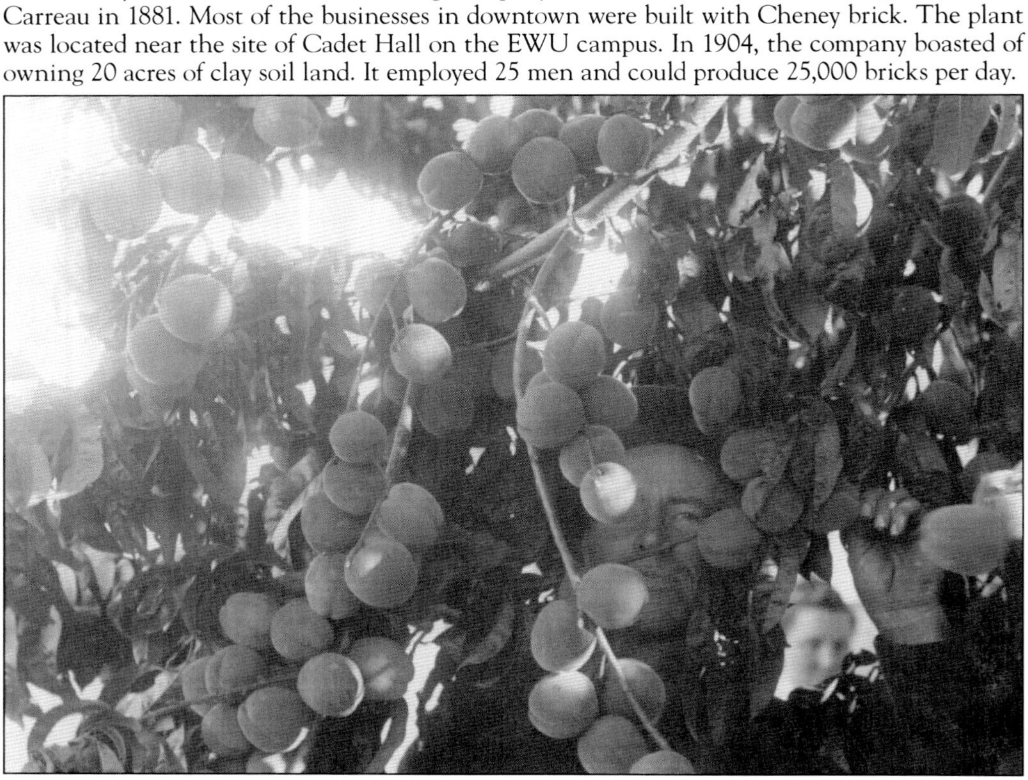

The dry-land fruit orchard industry thrived until about 1913, when drought and the emerging irrigated orchard business in Wenatchee killed it. Apples, pears, peaches, apricots, and cherries were shipped to Spokane and Seattle. Remnants of those orchards still dot the countryside. In this 1914 photograph, Anton Ottomeier peaks out from among the branches and his daughter, Maimie, is seen behind his arm.

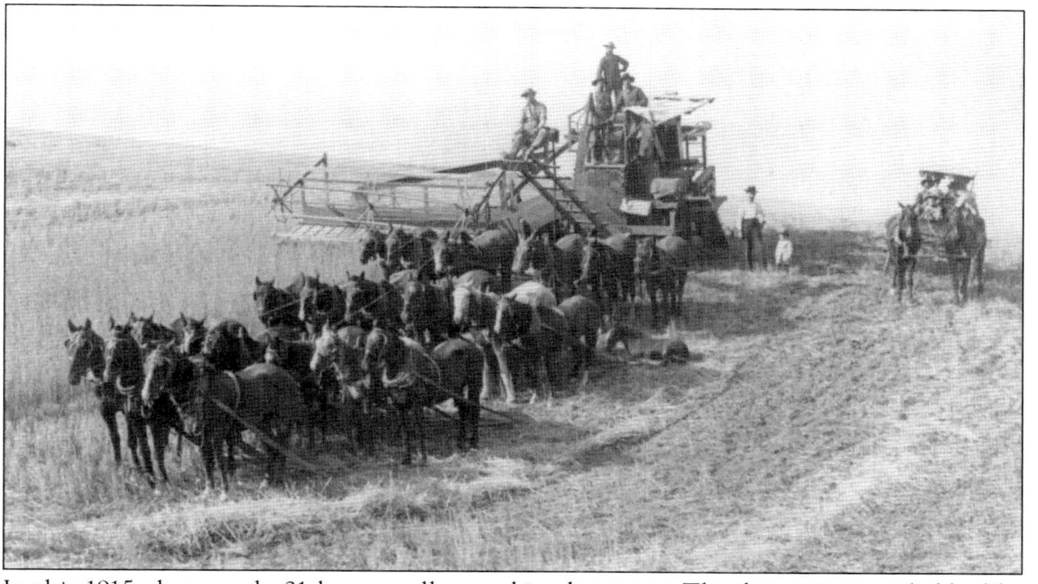

In this 1915 photograph, 21 horses pull a combine harvester. The driver sits on a ladder-like platform that was slanted out over the last row of horses. This design was not well suited to the steep Palouse hills, as the team dropped out of his sight on the hill crests, and his platform sank into the team in the valleys. Note the young horse lying near its mother.

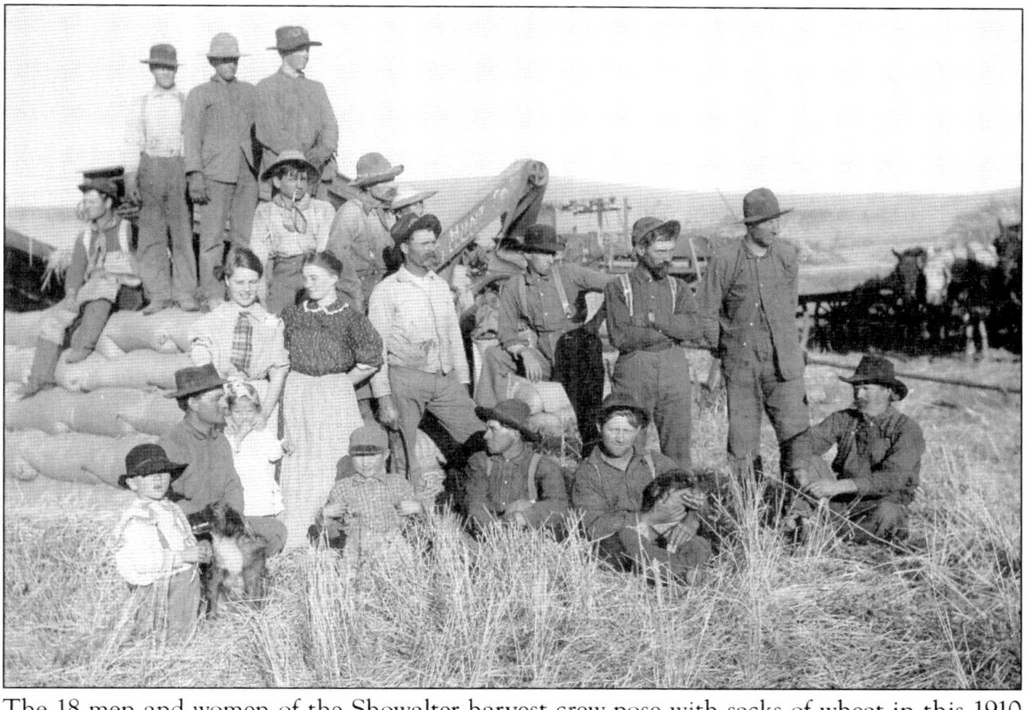

The 18 men and women of the Showalter harvest crew pose with sacks of wheat in this 1910 photograph by A.A. Ames. Standing at left in the round hat is Otto Schmitt; George William Showalter is seated at center front with his head turned, and the woman in the dark print dress with apron and white lace collar is Etta Harris Showalter, wife of Marshall Showalter.

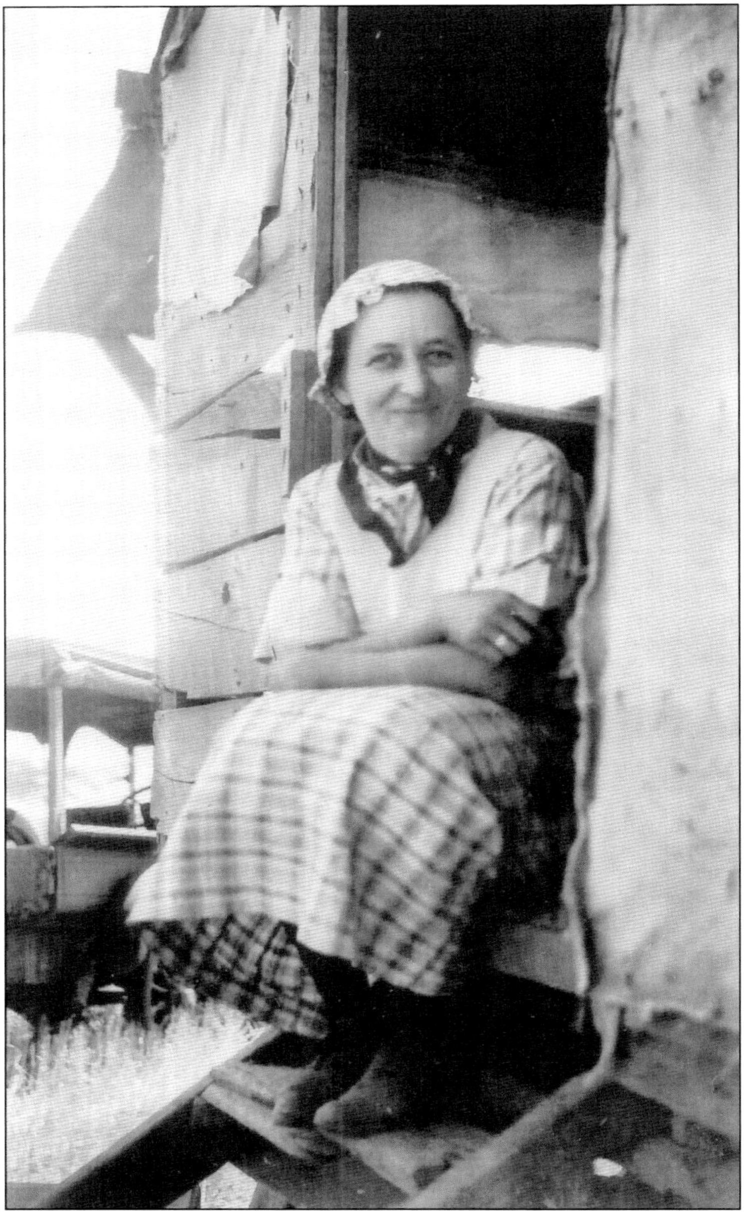

Mary Showalter is seated in the doorway of the cook wagon, which was set up near the thresher. Usually run by two to three women, the cook house had a stove at one end and tables with benches along the sides. It had a window or removable slants for ventilation. Preparing meals was hot, sweltering work. The cook was up at 3:00 a.m. each morning to fire up the stove and get the breakfast ready by 5:00 a.m. so the men could be in the field by daybreak. Her workday did not end until 10:00 or 11:00 p.m. The women prepared bread, biscuits, vegetables, meat, potatoes, and gravy for up to 30 very hungry men. They served four meals a day: breakfast, dinner, supper, and a lunch of sandwiches, along with a morning and afternoon coffee break. Harvest time was also a prime opportunity for farm girls to meet young men during meals or when riding out to deliver sandwiches in the field.

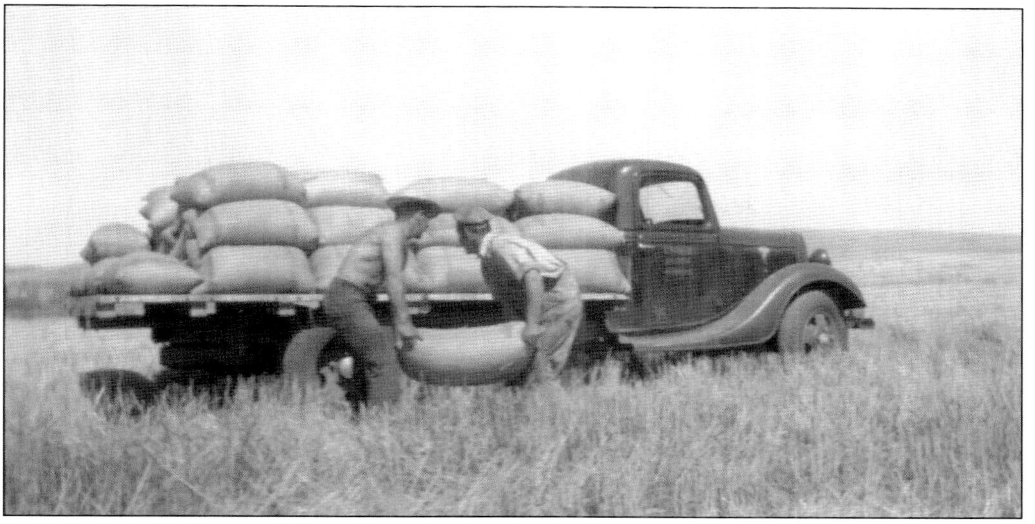

In 1940, Jack Philleo and Wisey Carey load sacks of wheat onto their 1935 Ford truck. A sack-sewer stitched a double half hitch around one end of the bag to form an ear on the sack. He then stitched nine to eleven stitches across the top, finishing with two more half stitches, making a second ear and closing the sack. A sack of grain typically weighed around 130 pounds.

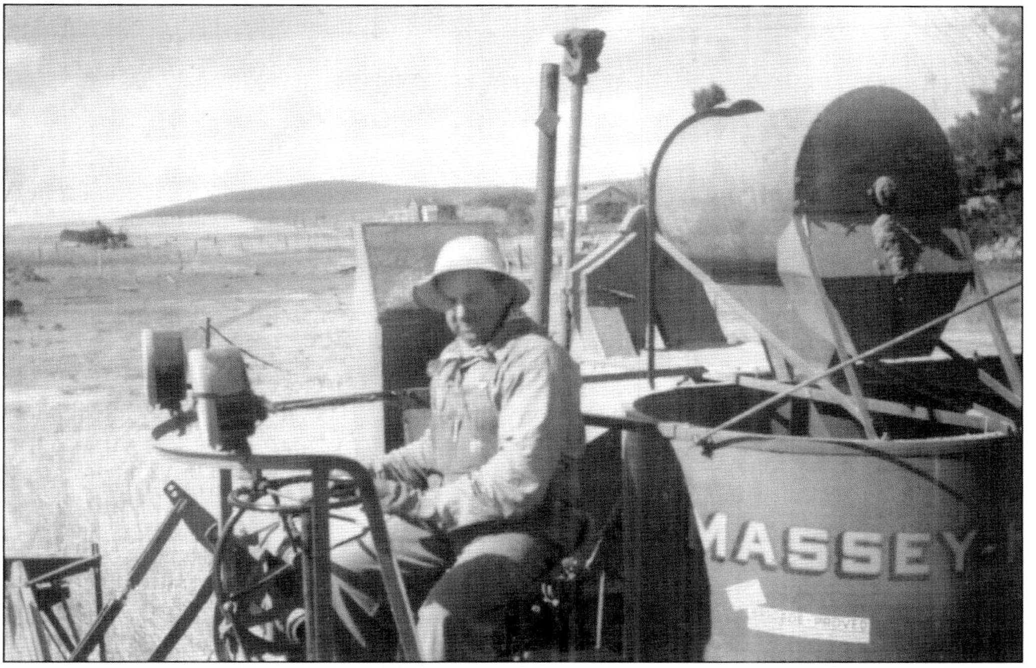

Carl O.C. Johnson is shown here in his Massey-Harris combine in August 1946. He owned the first self-propelled combine in the area. With the tractor incorporated into the machine along with a grain storage bin, the modern combine was born. With large capacity grain tanks on board, each combine driver could harvest over 100 acres a day. (Courtesy of Margit Johnson.)

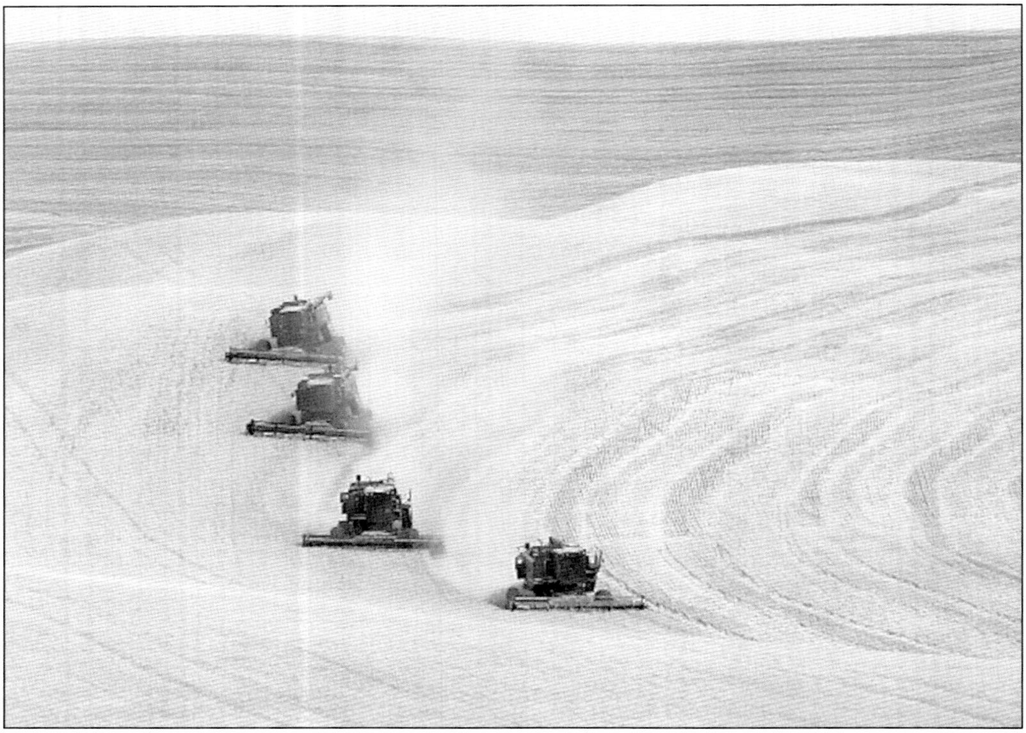

In this 2007 photograph, four combines make quick work of harvest on the Bafus place south of Cheney. The large harvest crews that fueled the economies of small towns are now gone; there are no more sack-jigs, sack-sewers, pick-up men, header-drivers, teamsters, strawbucks, forkers, engineers, firemen, hoedown men, roustabouts, tankees, cook wagon crews, or warehouse loaders.

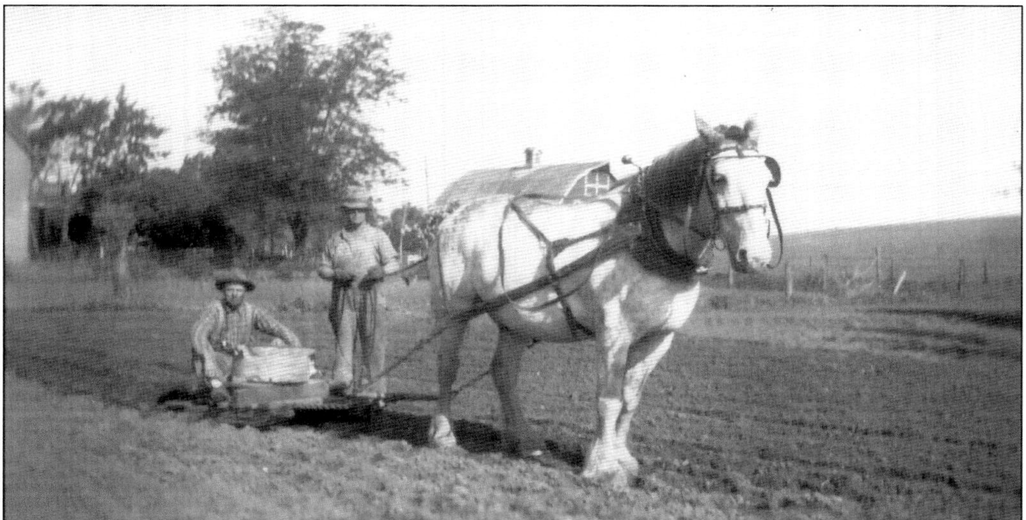

Edwin Philleo, standing, and an unidentified farm hand are shown here planting a field of potatoes. Cheney grocers contracted with farmers to provide produce and eggs for their stores. Everything from corn, turnips, cabbage, and spinach to tomatoes, watermelon, peaches, and apples were supplied by local farmers. When it was not in season, it was not in the store.

Some of the earliest pioneers arrived driving a herd of cattle, which they could sell to the military. In those early days, cattle roamed freely, mixing with others through most of the year. Sometimes ranchers found they might gain a few head during roundup. It was difficult to dispute if the cattle were quickly branded. This unidentified fellow poses in his buffalo-hide chaps in the scablands near Williams Lake.

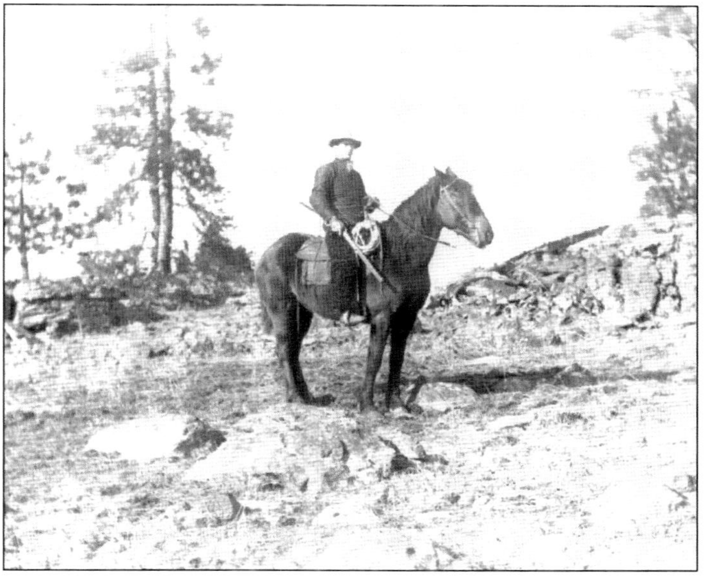

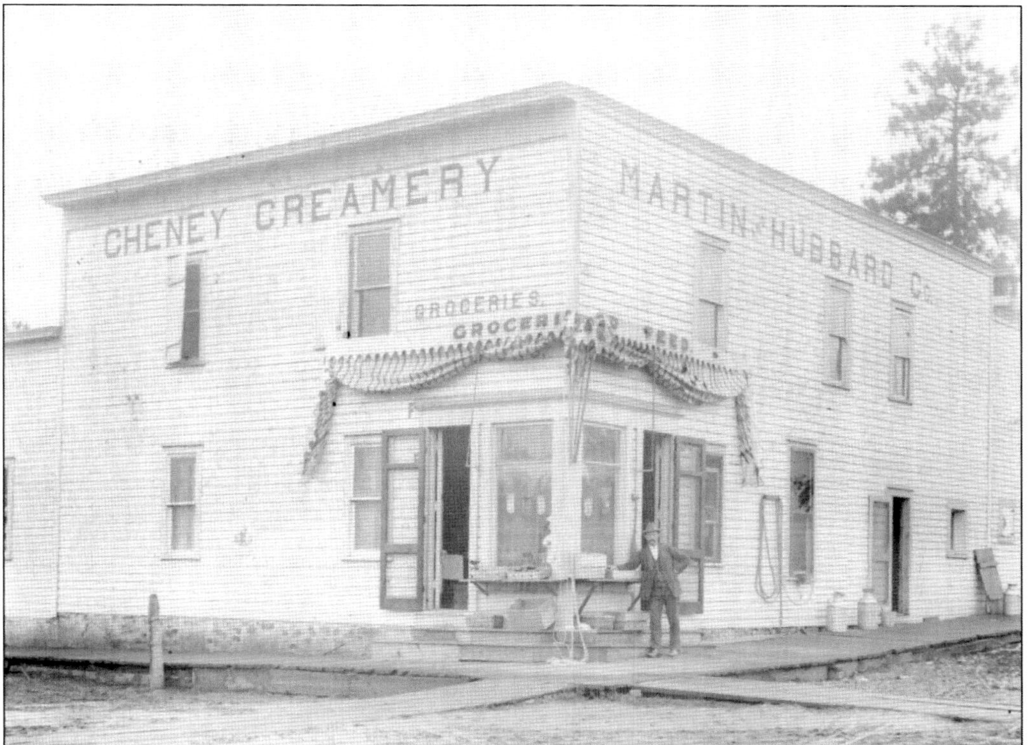

Frank Martin and Willis Hubbard established the Cheney Creamery in 1890 at Second and G Streets. By 1897, the company produced one-third of all the cheese in Washington, the largest producer in the state. The success was credited to German immigrant Frederick Reuter, who was hired as cheese maker. The Cheney Creamery closed in 1899, but Reuter opened his Cheney Cheese Factory in 1903 on Cheney Spangle Road.

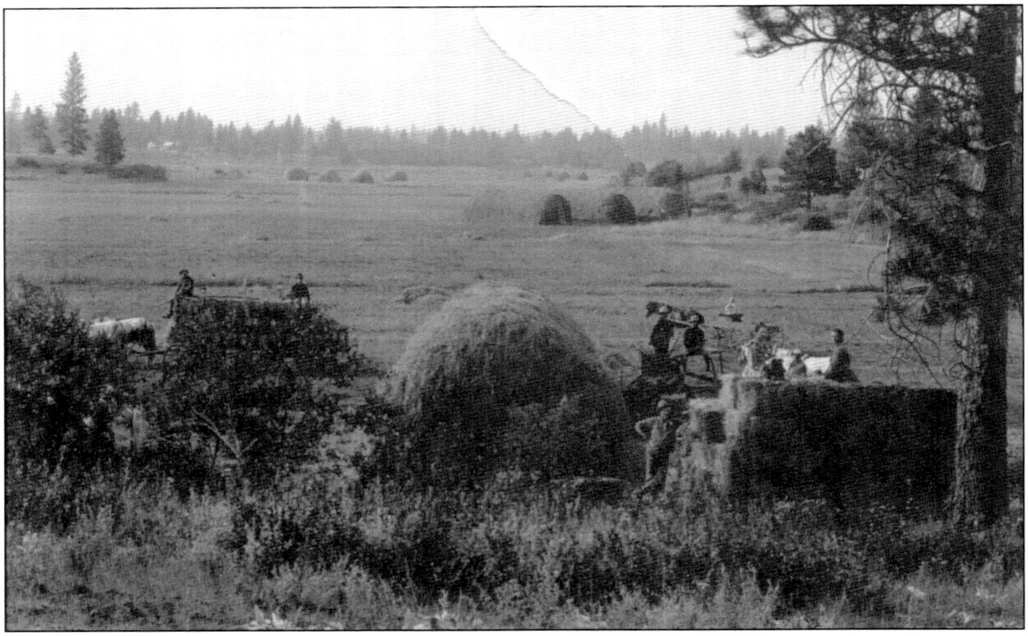

James Elmer Burbank's 150-acre meadow, shown here in 1906, was about half a mile south of Cheney. He and other farmers drained the shallow lakes to plant Timothy hay. It was cut and raked into large windrows, then taken to stacks or baled on buck rakes. Both stacks and bales can be seen here.

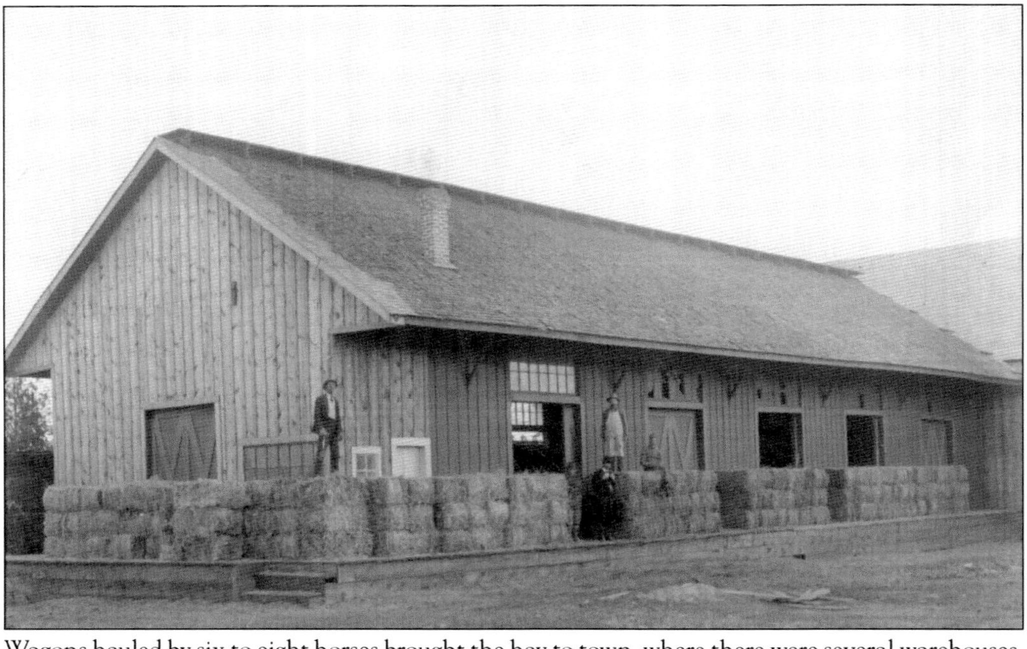

Wagons hauled by six to eight horses brought the hay to town, where there were several warehouses. The Burbank Hay and Grain Warehouse was located at the foot of G Street next to the Northern Pacific Railway track. This highly desirable Timothy hay was shipped to other eastern Washington towns, as well as Portland, Seattle, Idaho, Montana, and British Columbia.

Six

CHANGING MAIN STREET

When Laura Tyler and her husband, John, arrived in their wagon in October 1880, she later described a scene of scattered smoke columns rising from tents and cabins on the hill. She noted there was a blacksmith shop, a general store in a lean-to, and a newspaper press sheltered under a tree. The following year, as home to the Spokane County seat, Cheney's business district stretched from Pine to Union Streets.

Many of the staple businesses of the 19th and early 20th centuries have disappeared. There are no more livery stables, blacksmiths, wagon and saddle makers, no slaughterhouse, creameries, shoe repair shops, or furniture makers and undertakers.

Electricity and telephones first appeared in 1890. The electric company operated in the building known today as the Leifer Apartments.

Cheney had a number of early newspapers including Lucien Kellogg's *Northwest Tribune*, *Cheney Sentinel*, the short-lived *Cheney Leader*, and *Cheney Free Press*, which launched April 10, 1896.

There were a number of silent movie houses in the 1910s and 1920s. La Melodeon cinema, later renamed the Pix Theater, opened October 10, 1929, featuring the new "talkies." The cinema operated until 1964.

Rail was the primary means of moving people and goods after 1881, and the town was laid out in line with the track rather than the compass. Up until the freeway bypassed the town in 1964, the state highway went through Cheney, which had 13 gas stations at one time to serve motorists.

Banks, groceries, and hardware stores may change names, but they remain a staple of commerce. The Bank of America is the successor of financial institutions at First Street and College Avenue, going back to the Bank of Cheney in the 1880s. The Owl Pharmacy has changed locations, but it has an over 100-year history in Cheney.

Improved transportation and growth in Spokane closed Cheney's department store, clothing, and jewelry store. While the business community has struggled in recent decades to find a new niche, entrepreneurs are always willing to try new ideas.

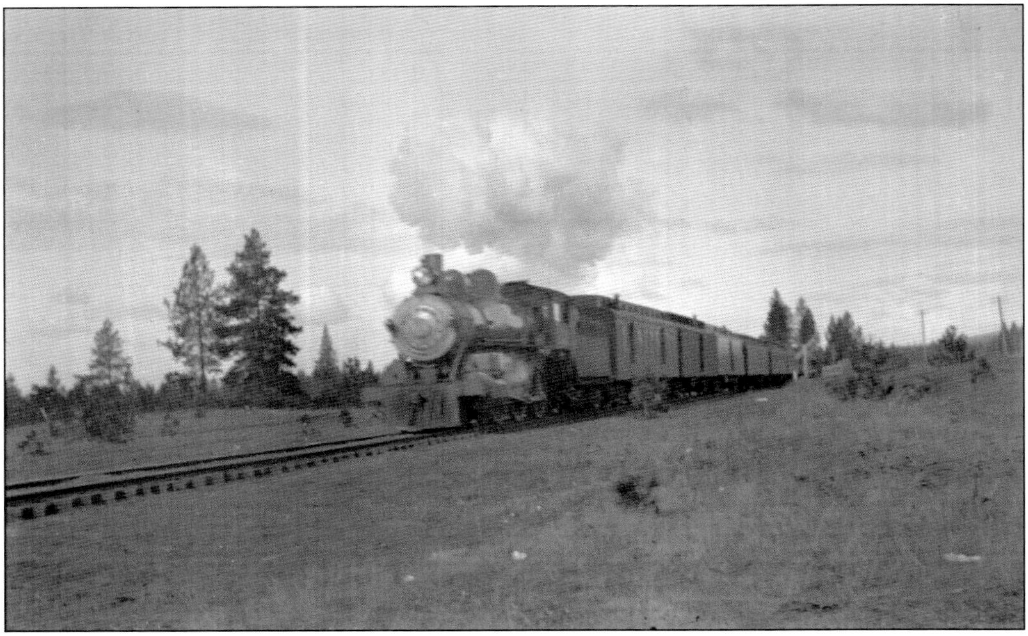

As the track bed was graded through Cheney in 1880, the town boomed with the promise of immigrants and commerce. The first passenger and freight trains began to operate as soon as the skeleton tracks were laid in June 1881. Over the next several years, train speeds increased as the tracks were improved, until the railway could boast that one could travel to Portland, Oregon, in less than a day.

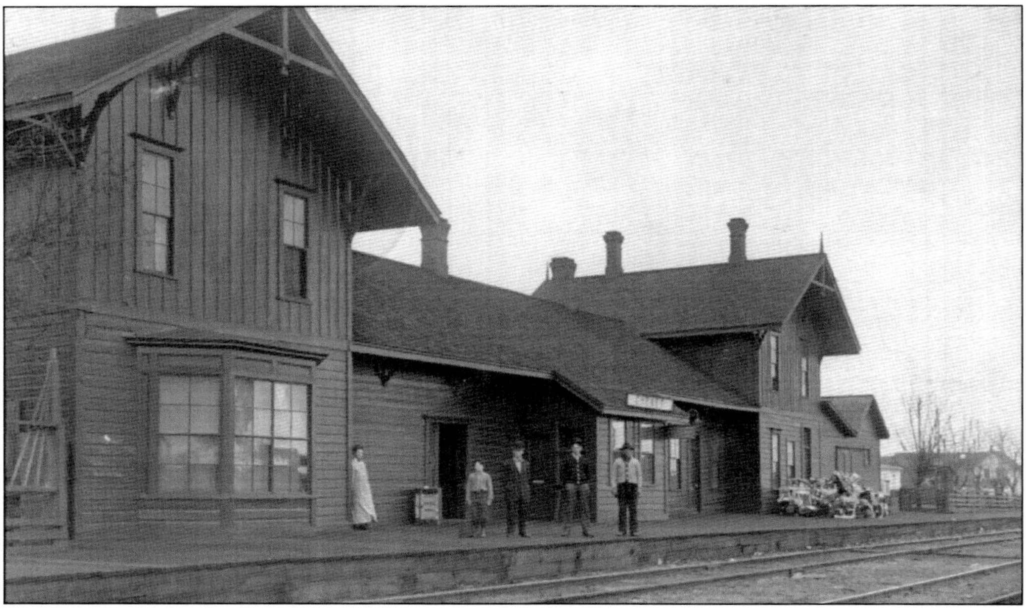

The Northern Pacific Railway depot at the foot of E Street, now College Avenue, was completed in 1881. The depot served as the gateway to Cheney, bringing people, orders from the Sears and Roebuck catalog, horses and livestock, or oranges from California as a special treat at Christmas. This postcard photograph is from 1910.

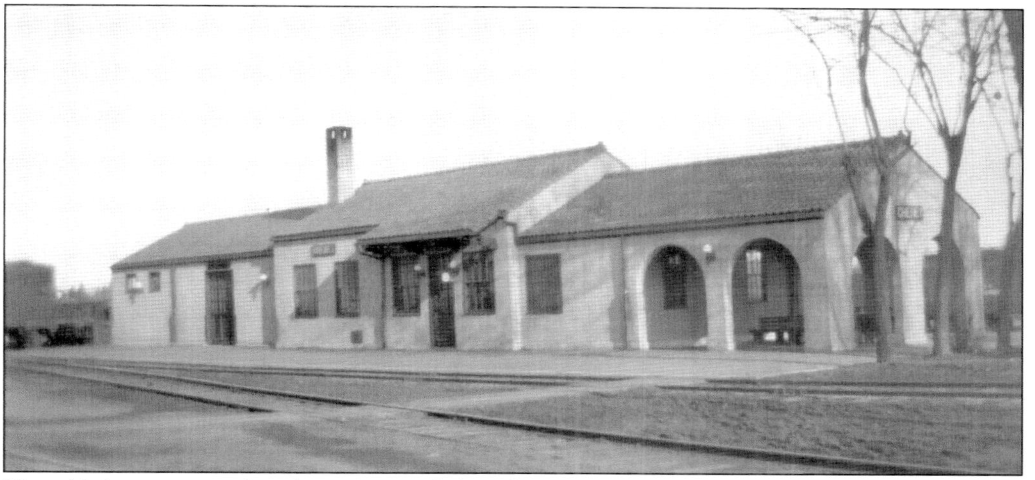

The old depot was replaced in 1929, and the *Cheney Free Press* boasted, "The depot is Spanish style in stucco with a tile roof and red brick platform. There is an arch-roofed outside waiting room, an inside waiting room, business and telegraph office, and baggage room. The freight platform is the same elevation as [the] car doors, so that freight may be trucked directly to the baggage room without any lifting."

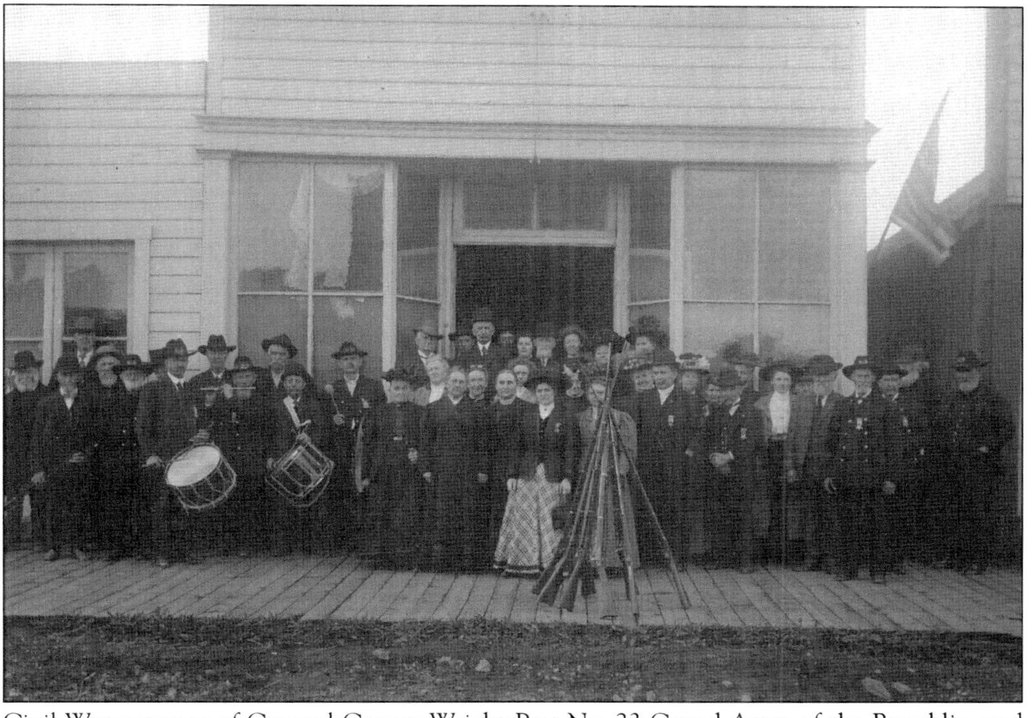

Civil War veterans of General George Wright Post No. 23 Grand Army of the Republic, and its auxiliary, Women's Relief Corp General George Wright Corp No. 8, pose in front of their meeting hall around 1890. The hall was on the north side of First Street between F and G Streets, where a bank parking lot is today. The building also housed the office of the *Cheney Sentinel* newspaper.

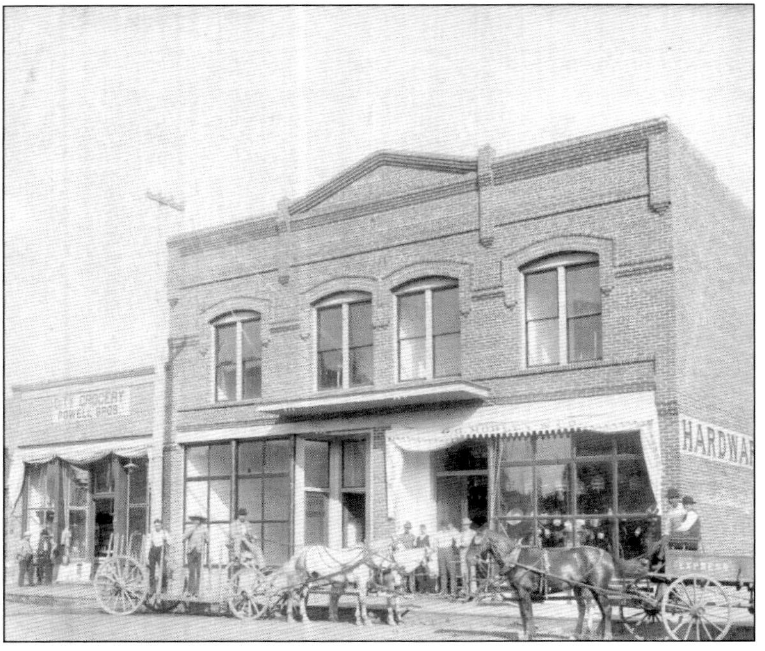

This photograph was taken to commemorate the grand opening of the G.G. Mobley and Company hardware store in the newly completed Pomeroy building at 407–411 First Street on July 3, 1891. George Gayle Mobley stands at left in front of the door. Mobley closed his store and moved his family to Canada in 1897. The brick building next store is the City Grocery, operated by the Powell brothers.

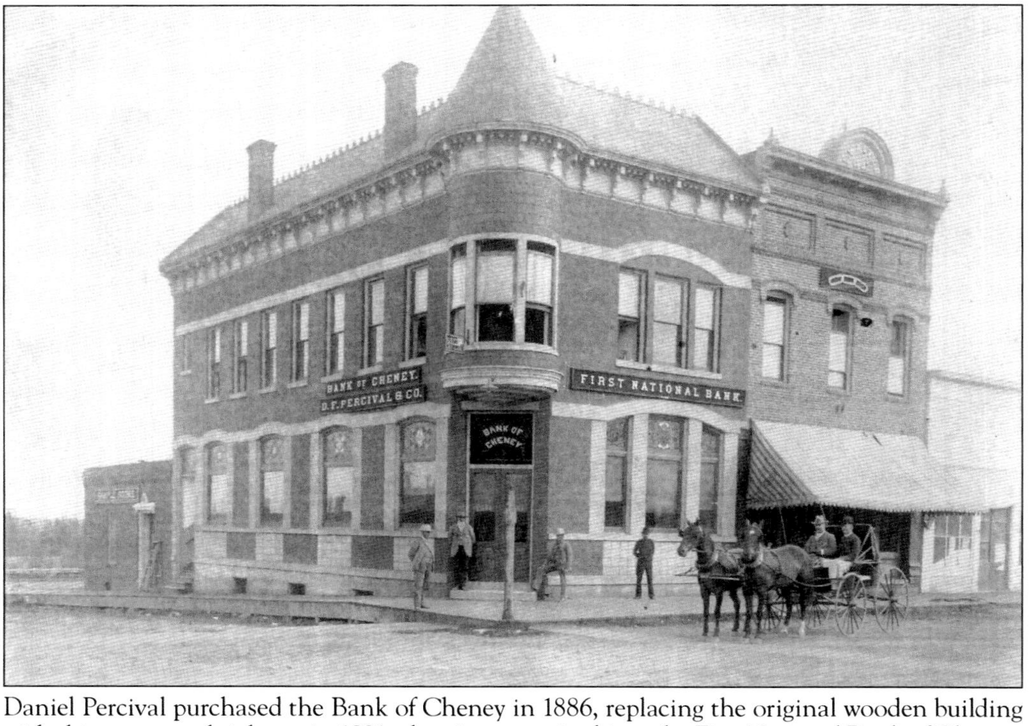

Daniel Percival purchased the Bank of Cheney in 1886, replacing the original wooden building with this two-story brick one in 1891 when it reorganized into the First National Bank of Cheney. The sign on the second-story turret window advertises DeWitt H. Fisk, attorney at law. Next door is Louis Walter's Harness and Saddlery. Behind the bank, sample rooms were available for rent to businessmen to show their wares.

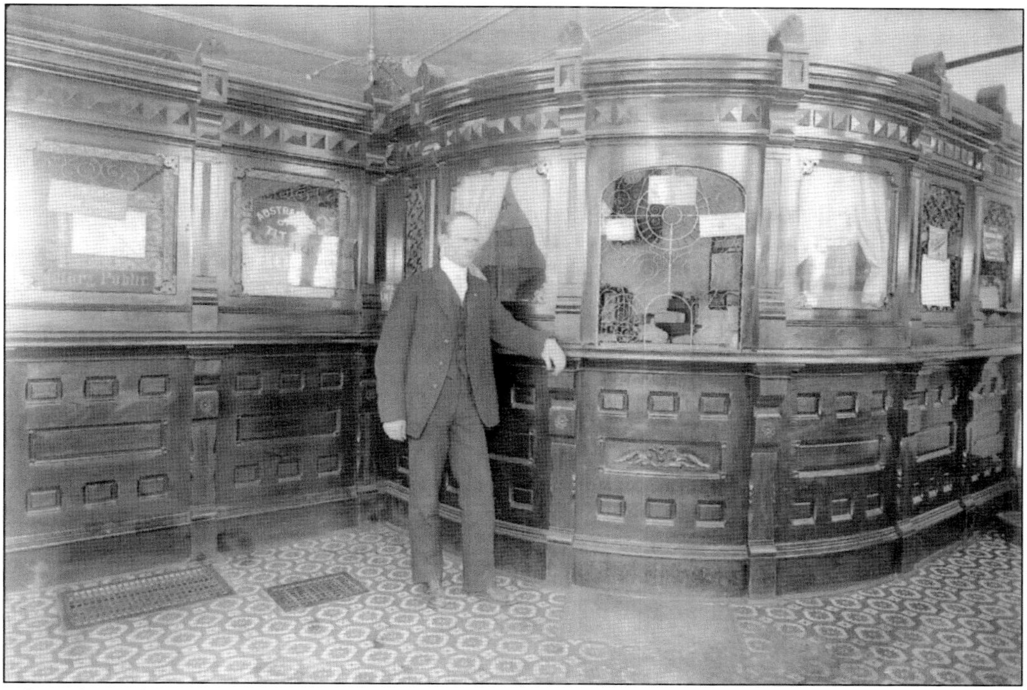

Edward Franklin Betz posed for this photograph inside the National Bank of Cheney when he became president in 1908. The Bank of Cheney later merged to become part of SeaFirst Bank and then, a branch of Bank of America. From the earliest days of Cheney to today, a bank has operated on the corner of First Street and College Avenue.

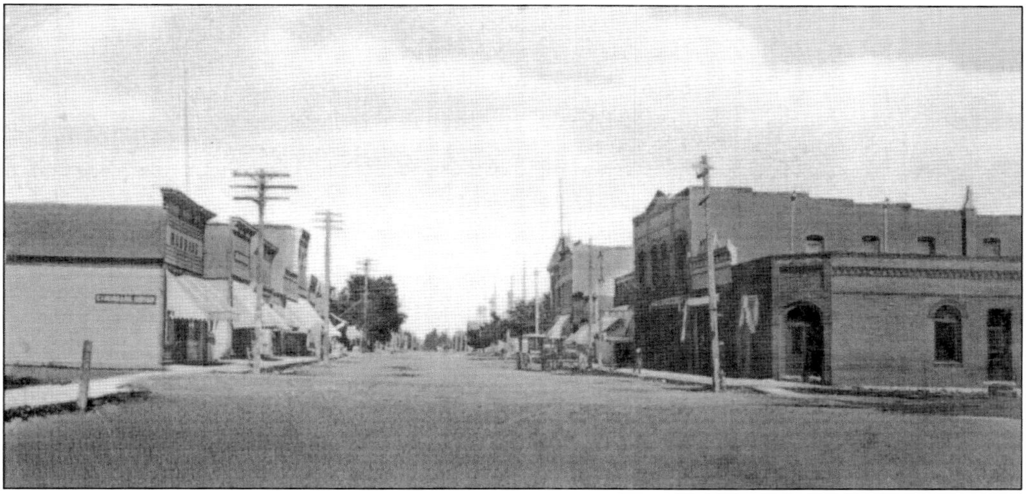

This postcard view looking east on First Street from F Street around 1900 shows C.I. Hubbard's Grocery on the left and the post office in the one-story corner brick building on the right. Note the line of poles carrying electricity and telephone lines through the business district. Most businesses had phones by this time, though many residences did not.

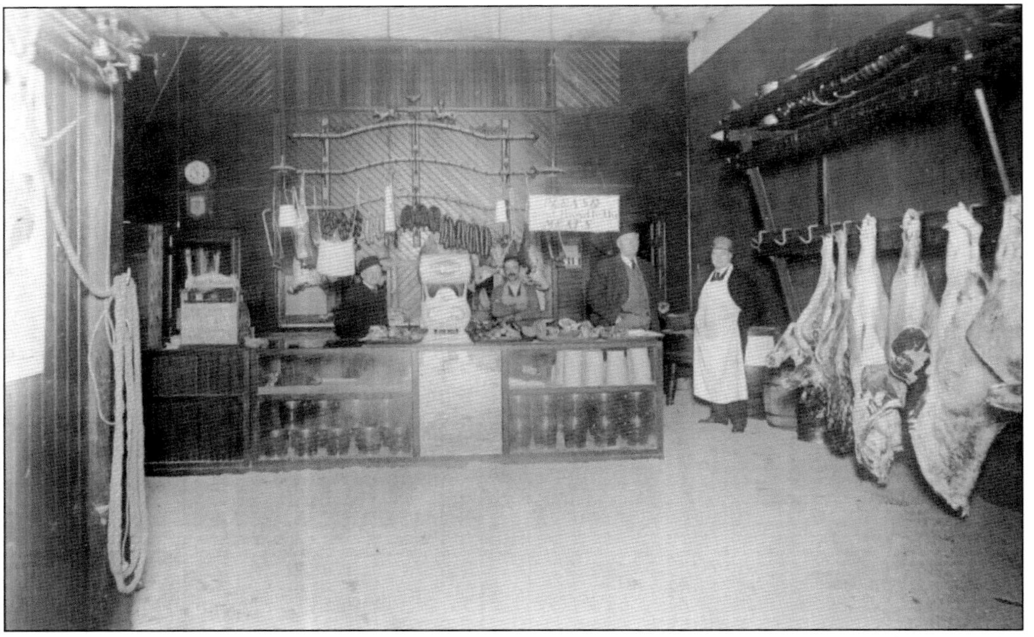

James Elmer Burbank, of Burbank Hay and Grain Warehouse, is standing, second from right, inside either O.B. Royce's or A.J. Mill's meat market around 1900. Cheney had at least two meat markets through the 1940s. The Holmes brothers' meat market of the 1960s was the last market offering local beef, lamb, and pork to residents.

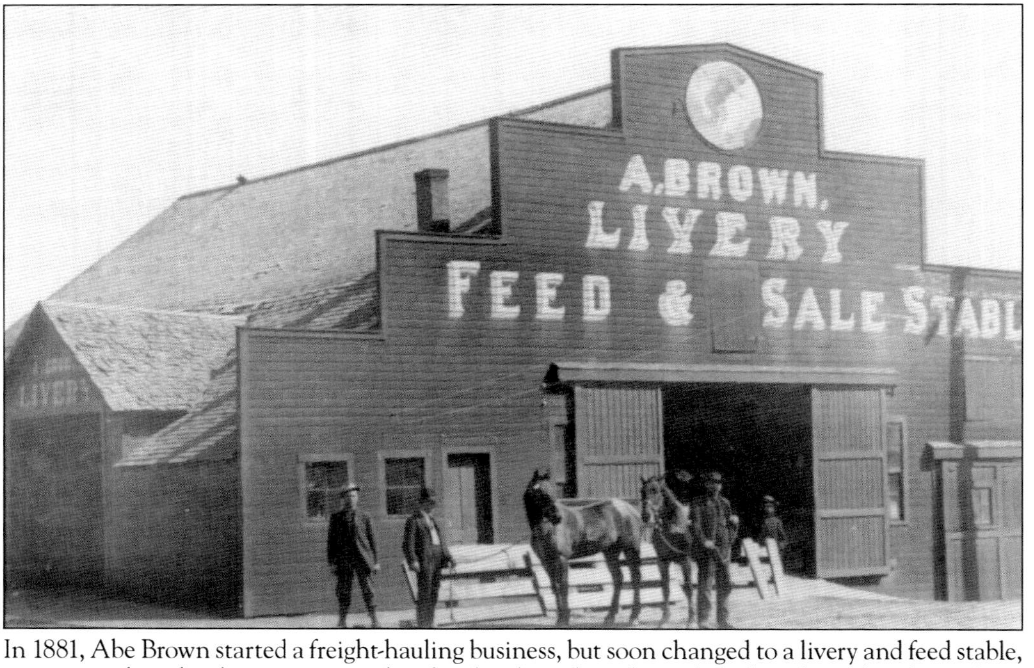

In 1881, Abe Brown started a freight-hauling business, but soon changed to a livery and feed stable, catering to long-haul wagon trains that freighted goods and people before the railroad spur lines were laid. He is holding a horse lead at the center of this photograph from about 1890. His stable was located at the corner of Second and F Streets. It burned down in 1916.

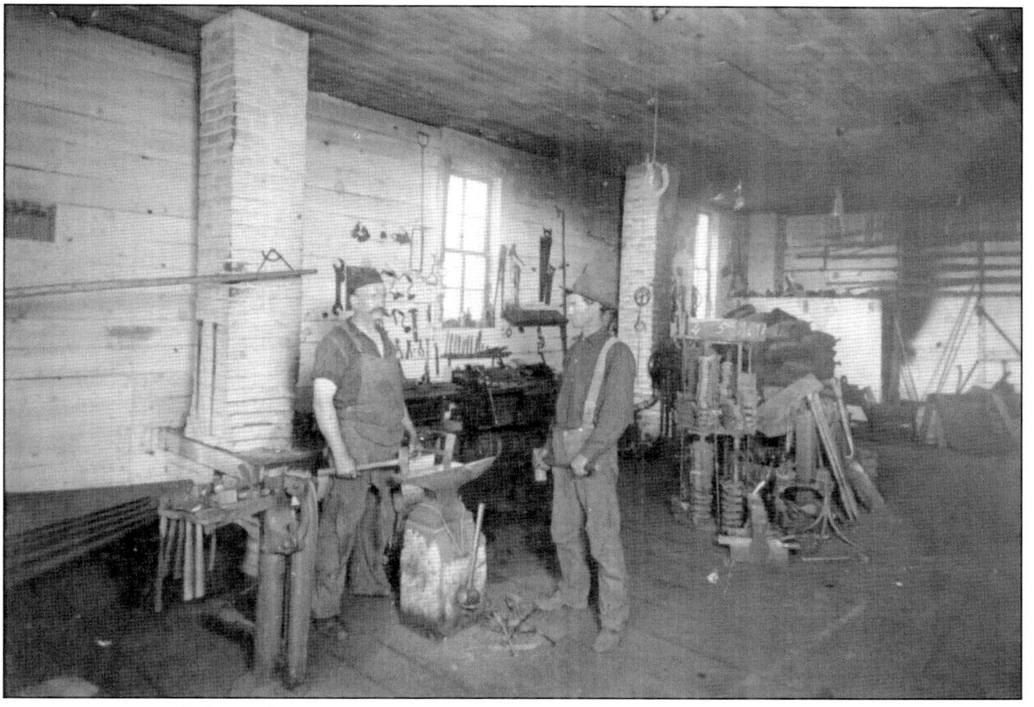

Pete C. LaCasse (left) and Alva Briner stand inside the People's Horseshoeing Shop at Second and F Streets around 1908. With the advent of automobiles, LaCasse converted much of his business to repairing cars in the early 1910s, though his blacksmithing skills were used for many more years in keeping farm equipment operational. The Owl Pharmacy stands on the site today.

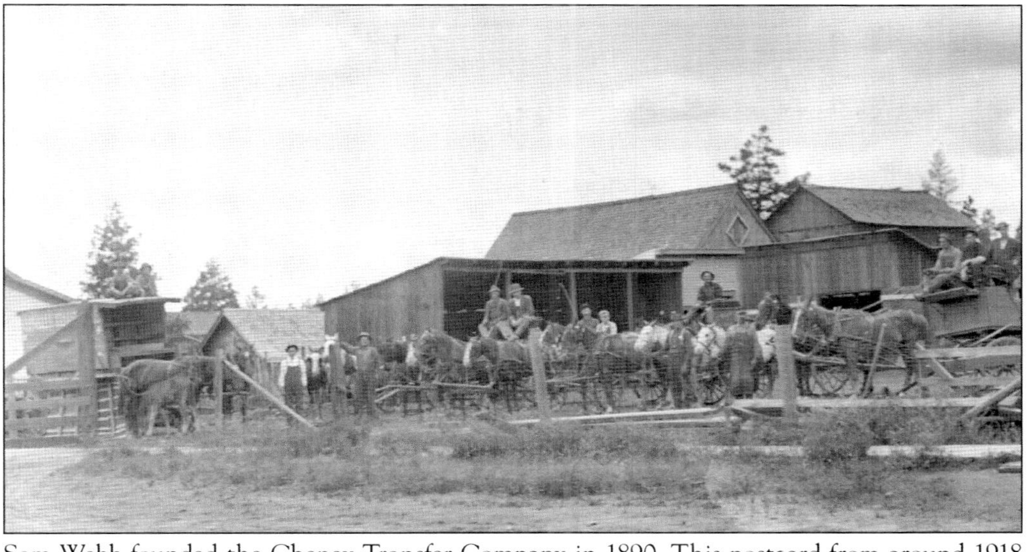

Sam Webb founded the Cheney Transfer Company in 1890. This postcard from around 1918 shows the draying operation located on Third Street near Union Street. His company hauled freight from the railroad station to businesses, as well as serving as the moving van of the day to move households. Sam Webb started the first bus line to Spokane in the 1920s, and served as a county commissioner in the 1930s.

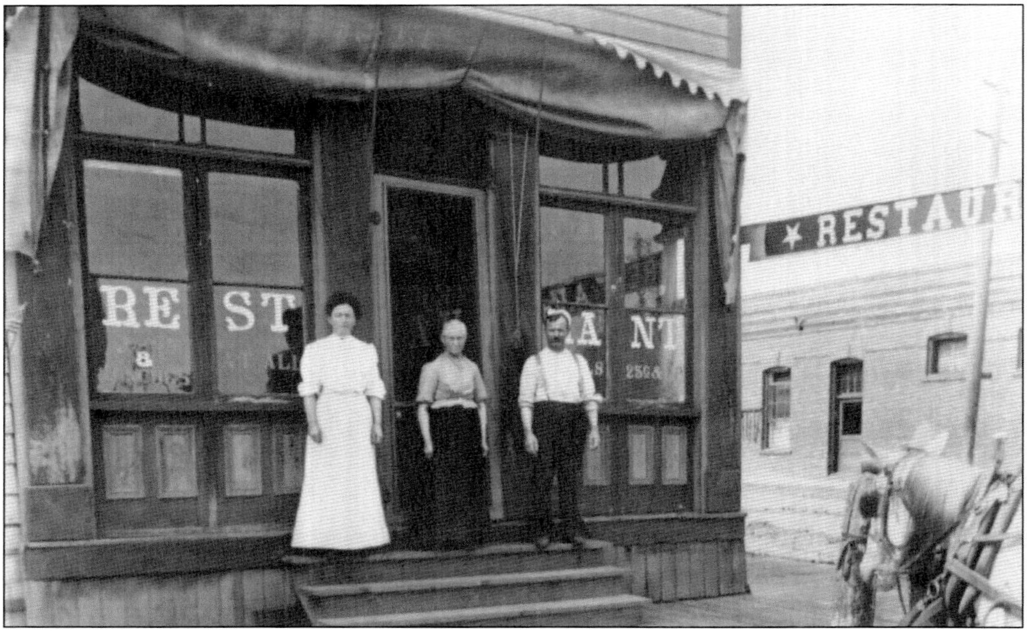

The owners of the Star Restaurant pose on the front steps of their establishment around 1904. The restaurant was on the corner of First and F Streets, where the Owl Pharmacy parking lot is today. Restaurants and lunch counters were found throughout the business district on First Street and on Railroad Street facing the tracks. (EWU 007-0584_2-38-1.)

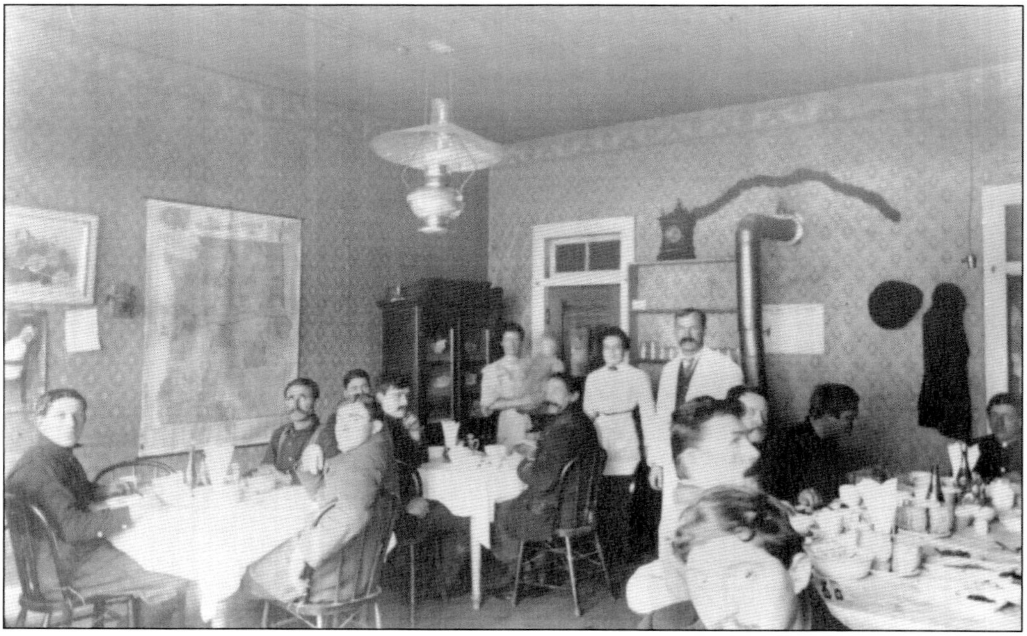
Single men living in boarding houses or light-housekeeping rooms ate one or more of their daily meals in a restaurant, such as the Star, pictured here. Most restaurants and lunch counters offered a kind of prepaid card. Each 10¢, 15¢, or 25¢ meal was punched or marked when purchased. Single women did not eat in restaurants on their own. (EWU 007-0584_2-38-2.)

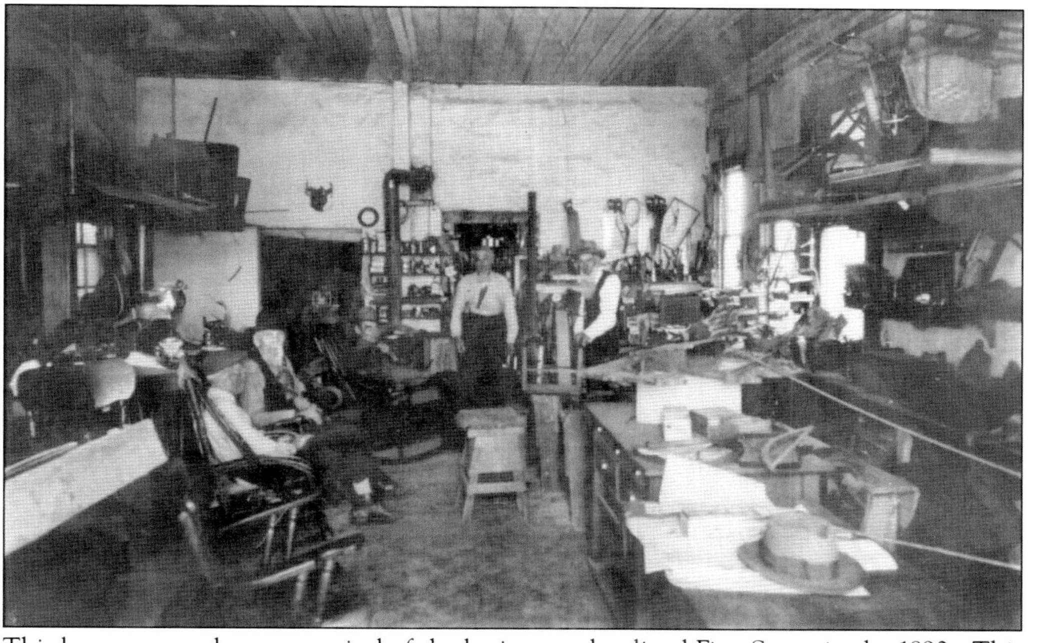

This long, narrow shop was typical of the businesses that lined First Street in the 1890s. This secondhand store was owned by John Garner, standing at center near the stove. It was located on the south side of First Street near G Street. During the mid-20th century, a Union 76 gas station occupied the location. (EWU 007-0584_2-26-1.)

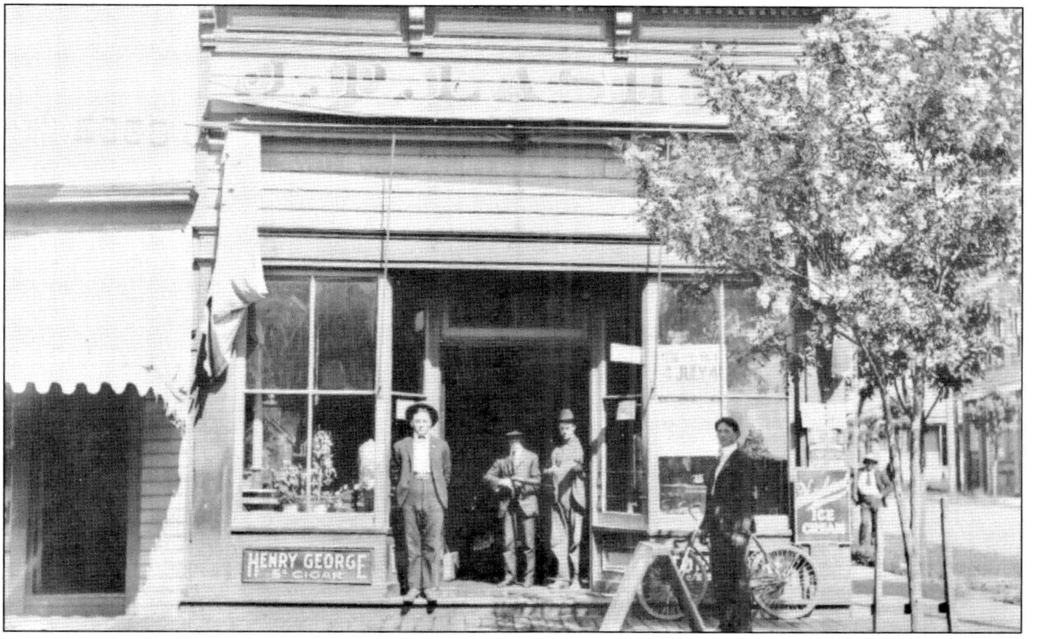

John Patrick Lasher stands at right with a bicycle in front of his store at 424 First Street around 1904. His three associates are unidentified. J.P. Lasher's was a confectionery store that sold candy, fruit, ice cream, school supplies, books, magazines, notions, jewelry, cutlery, tobacco, cigars, Rambler and Crescent bicycles, and other sporting goods.

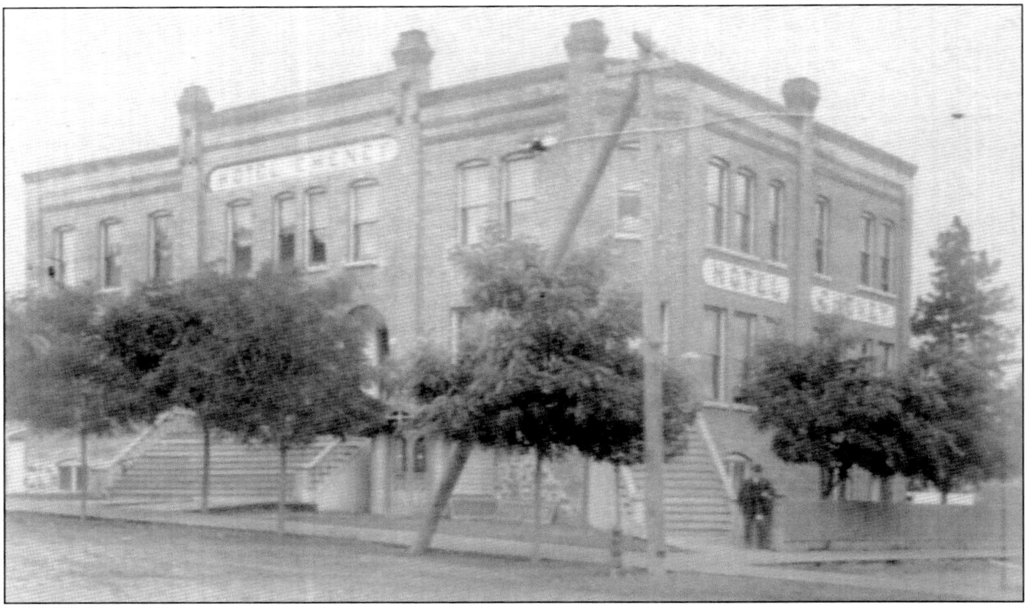

The Hotel Cheney was built in 1891 south of First Street on Normal Avenue (now College Avenue) adjacent to the Northern Pacific Railway depot. This was the premier hotel in Cheney in the early days. The hotel was converted into apartments by the government during World War II. It burned to the ground in 1956, and the foundation was paved over by the Cheney Chamber of Commerce in 1971.

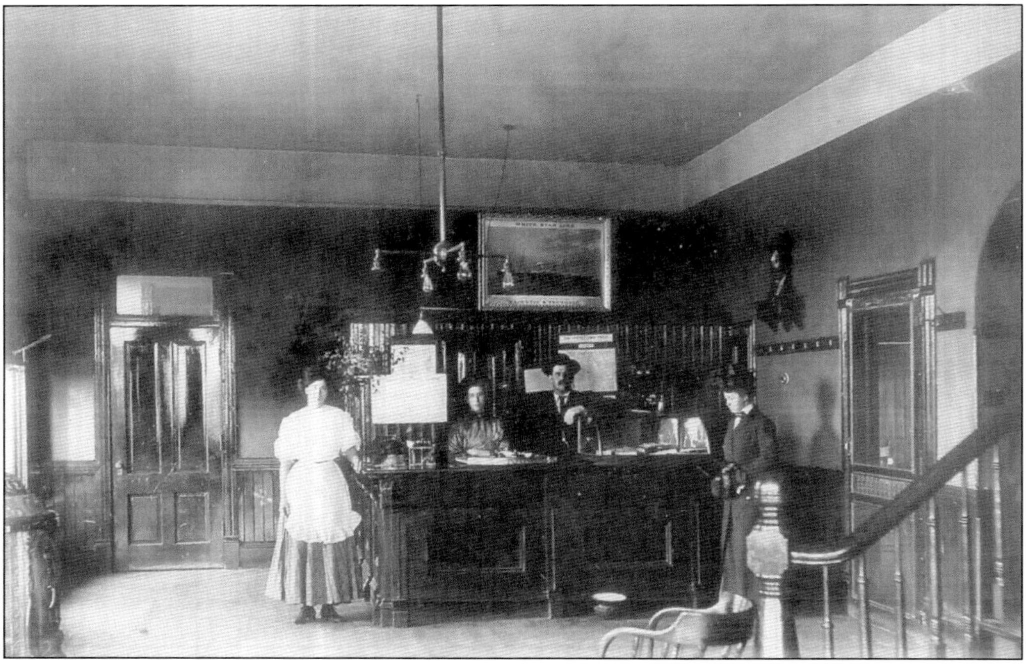

Zettie Fink West and her husband, John Nelson West, stand behind the counter in the lobby of the Hotel Cheney about 1909. The two were managers of the hotel. Note the wood stove at far left. The archway leading into the hotel dining room is at far right.

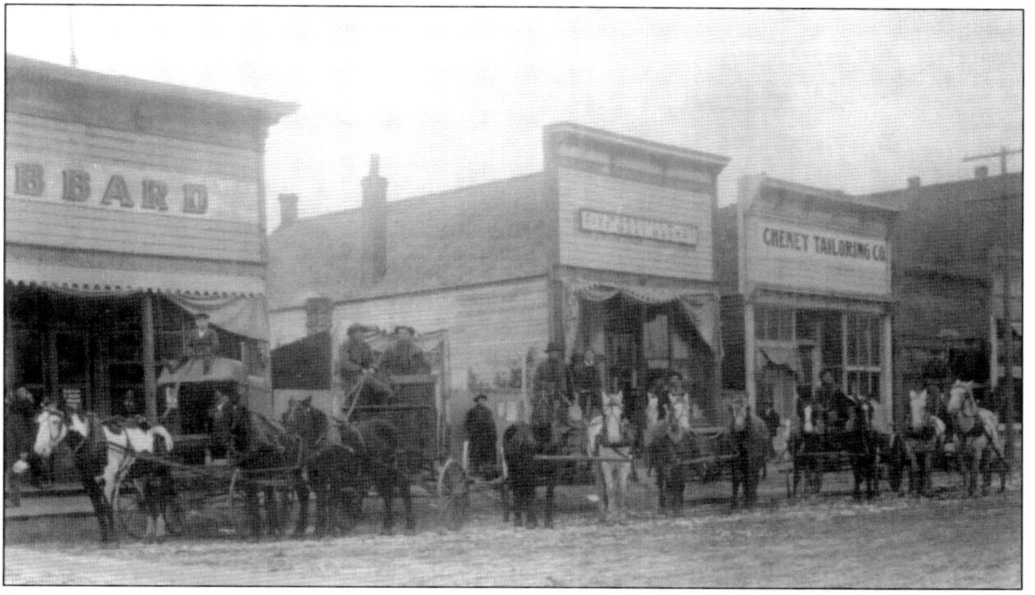

Six wagons pose on First Street in this view from around 1901. Hubbard sold groceries, sporting goods, and hardware at the corner of First and F Streets. The small building is Emma L. Shearer's millinery shop, followed by the City Meat Market. James Minnick's was a jeweler and optometrist, as well as the telephone switchboard operator. A.L. Ames's Cheney Tailoring Company is followed by Houck and Monk, a general merchandise store.

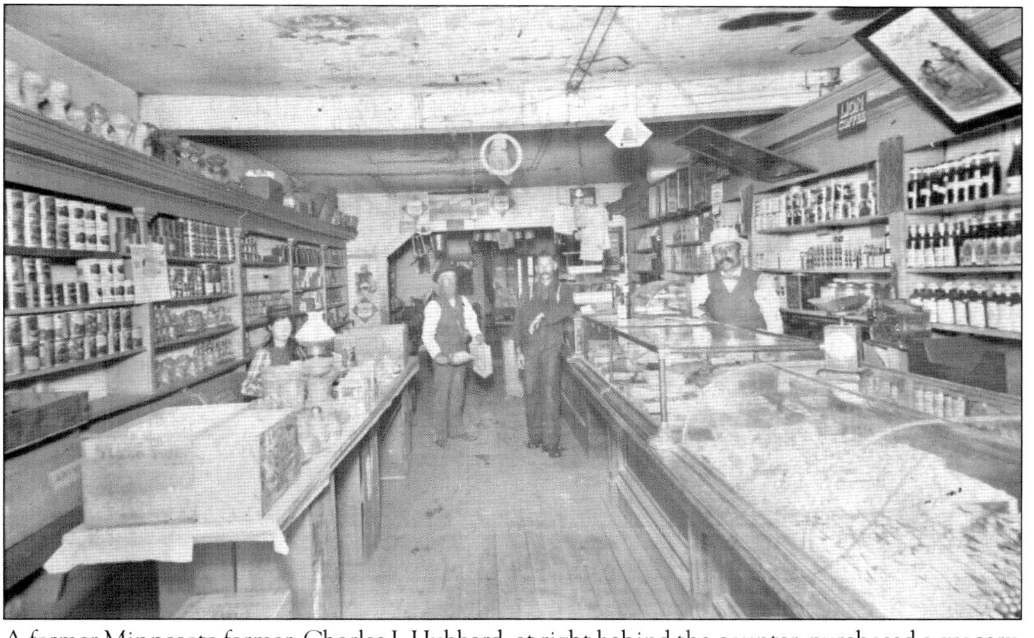

A former Minnesota farmer, Charles I. Hubbard, at right behind the counter, purchased a grocery, hardware, and sporting goods store at 402 First Street in 1900. His store burned in 1902, and he rebuilt in brick. When automobiles became available, he added auto parts to his inventory. Hubbard retired about 1930, and the building became a Safeway grocery, and later, Hansen's Hardware store. (EWU 007-0584_2-7-1.)

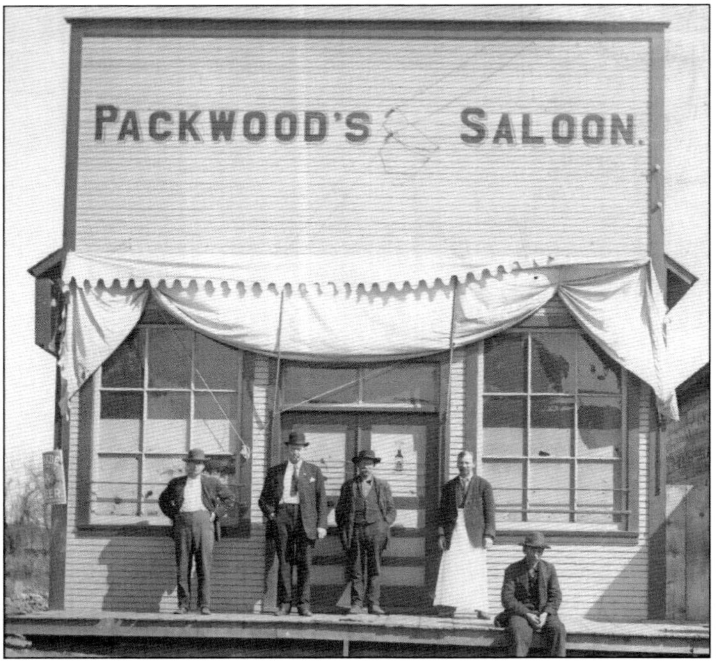

Bartender Henry Prehn, in the apron, stands in front of Packwood's Saloon around 1905. In order to protect the morals of the Normal School students, saloons were ordered to move off First Street, and Packwood's relocated south of the Northern Pacific Railway tracks on today's Cheney Spangle Road. A little farther south, off the road near the tree line, was a house of prostitution.

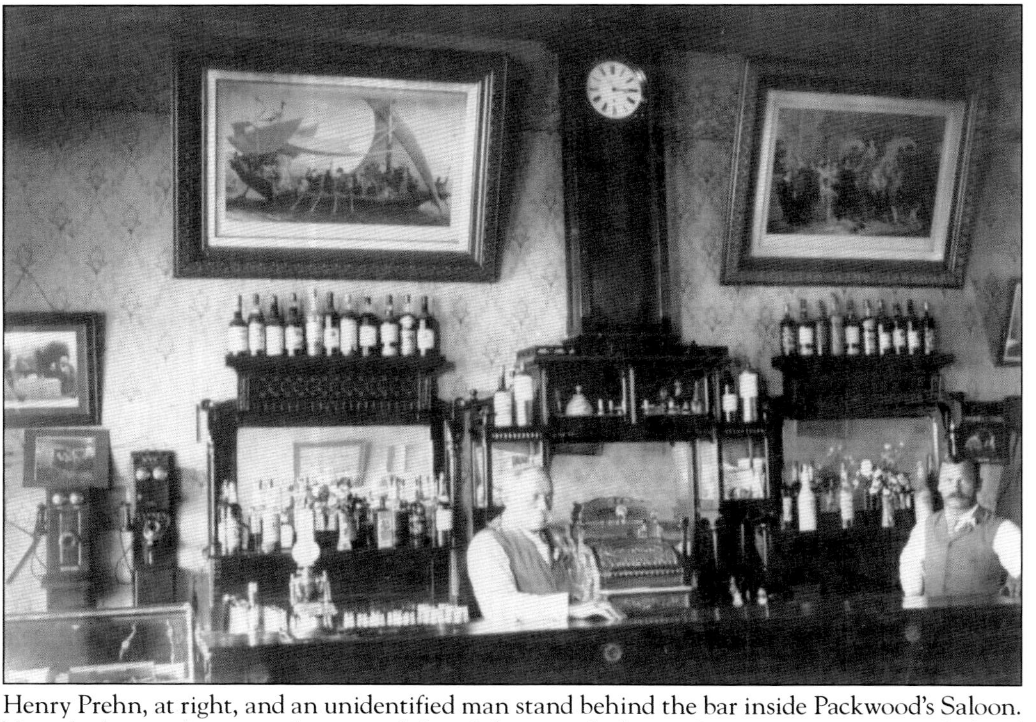

Henry Prehn, at right, and an unidentified man stand behind the bar inside Packwood's Saloon. Note the boxes of cigars in the case at left and the two telephones. In 1910, voters approved a local prohibition, and all liquor production and sales within Cheney were banned. This was six years before Washington state outlawed liquor sales, and nine years before the national prohibition. Prohibition was repealed in 1933.

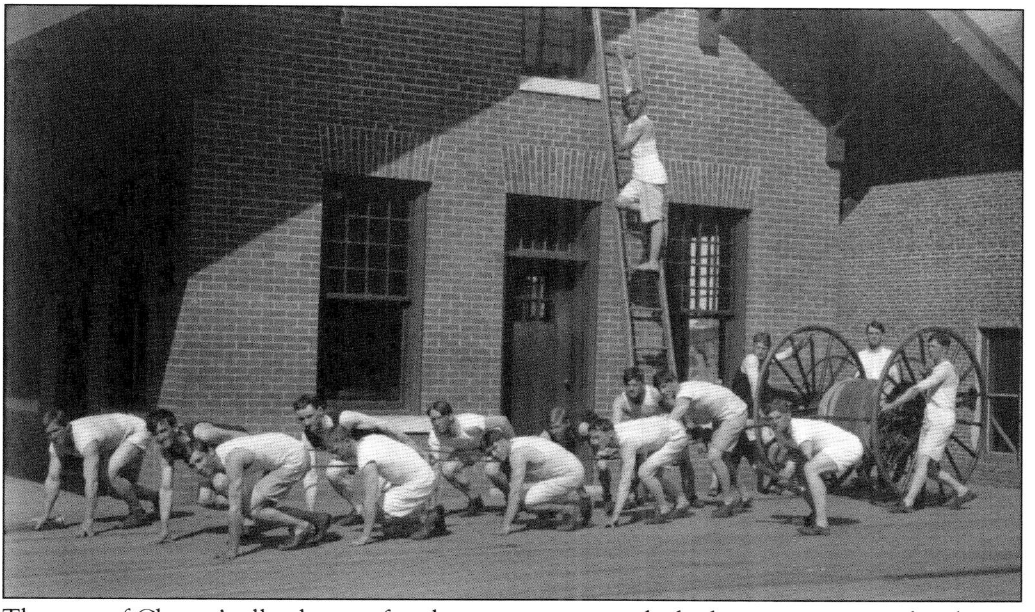

The men of Cheney's all-volunteer fire department pose with the hose cart next to the electric train depot around 1915. In 1882, a subscription-based fire company organized, but by 1891, the city had a well-organized volunteer fire department. The city began to provide the equipment for the department in 1915. It was not until the 1960s that the Cheney Fire Department had any paid staff.

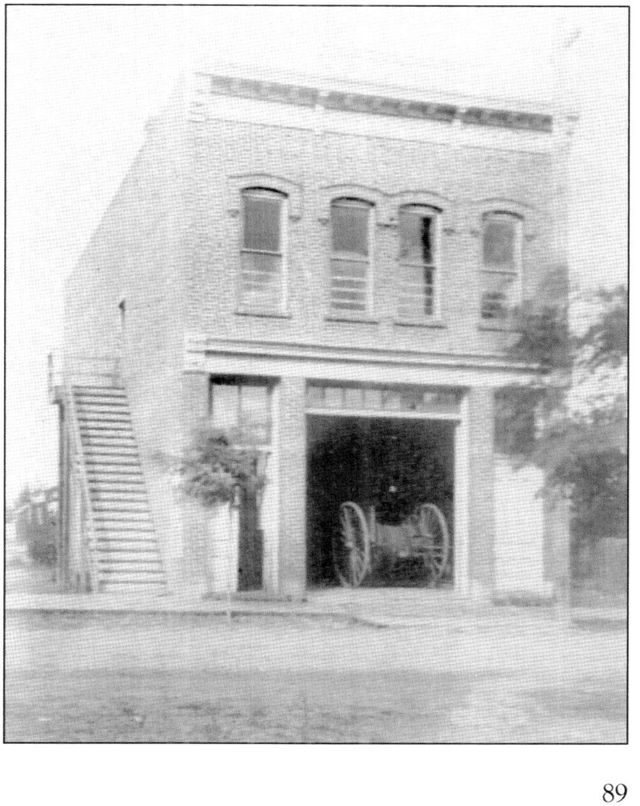

On October 24, 1890, the fire department, city hall, and jail building at 111 Normal Avenue was dedicated. The city offices were located on the second floor. The first city hall office, located on the second floor of a store on First Street, was destroyed in the 1883 fire. City offices temporarily moved to the second floor of the Griswold building at 416 First Street before moving into this building.

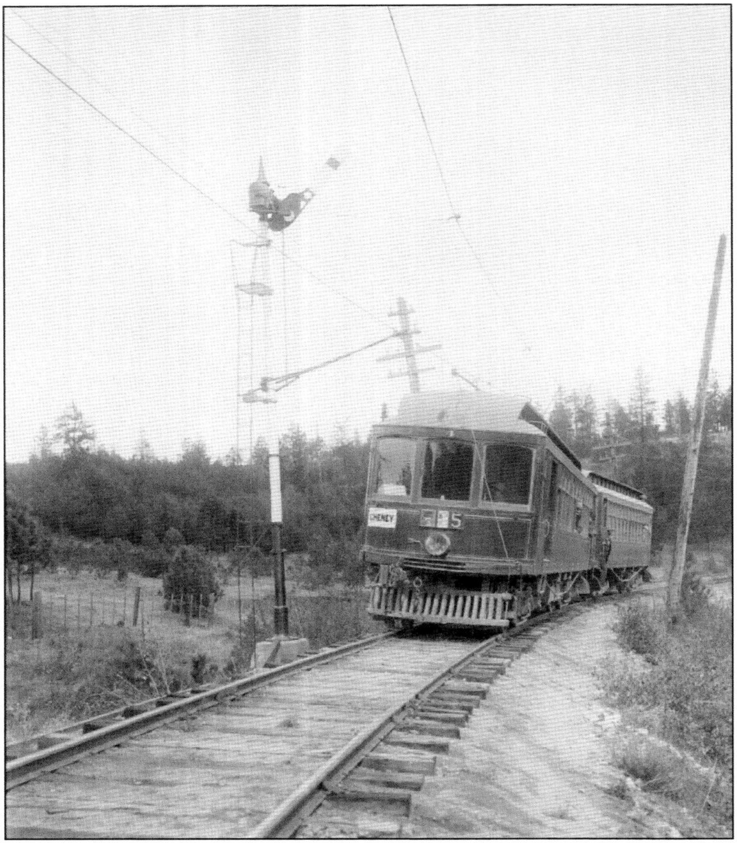

The two-car interurban electric train traveled 19.5 miles from Spokane to Cheney in 55 minutes. The lead car held the motorman's compartment, baggage compartment, a small smoking section, and a non-smoking compartment. The trailer car had a small toilet room. The fixture was open to the track and could only be used outside of the city while the train was moving.

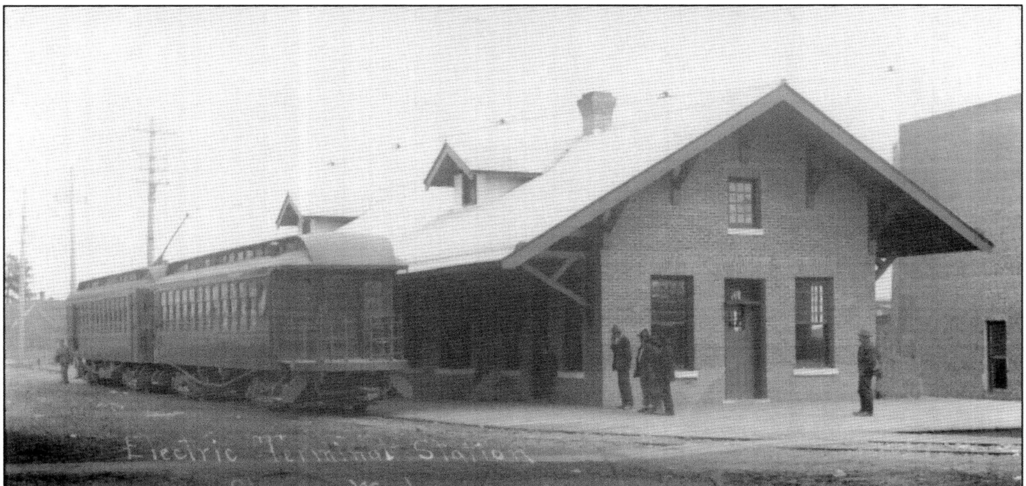

The Cheney Electric Train Depot on Second Street at the corner of Normal Avenue opened in December 1907. The two-car trolley is parked in front in this postcard from around 1915. Electric train service ended in March 1922. The old depot was subsequently used as a bus station, laundry, nursing home, antique market, and, most recently, as a Mexican restaurant.

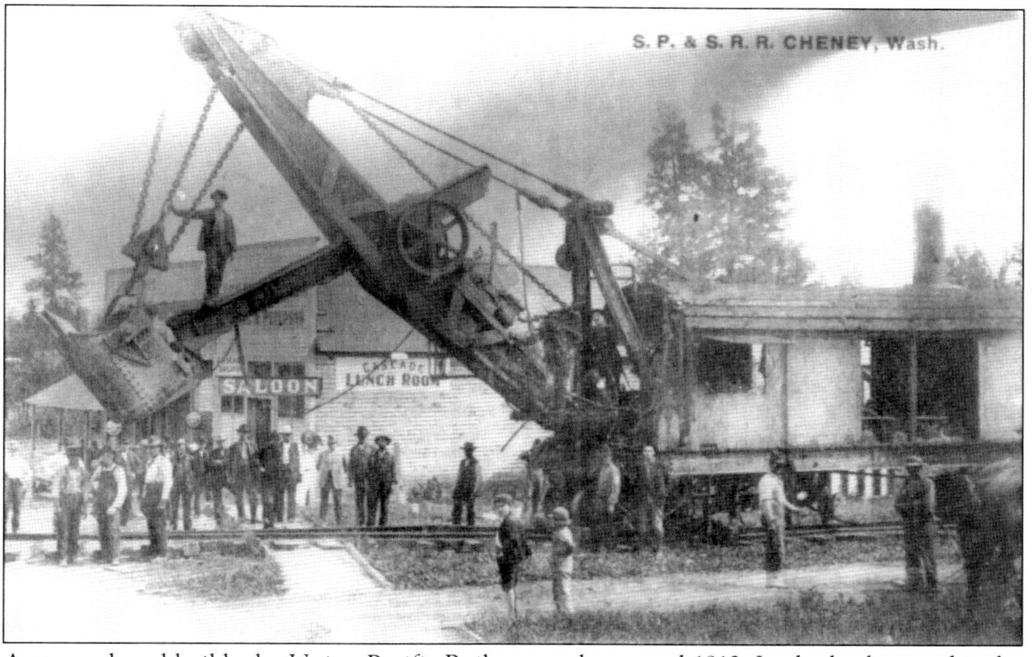

A steam shovel builds the Union Pacific Railway tracks around 1912. In the background is the Cascade Lunch Room and Saloon, which was located on the east side of today's Cheney Spangle Road. The Union Pacific was the third railroad built through Cheney after the Northern Pacific in 1881 and the Spokane, Portland & Seattle in 1908. The SP&S track bed became the Columbia Plateau Trail in 1991.

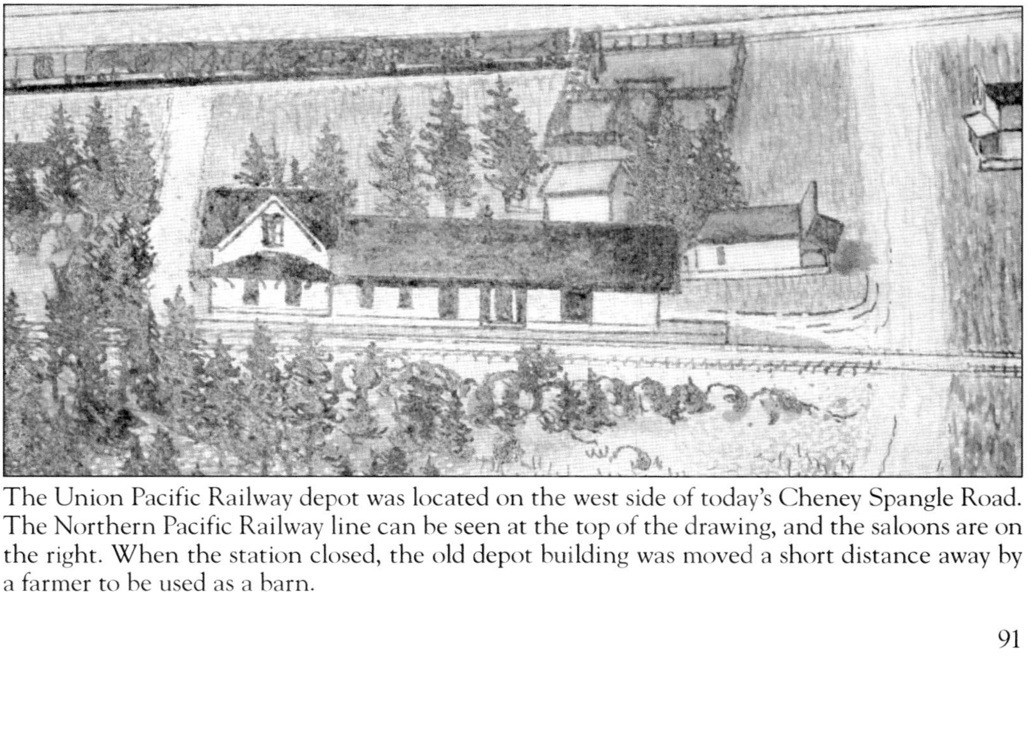
The Union Pacific Railway depot was located on the west side of today's Cheney Spangle Road. The Northern Pacific Railway line can be seen at the top of the drawing, and the saloons are on the right. When the station closed, the old depot building was moved a short distance away by a farmer to be used as a barn.

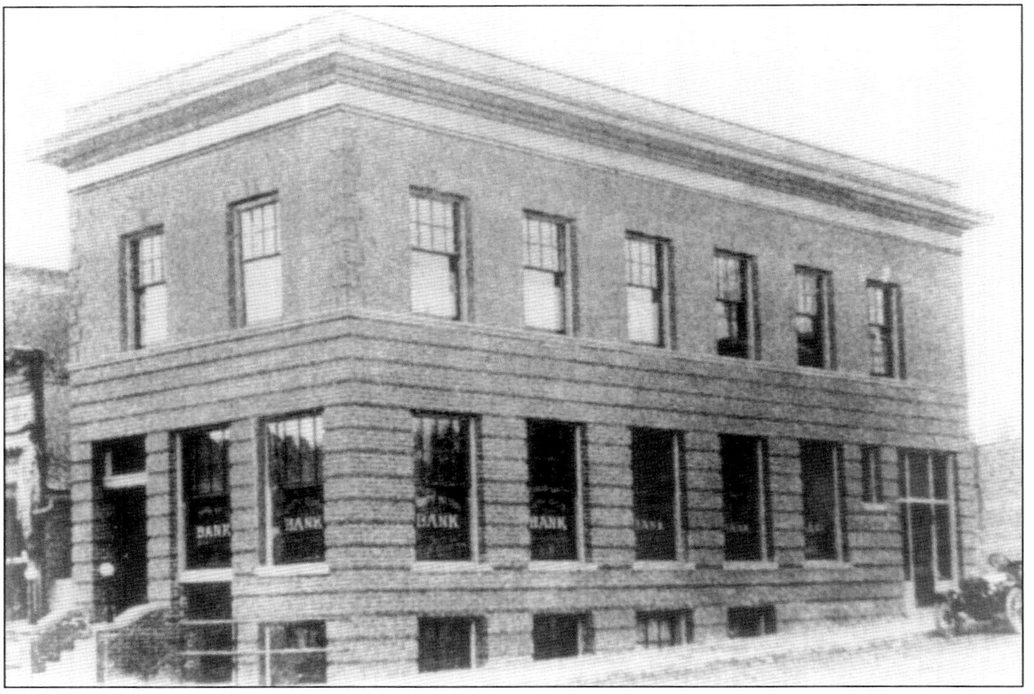

The Cheney State Bank opened on October 22, 1906. It reorganized as the Security National Bank and moved into the first level of the Masonic building on the corner of First Street and College Avenue in 1910. William Sutton was the bank's president. The bank closed December 31, 1931, a casualty of the Depression. The old bank safe is still in the basement of the building.

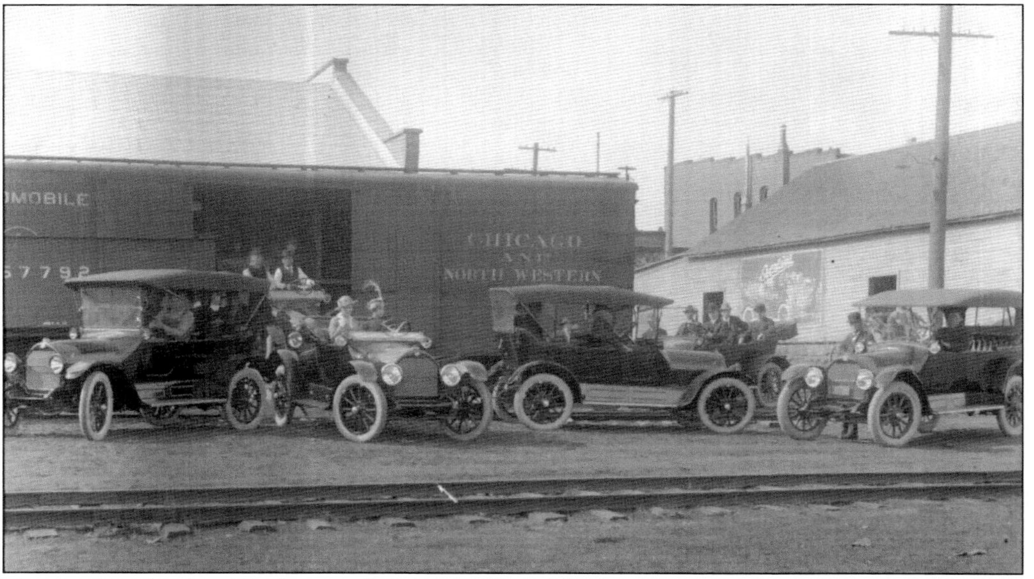

The first Overland and Ford automobiles arrived by rail for the Charles A. Ratcliffe dealership in 1912. This photograph shows Emery E. Garberg (passenger) and Frank M. Martin driving an automobile out of the train car. In the foreground, Lawrensa Garberg is driving the convertible with Clara Everson beside her. The Ratcliffe Ford dealership was a fixture on Second Street until 2003.

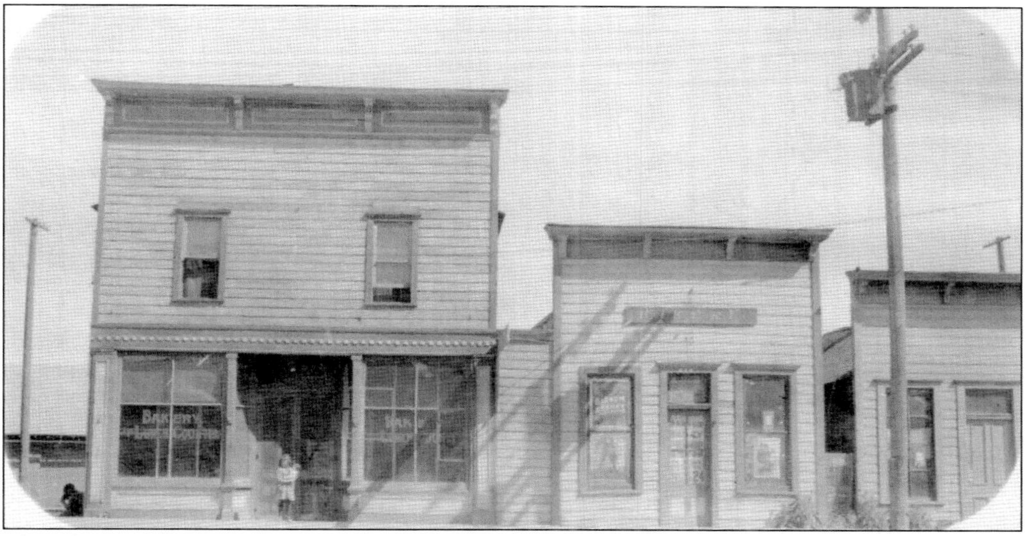

The Cheney Bakery, located at 313 First Street, was established by J. Eugene Roos in 1899. The family living quarters were upstairs. In 1904, Eugene purchased the Chinese laundry next door and moved his ovens there to make room for a dining room at the back of the bakery, as well as to keep the heat down in the living quarters.

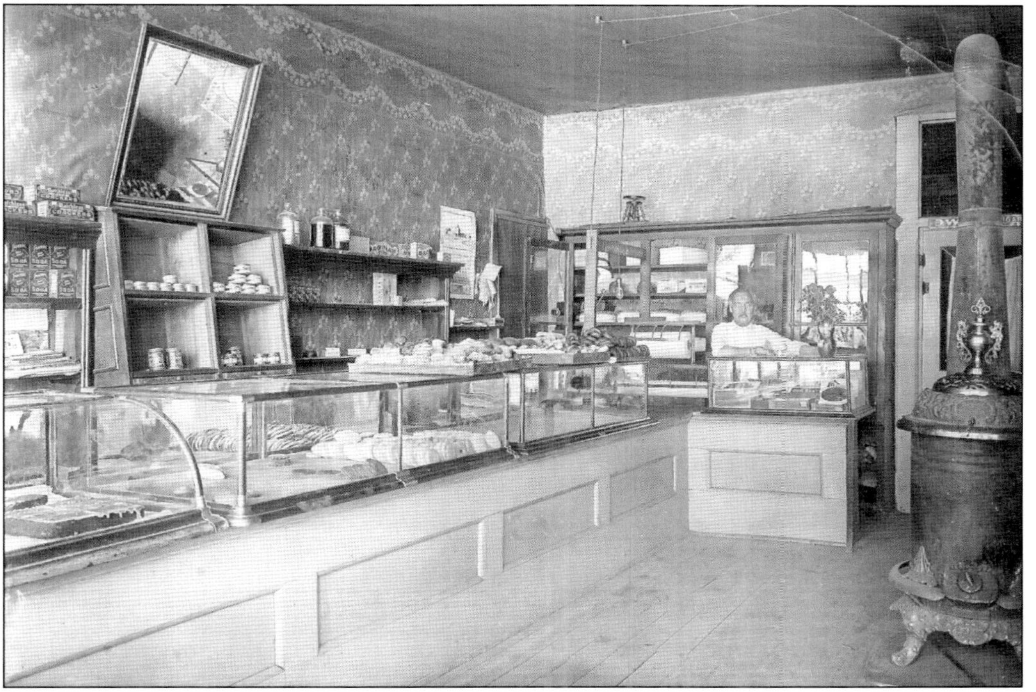

This photograph, taken around 1919, shows Eugene Roos inside the Cheney Bakery. Along with the cases of baked goods, there was a lunch counter in the store. Note the pot-bellied stove at right. Eugene retired in 1922, first leasing the bakery, and then selling it in 1924 to Konrad Lauff.

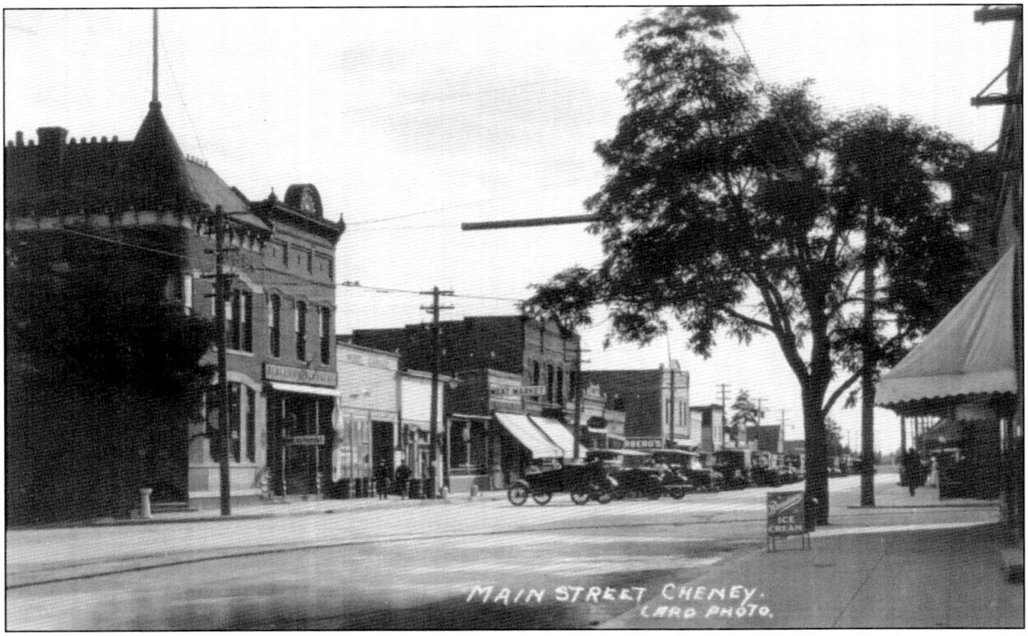

This was the view west on First Street in 1920. The National Bank of Cheney sits at the corner of First Street and College Avenue. The sign for Louis Walter's Harness and Saddlery is still on the building next to the bank, but a new sign for automobile tire repair has been added. The Model Garage, a meat market, and Garberg's Hardware store can be seen farther down the street.

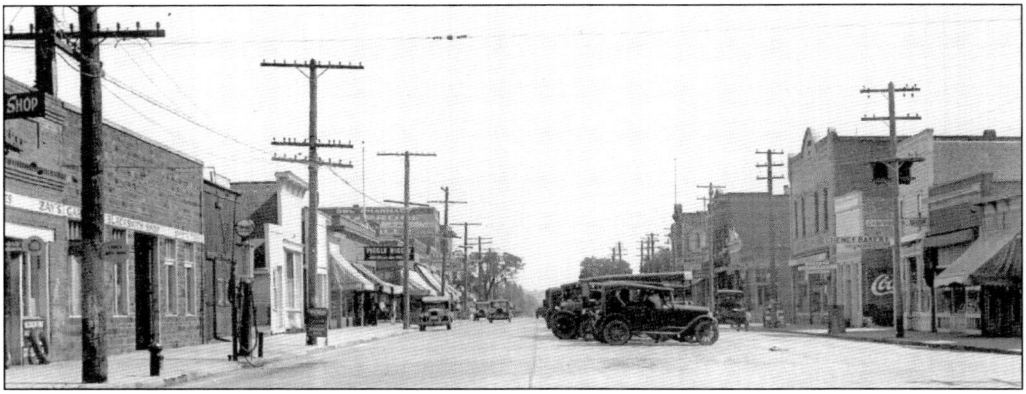

This view of First Street was taken from G Street looking east on July 8, 1927. On the left is Ed Zay's Garage with signs advertising bicycle tires, a gas pump, and a ladies restroom. Farther down the street are the Piggly Wiggly grocery, Ted's Ice Cream and Candy, a meat market, and Owl Pharmacy. On the right are Campbell's Shop, the Cheney Bakery, a restaurant, and another meat market.

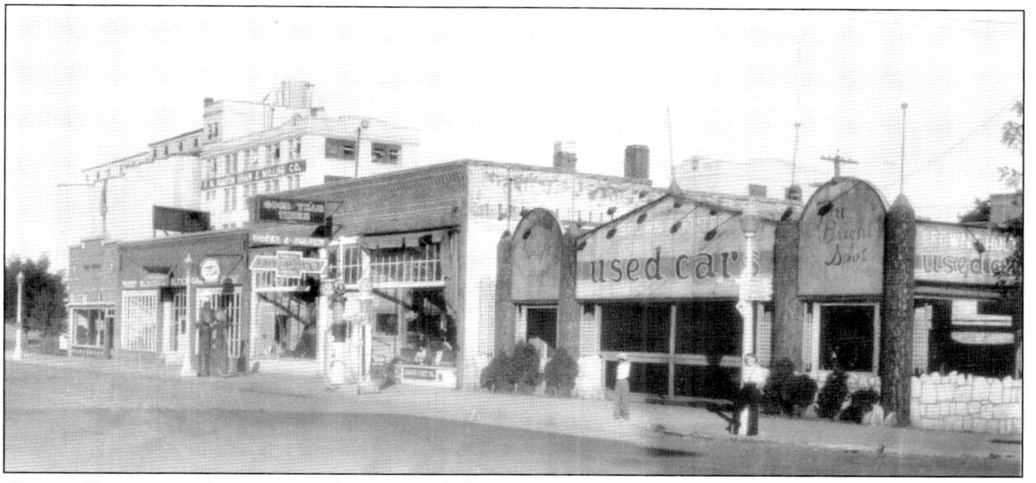

George Brown and Norman Holter opened their Chevrolet dealership October 1, 1920, occupying most of the 500 block on the south side of First Street. They also sold Dodge, Studebaker, and Maxwell cars at one time. The family sold the dealership in 1974; a decade later, it moved to North First Street before closing in the 1990s. This 1935 view shows the post office at the end of the block.

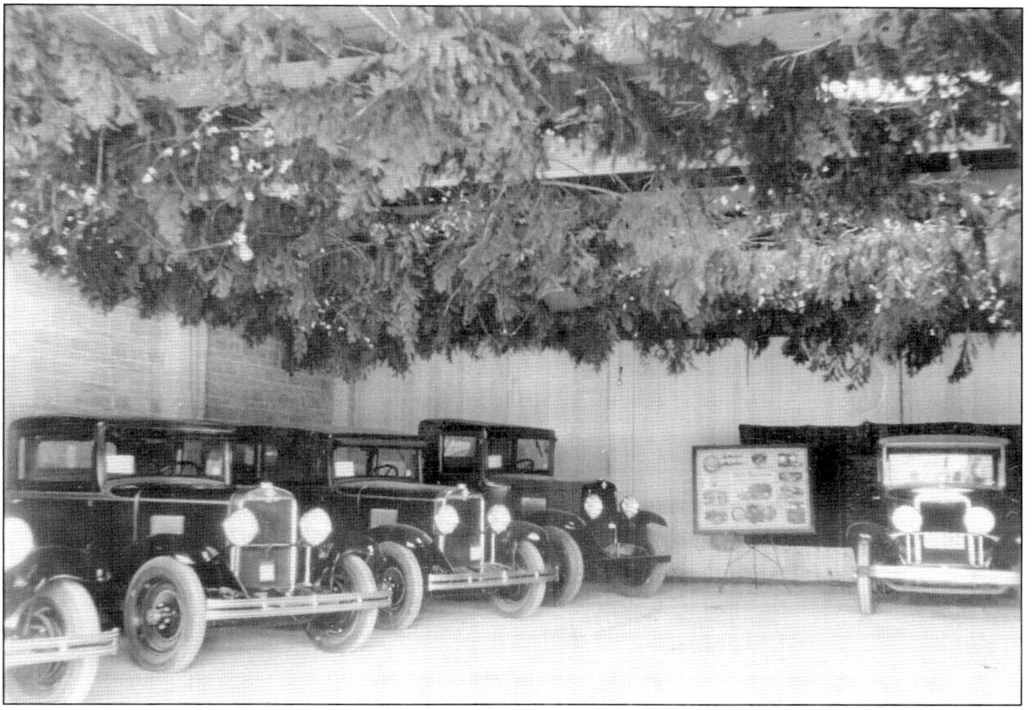

New cars line the Brown and Holter showroom around 1930. Martin Holter took his father's place with the firm in 1926. Nolan Brown succeeded his father, George, after graduating from Washington State College. He also served as Cheney's mayor from 1956 to 1966. The dealership was sold to Roy Leland and Tom Beatty in 1974. Gary Anderberg purchased the company in 1981.

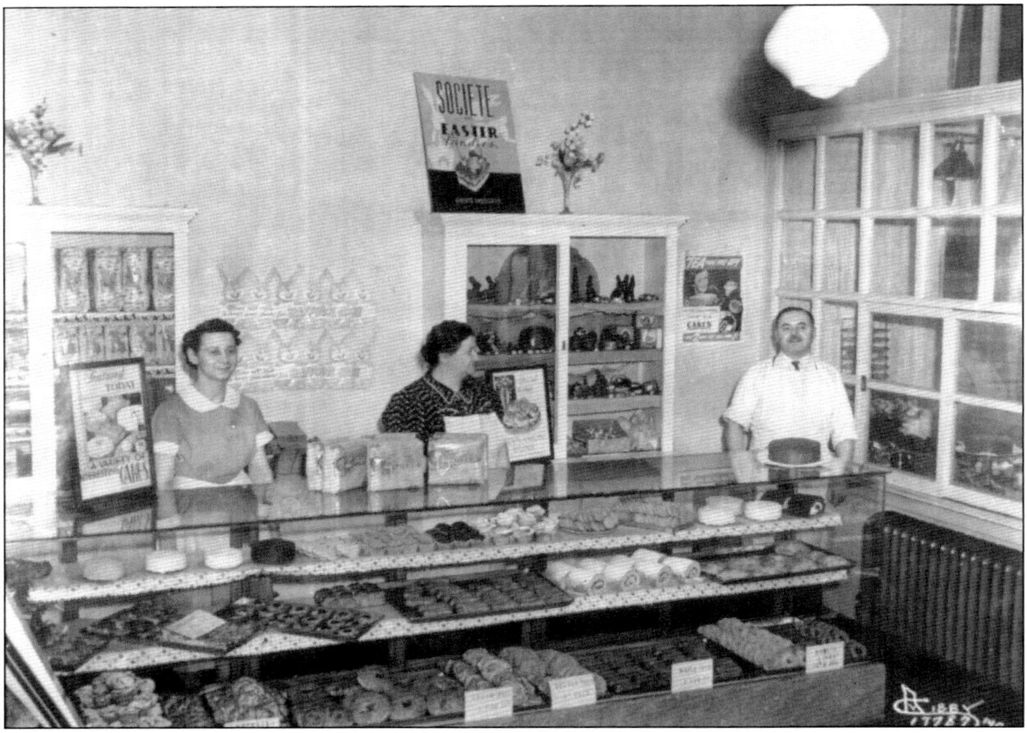

Konrad and Marie Lauff leased the Cheney Bakery and Café from Eugene Roos in 1922. Two years later, they purchased the business. This 1935 photograph shows Margaret Lauff with her parents behind the bakery counter. In 1939, actress Bette Davis had dinner in the café while traveling incognito with friends to Mount Rainier. She stayed overnight at Johnson's Auto Camp.

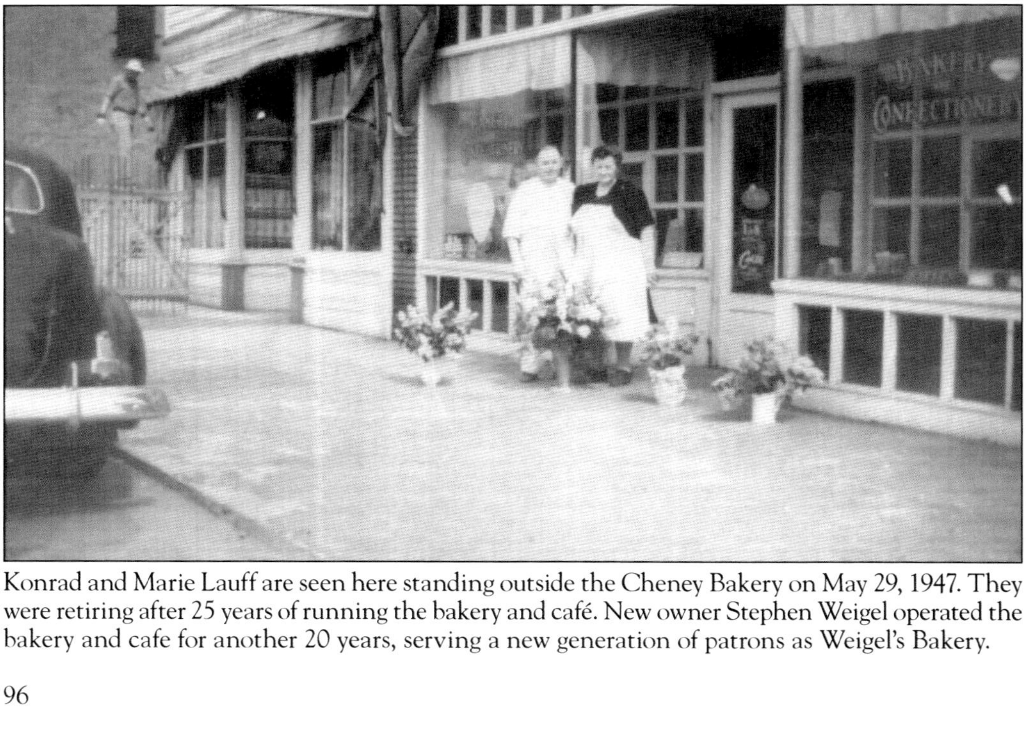

Konrad and Marie Lauff are seen here standing outside the Cheney Bakery on May 29, 1947. They were retiring after 25 years of running the bakery and café. New owner Stephen Weigel operated the bakery and cafe for another 20 years, serving a new generation of patrons as Weigel's Bakery.

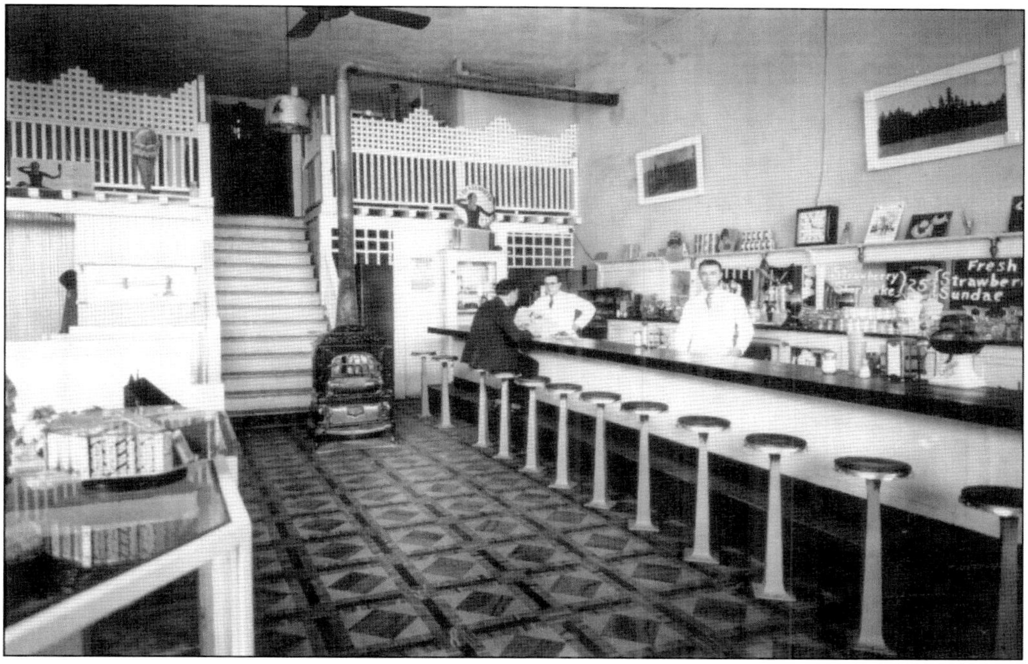

A customer could get strawberry shortcake or a fresh strawberry sundae for 25¢ in April 1932 at Sweets N' Eats. Kyle Pugh Sr. is standing behind the counter toward the back with the customer. He later served as superintendent of utilities for the city. Note the potbelly stove for heat between the counter seating and booths on the left.

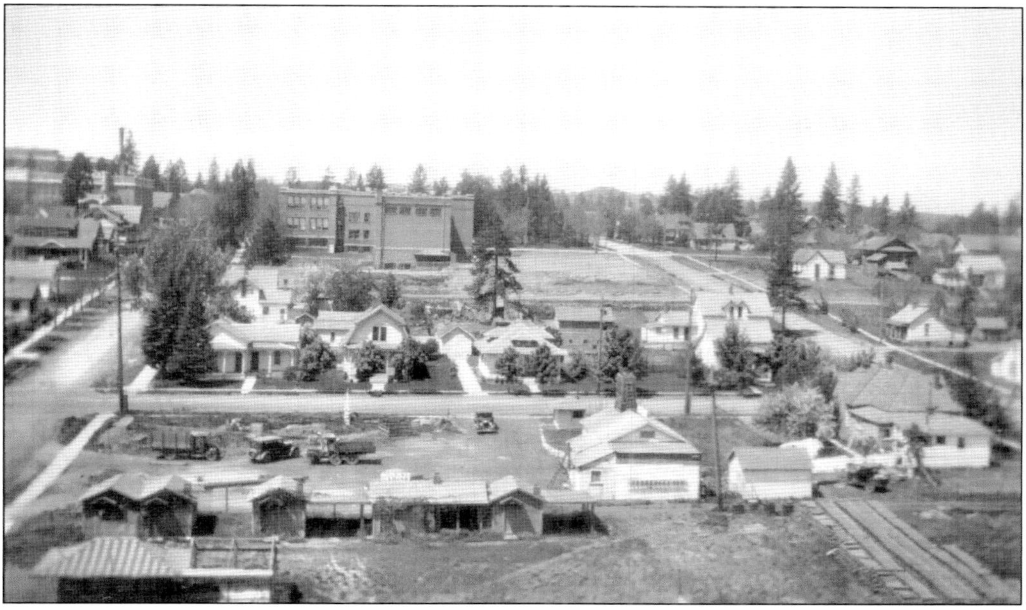

The view up the hill between D and C Streets around 1930 shows Johnson's Auto Camp in the foreground. Behind it, trucks and cars are parked on the site of today's city hall. Farther up the hill is the 1913 high school, which was serving as the junior high by the time of this photograph. At far left is the new high school.

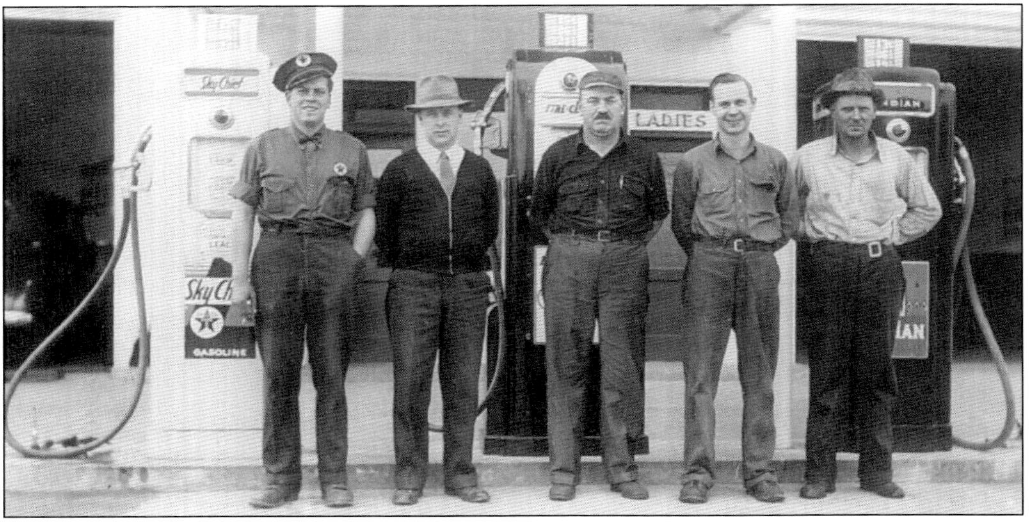

On June 1, 1934, Lloyd Holladay opened his Texaco Service Station and the Cheney Motor Company Plymouth dealership at 308 First Street in the location of the former Zay's Garage and Blacksmith Shop. The employees are, from left to right, Lyle Graham, Holladay, Earl Fish, Al Easton, and unidentified.

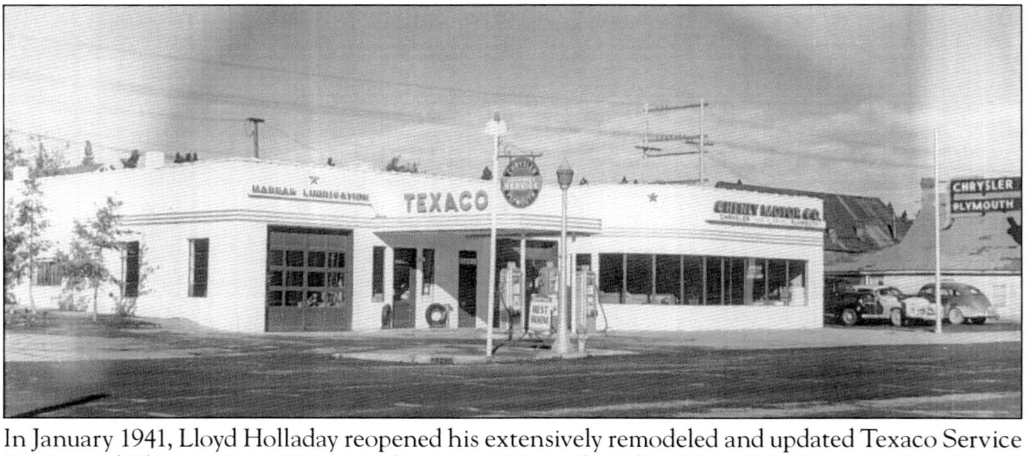

In January 1941, Lloyd Holladay reopened his extensively remodeled and updated Texaco Service Station and Cheney Motor Company showroom. He purchased and demolished two wooden pioneer-era buildings to create his used car lot in 1948, shown at far right. Lloyd's Plymouth dealership closed in 1968. The building was demolished to make way for a Lincoln Savings Bank.

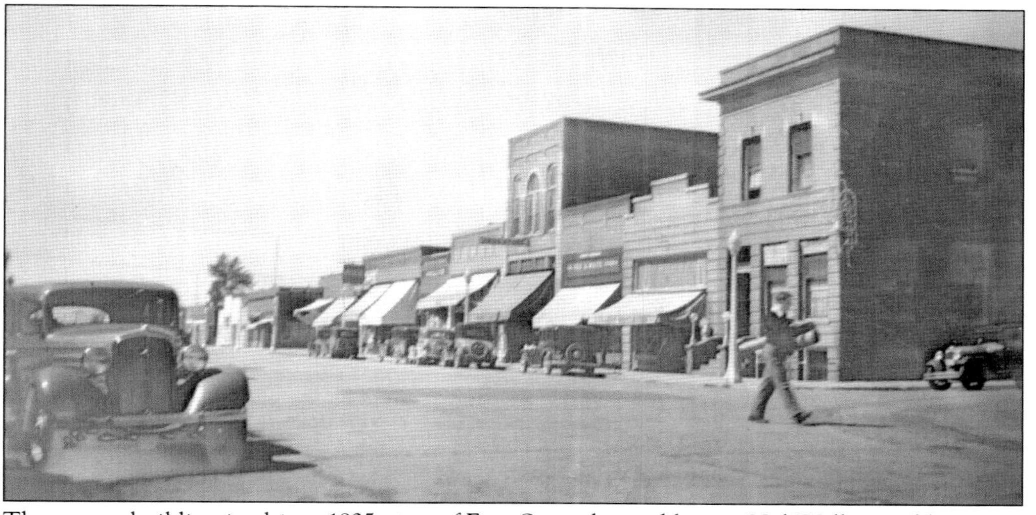

The corner building in this c. 1935 view of First Street housed lawyer Hal Walker and longtime dentist Dr. William Bernard. Next was Charles Bernard's Men's Store, followed by Gibson's Red and White Grocery. The two-story building was Casey's Store, followed by Owl Pharmacy, and Kelly's Tavern. Other stores on the street included Selner's Jewelry Store, Carr's Cash Store, Ted's Sweet Shop, Safeway, and Bair's Grocery.

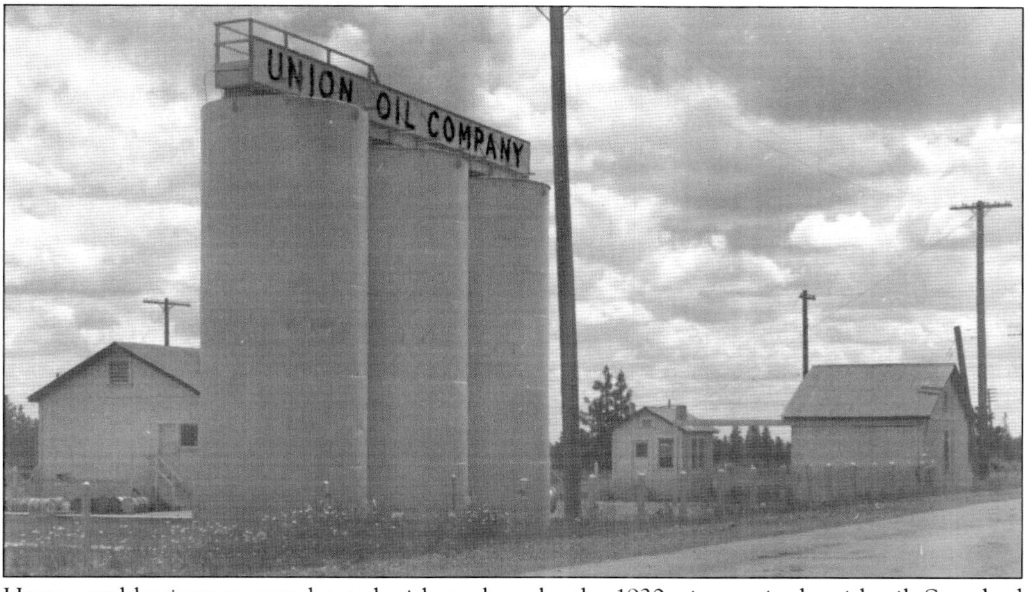

Homes and businesses were heated with coal, or, by the 1930s, increasingly with oil. Standard Oil, Shell, and Union Oil all had storage and distribution facilities south of First Street near the railroad tracks. The companies fueled the five service stations in town and delivered oil to fill the home heating tanks of residents.

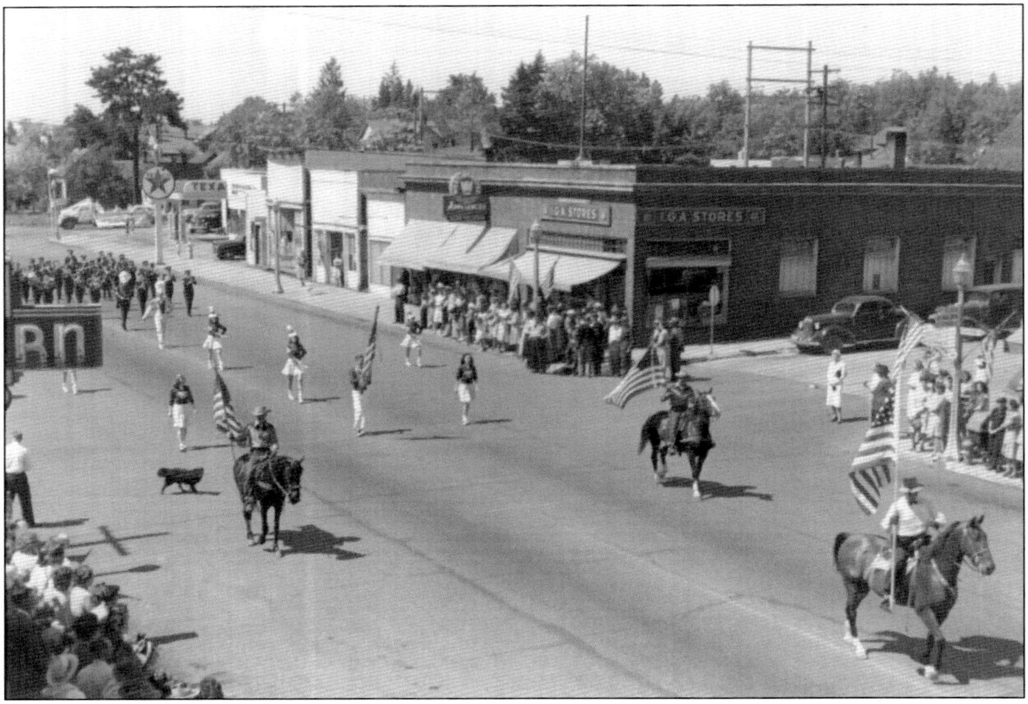

People lined the street for the May Day Festival parade around 1945. Looking west from F Street, one can see Marion Bair's IGA Grocery, Ray Wargi and Martin Tollefson's electrical and appliance store, and Lloyd Holladay's Plymouth dealership and Texaco Service Station at the far end of the block at G Street.

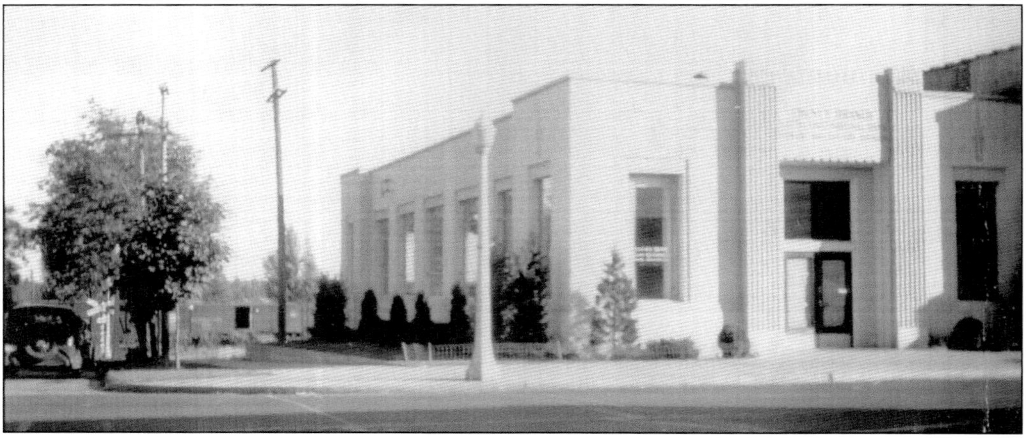

After 51 years, the old Bank of Cheney on the corner of College Avenue and First Street was replaced with this beautiful white building. Customers were invited to the grand opening of the Cheney Branch of Spokane and Eastern Division Seattle–First National Bank on Saturday, April 11, 1942.

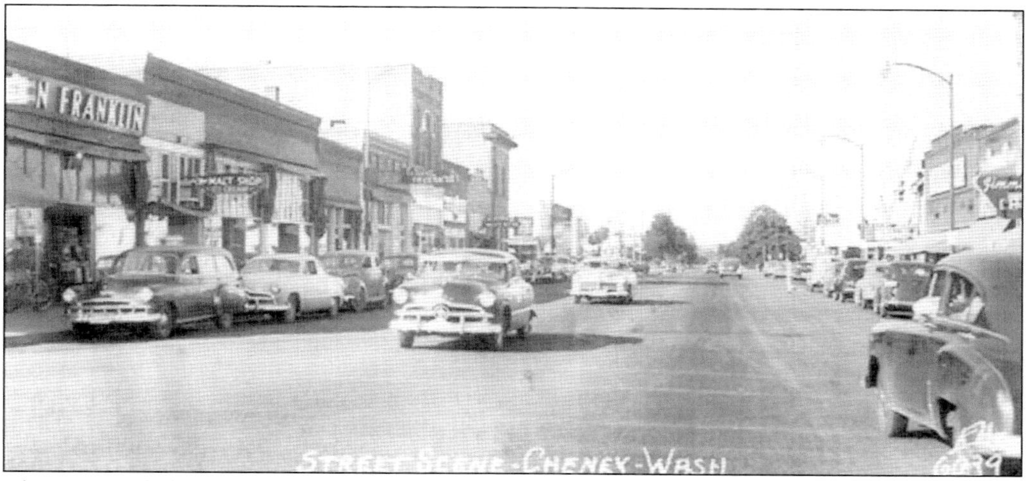

This postcard photograph of First Street, taken from F Street around 1950, shows Ben Franklin, the Malt Shop, Selner's Jewelry, and Kelly's Tavern on the left. Farther down the block are the Owl Pharmacy, Gibson's Grocery, and Olsen's Menswear. On the right, stores include Rollie's Cafe, Bill's Tavern, Pastime Tavern, Jimmie's Cafe, Melron's Department Store, Gem Meat Market, Pix Theater, and SeaFirst Bank.

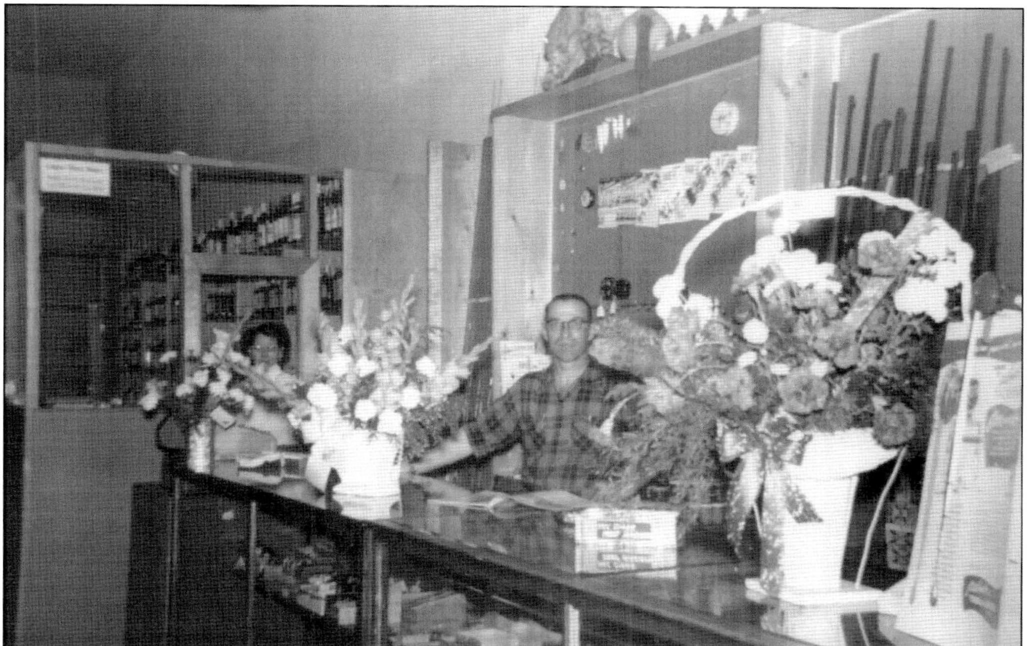

John and LaVina Davis, shown here behind the counter, operated Davis Sporting Goods at 113 F Street starting about 1948. In 1952, they moved to 508 First Street, where they continued to supply hunters and fishers until the early 1960s. Inside their business was also Cheney's liquor store.

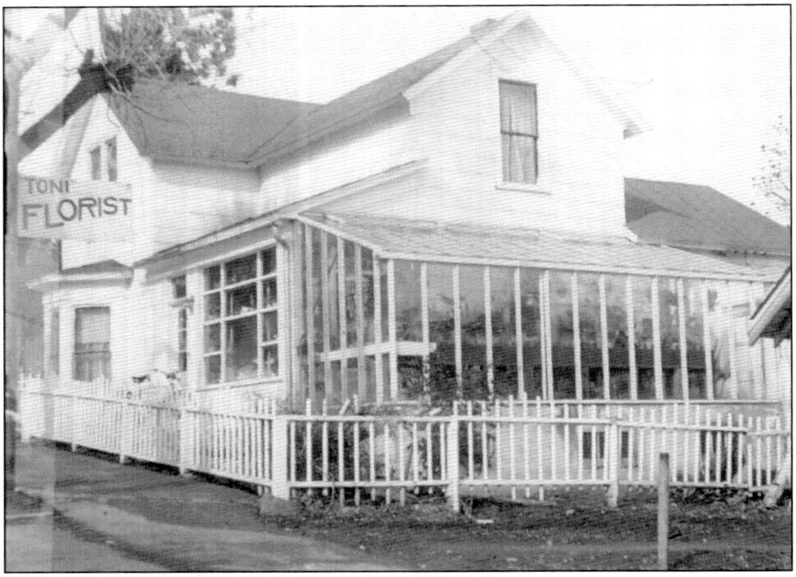

Toni Pugh opened a flower shop about 1948 that was attached to the family's home at 213 D Street, shown in this photograph from 1950. The small shop was packed with flowers and house plants, as well as a variety of cactus. She retired and sold her stock to Chet and Bea Johnson of Chet's Flowers around 1958.

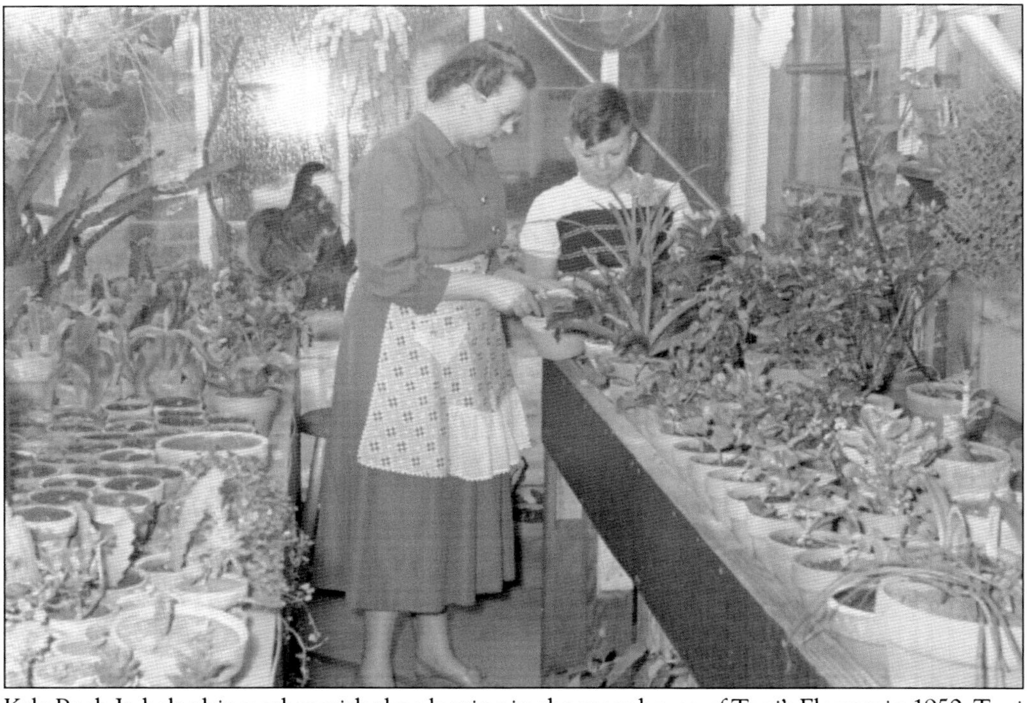

Kyle Pugh Jr. helps his mother with the planting in the greenhouse of Toni's Flowers in 1950. Toni Pugh created bouquets, corsages for proms, and hanging baskets of houseplants, and stocked seeds for the home gardener in her small nursery and shop. Note the family cat on the bench at left.

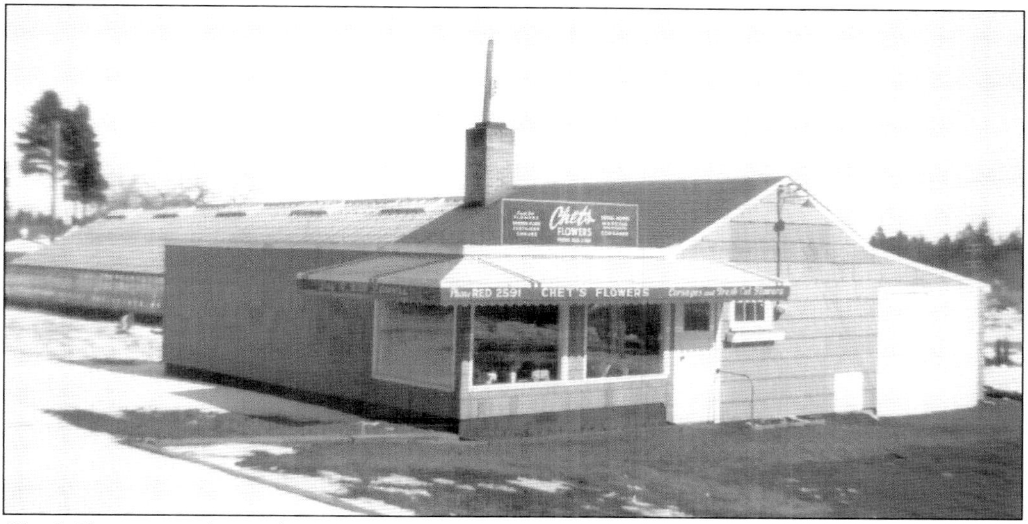

Chet's Flowers was located at First and Pine Streets. Chet and Bea Johnson built the greenhouse and business around 1951 after he worked at the Spokane Greenhouse in Marshall for a number of years. The front building housed the retail shop, as well as the steam heating plant and stoker. The attached greenhouse in the rear was made with glass panes fitted in place with a special pliable putty.

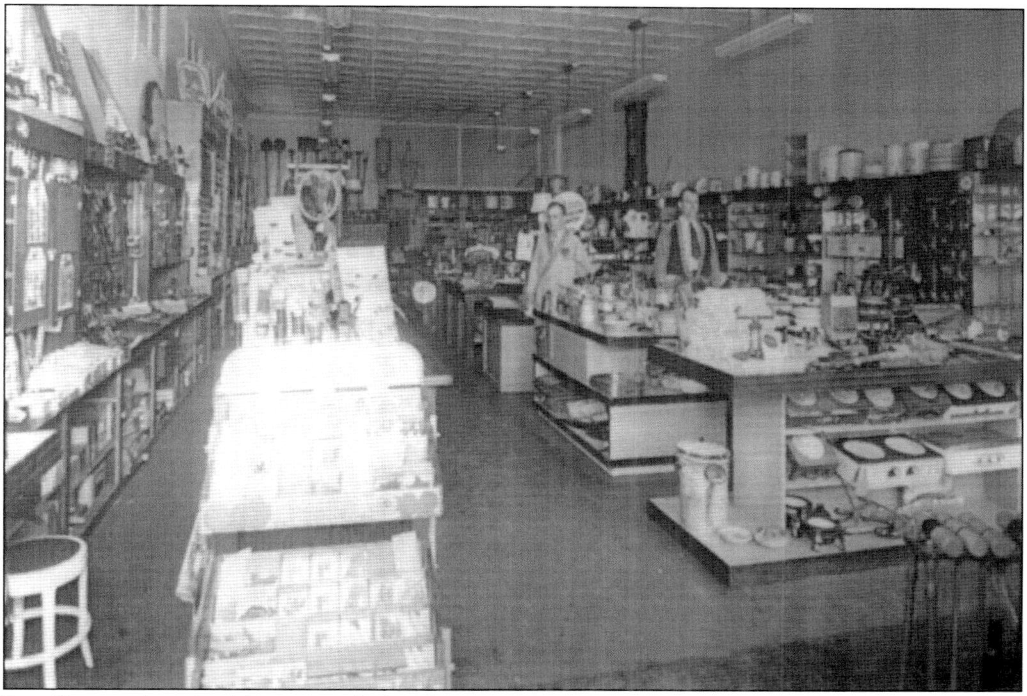

Roy Hansen bought Abe Bottorff's hardware store in November 1938. William Bernard, shown here with Roy Hansen, had worked at Bottorff Hardware for a number of years. The hardware store was originally located in the Odd Fellows building at 321 First Street. In 1941, Hansen and Safeway grocery swapped locations, with the hardware store moving into 402 First Street. This photograph was taken shortly after the move.

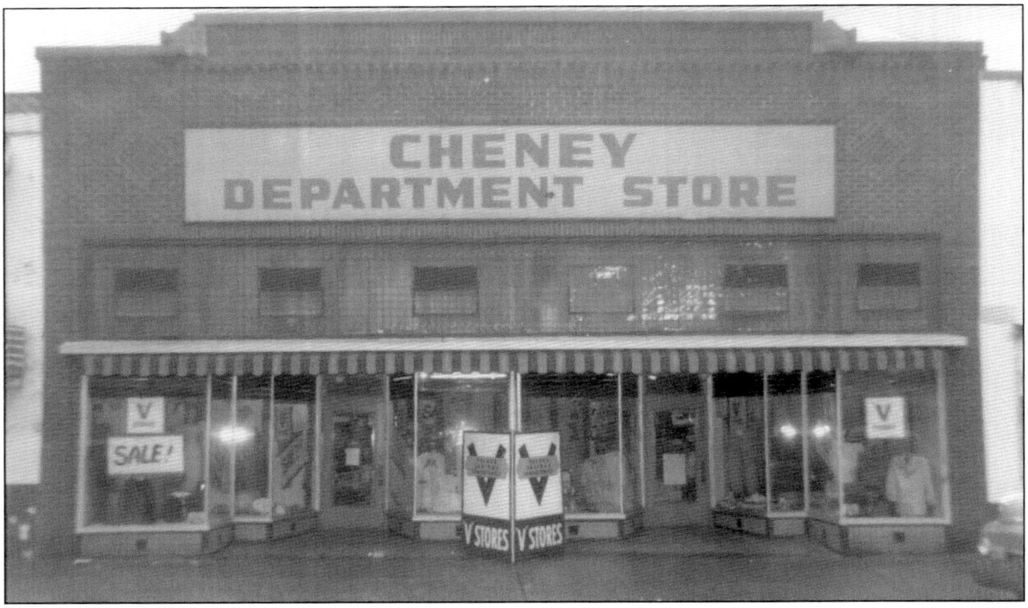

Elbert "Wag" Wagoner purchased Melron's Department store in 1951. The Cheney Department Store, also called the V Store, was located at 415 First Street. The store was originally built around 1929 as a J.C. Penney store. This photograph is from 1959. Wagoner retired in 1978. The building was later demolished for a parking lot.

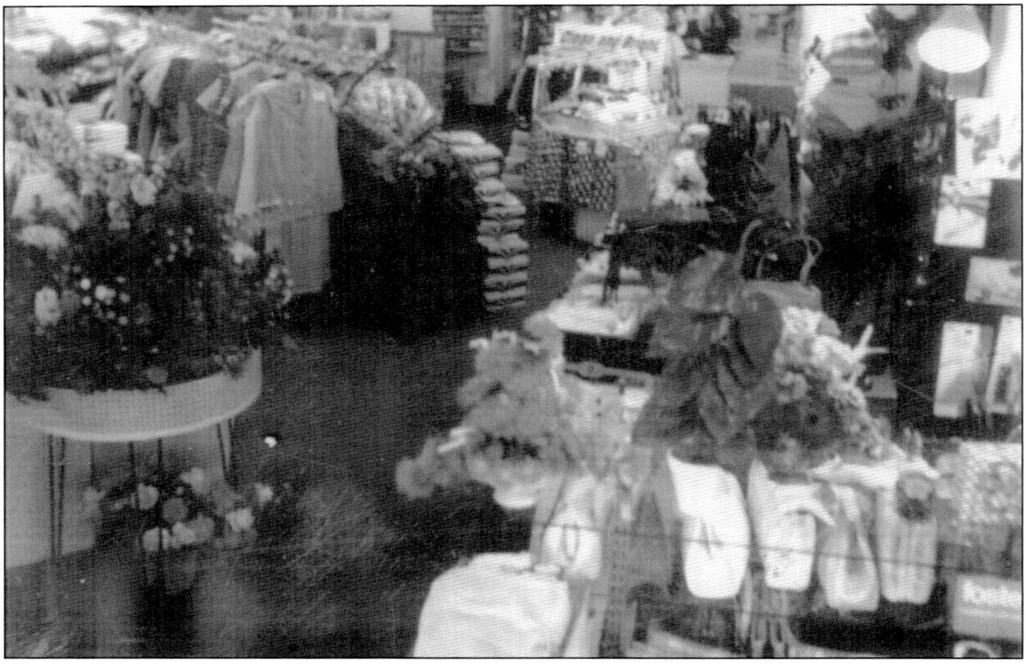
This 1965 photograph shows just a small selection of the items shoppers could find in the Cheney Department Store. It was a full-scale department store with clothing and shoes for men, women, and children. One could find everything except furniture to make a home, including housewares, fabric, and toys.

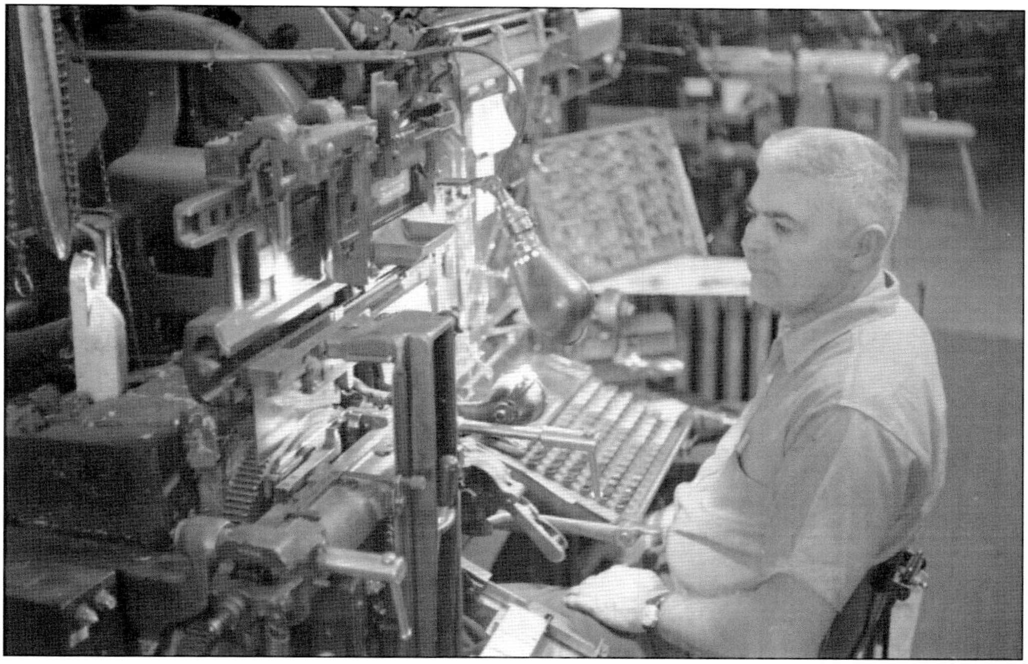

John Early sets type inside the *Cheney Free Press* office on First Street in the early 1960s. Established in 1896, the *Free Press* opened after the *Northwest Tribune* left town, but faced competition from the *Cheney Sentinel* for several years. By 1900, the *Cheney Free Press* was the only newspaper in town and has been producing a weekly paper ever since. (EWU-SPC-WWP 002-548_57-D-1.)

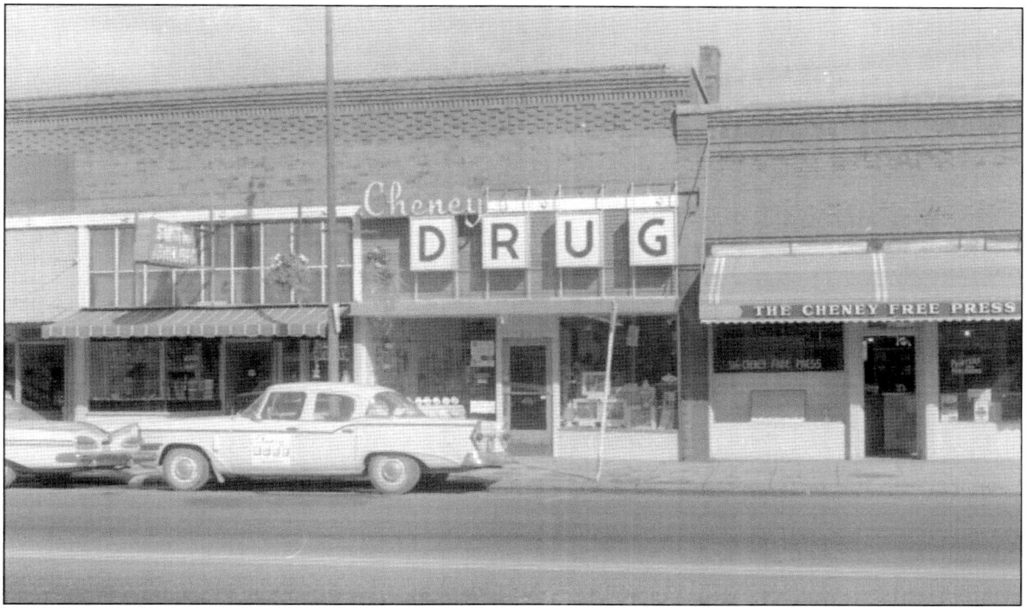

This photograph from the early 1960s shows Smith Jewelers at 408, the Cheney Drug Store at 410, and the Cheney Free Press at 412 First Street. The Malt Shop is partially visible on the left. Claude Murray and Bill Colbert opened the Malt Shop in 1946, taking over Jimmie's Fountain Café location from Jim Crawford. (EWU-SPC-WWP 002-0548_31-D-4.)

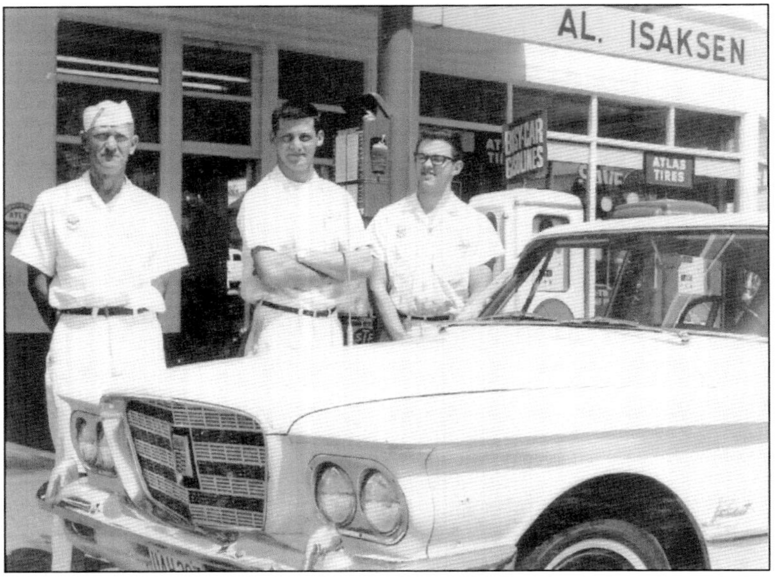

Al Isaksen's Chevron Service Station on the corner of First and D Streets was one of 13 gas stations in Cheney. Employees wore white uniforms when this photograph was taken in 1964. From left to right are Al Isaksen, Bob Heehn, and Harold Ott. Today, the Cheney Federal Credit Union parking lot covers the site of the old Chevron station.

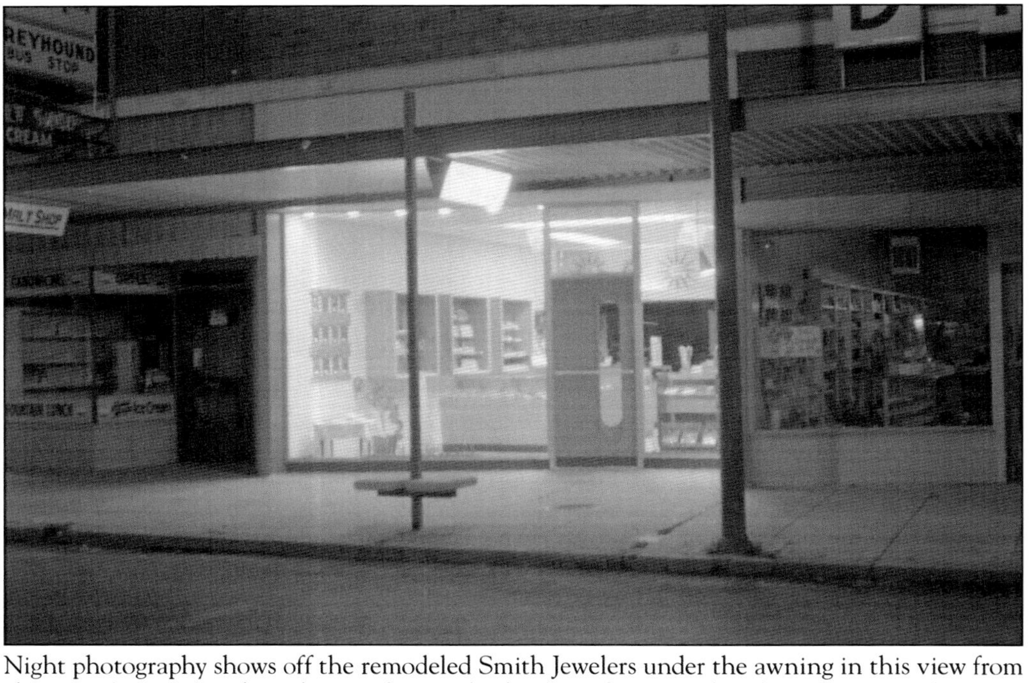

Night photography shows off the remodeled Smith Jewelers under the awning in this view from about 1967. Pete Smith took over the jewelry business from Frank Selner in 1952. Selner had purchased the jewelry and optometry business from James Minnick in 1920. He had been the town's jeweler, optometrist, and watchmaker since 1890. Pete Smith retired in 1976. (EWU-SPC-WWP 002-0-548_51-G-3.)

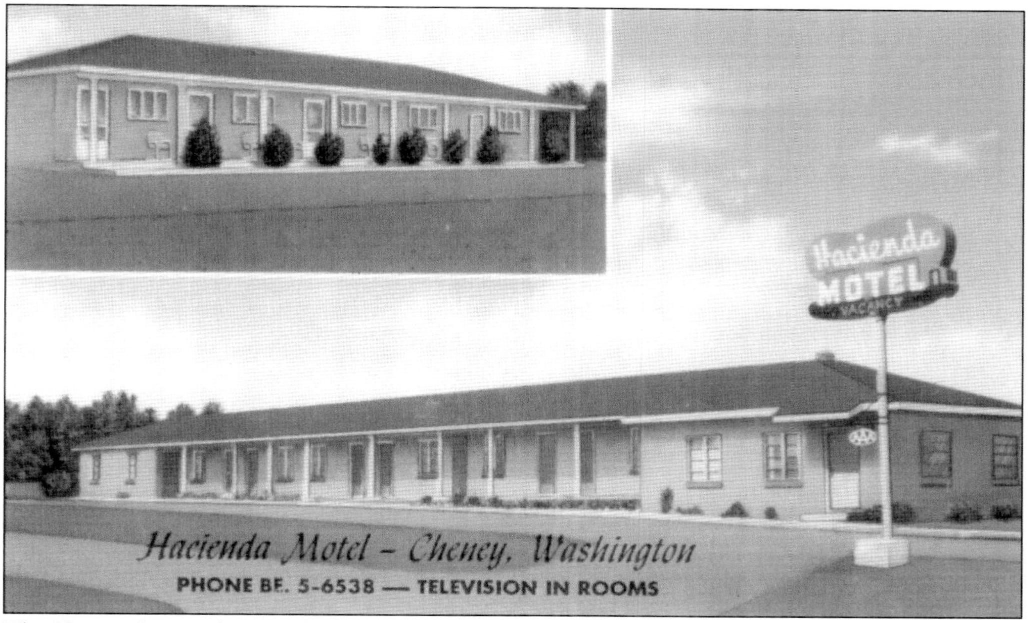

The Hacienda Motel opened at 304 West First Street, five blocks west of the city center on State Highway 10 about 1953. The motel owners boasted on this postcard from the early 1960s that each room had a television. In the late 1980s, the motel was renamed the Rosebrook Inn. It is known today as the Rosebrook Apartments.

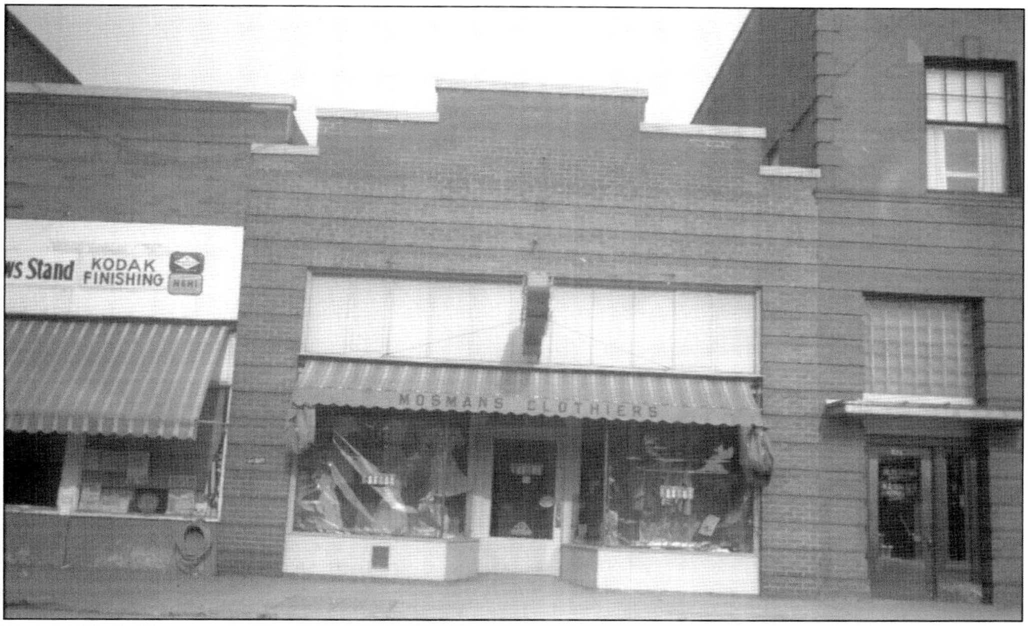

Bob Tubbs's Cheney Cycle and Magazine Shop appears at left in this photograph from about 1961. Harry Mosman opened his clothing store in 1957, taking over from Al and Buddy Olson, who in turn had bought out Elmer Hansen in 1949. Hansen had taken over the store from Charles Bernard, who began the long line of men's clothing stores at that address in 1933. (EWU-SPC-WWP 002-0548_68-I.)

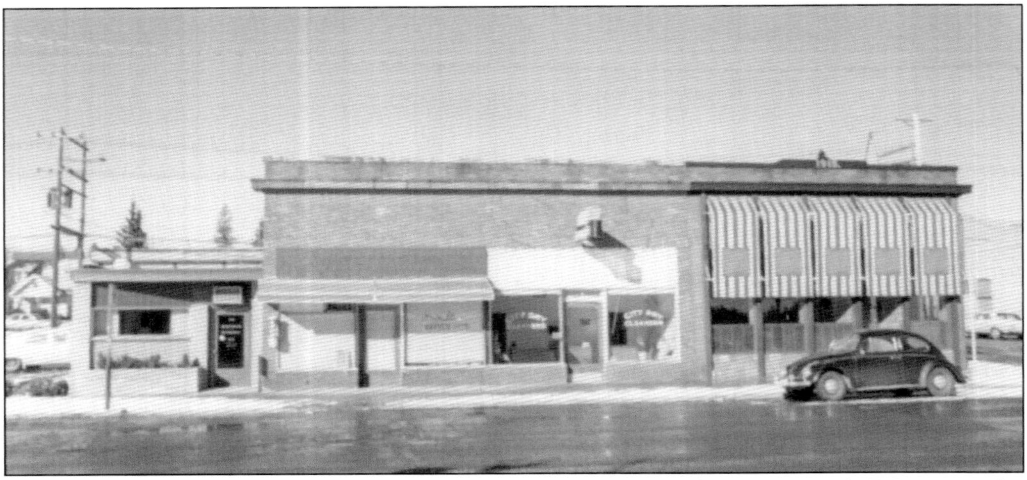

This 1971 photograph shows the north side of the 300 block of downtown with F Street at the far right. On the corner is Pizza Hut in the old Bair's Grocery building, followed by the City Dry Cleaners operated by Lyman and Nita Johnson, Shorty Goodwin's Barber Shop, and Merritt Johnson's Law Office.

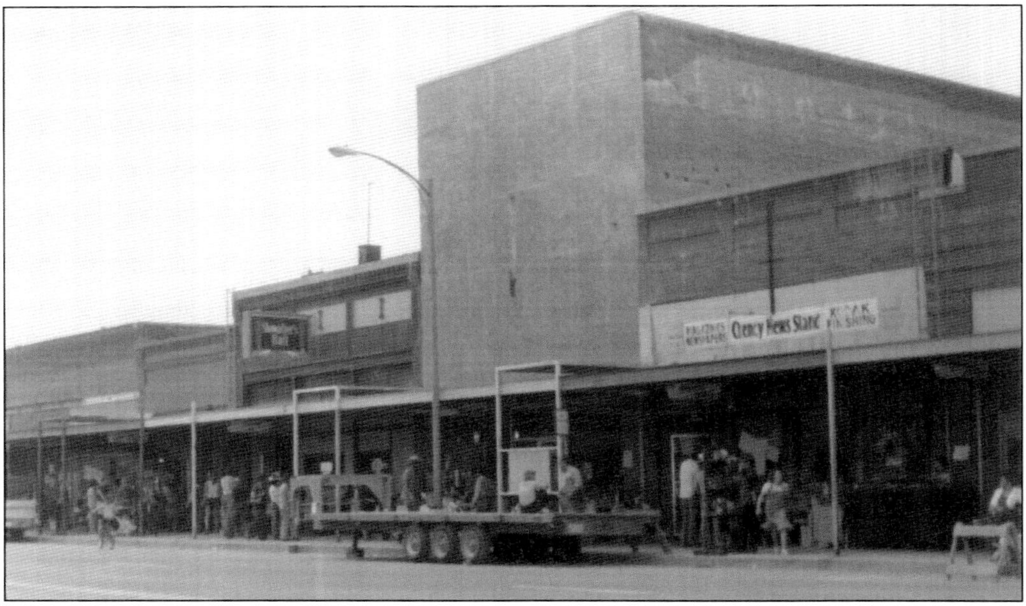

A few vendors are showing their wares under the awning on the north side of First Street as the rodeo street fair winds down on July 12, 1980. From the left, one can see Ellen Jones's Book and Brush, Smith Jewelers, New York Life Insurance, Showalter Hall Tavern, the Cheney Library, Robert's Sports under the old sign for the Cheney Newstand, and Harry Mosman's Clothing and Sporting Goods.

Seven

Times to Remember

For each generation of residents, there are events that stand out clearly. For some it was the fatal train wreck of 1916 or of 1955. For others, it was the firestorm of 1960, which destroyed the Tyler schoolhouse and sent showers of embers down on Cheney. For the pioneers, there were the fires of 1883, 1889, and 1890, which burned through the business district, or those that destroyed the Normal School in 1891 and 1912.

Residents remember where they were when the oil refinery next to the railroad tracks exploded in 1962, the Crescent Laundry was engulfed in flames in 1946, or the field house became an inferno in 1977. Most people can recall where they were and what they were doing in 1980 when day became night and ash rained down on everything during the eruption of Mount St. Helens. Since the ash coated everything, everyone participated in the cleanup of the community.

Each generation also has stories to tell about a blizzard or the deep snows that stopped the world for a time, but provided youngsters with a magical time for play.

There were good times and joyful pastimes in the memories of each generation as well. There were the Fourth of July celebrations in pioneer times, the annual May Day festival, community fairs, and rodeos that brought people together. Crowds filled the Cheney Racetrack to watch people race horses, bicycles, or each other.

Summers were times for baseball, picnics, boating, fishing, and swimming. There was sledding in winter along with ice skating on the many ponds south of town. Local bands played for dances in the grange halls, schools, and country homes at all times of the year.

Early residents went to see the silent movies at the Rose Theater on College Avenue, while later generations flocked to see the latest Hollywood offering at La Melodeon, later known as the Pix Theater on First Street.

Other special moments include suffragette Frances Willard speaking here, preacher Billy Sunday stopping by to visit friends, President Truman's brief visit in 1950, and Launi Meili winning gold at the 1992 Olympics.

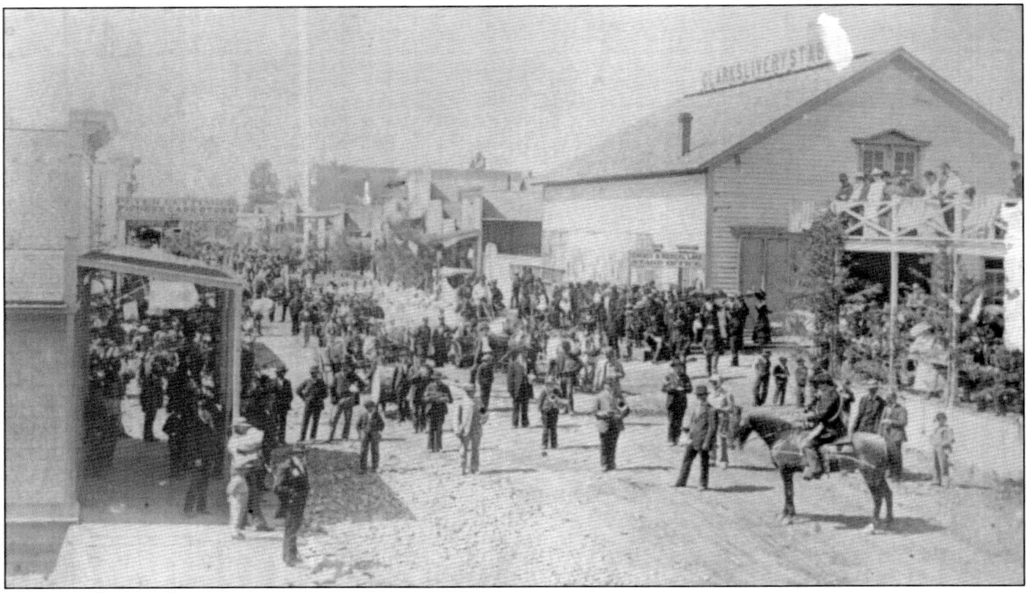

In one of the earliest photographs of Cheney, crowds line the streets for the Fourth of July parade in the Spokane County seat in 1884. Looking west from C Street, Peter Bettinger's Cash Store, on the left, also housed the post office. Clark's Livery Stable also served as the Cheney–Medical Lake stagecoach ticket office.

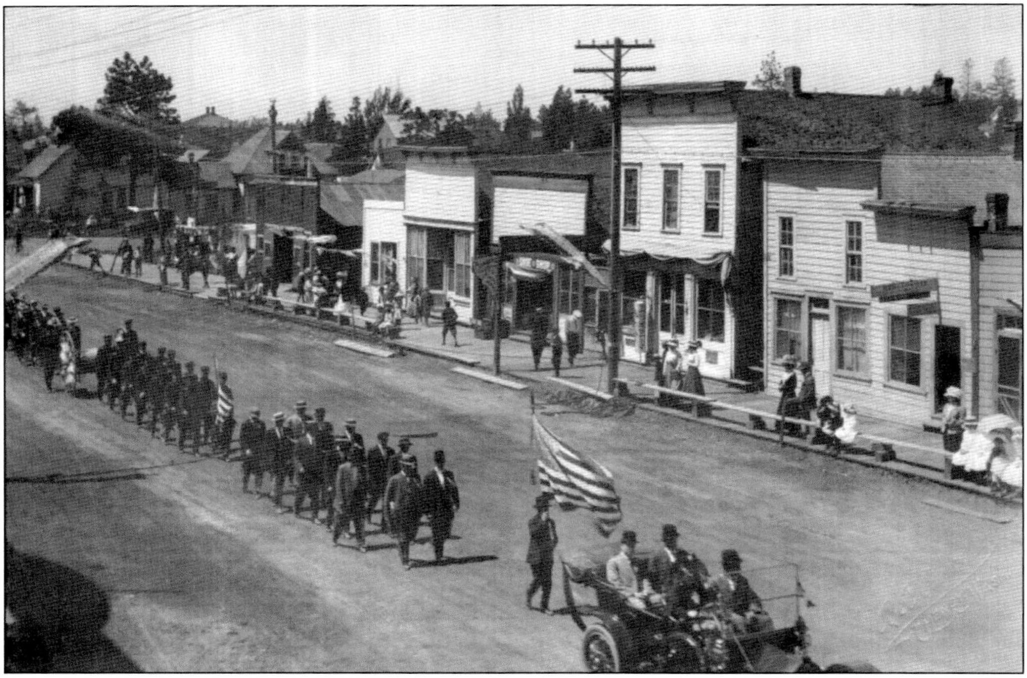

The May Day festival started in 1910. One of its main events was the parade, which wound down from Fifth Street, through downtown, and back up the hill to City Park. There are signs visible for a shoe shop, Plumbing, Steam Pipes and General Joining, and Money to Loan—First Class Real Estate. The store second from left at the end of the block was also the Grand Army of the Republic hall.

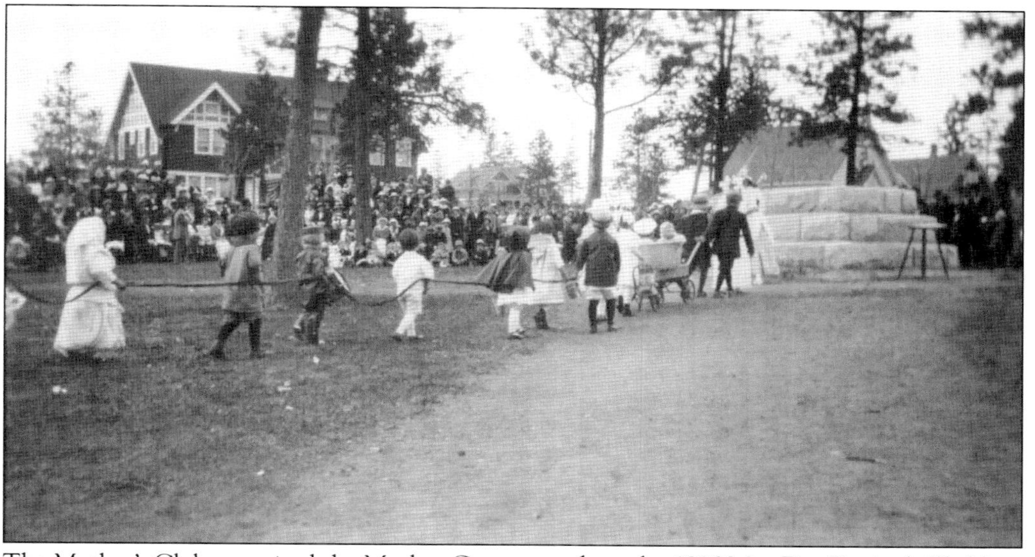

The Mother's Club organized the Mother Goose parade at the 1916 May Day Festival. Children are shown marching toward the granite pedestal that would later hold the war memorial in City Park. Those granite stones came from the foundation of the Normal School after it burned down in 1912. In the background is the home of Charles A. Ratcliffe, owner of the Ratcliffe Ford dealership.

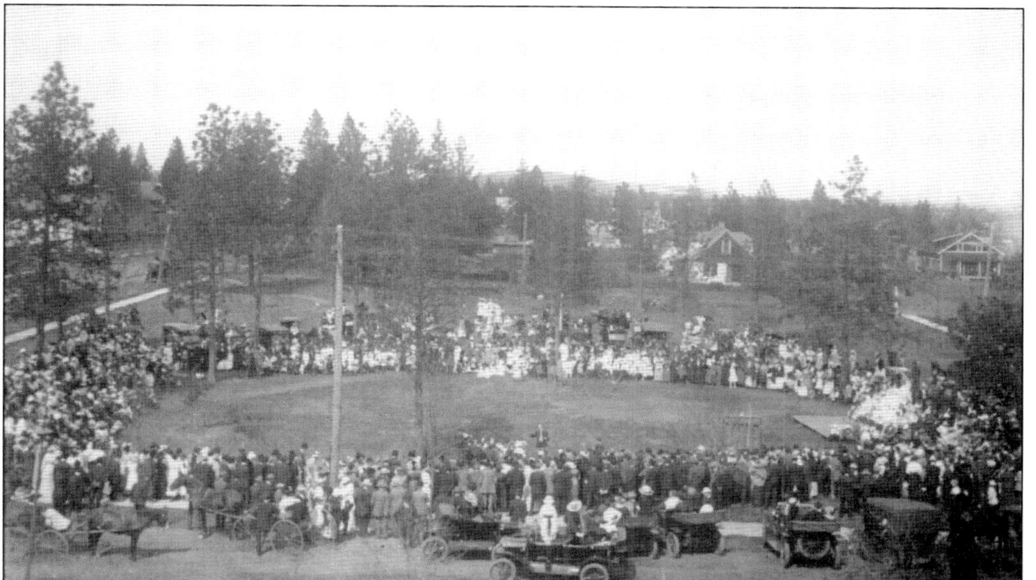

The crowd gathered at City Park (now Veterans Park) for the crowning of the May Day queen, speeches, dramatic performances, and games. The day was capped with a dance at the Normal School. The May Day festival was held annually until the outbreak of World War II. It was revived for short periods after the war, but never regained the popularity it once had.

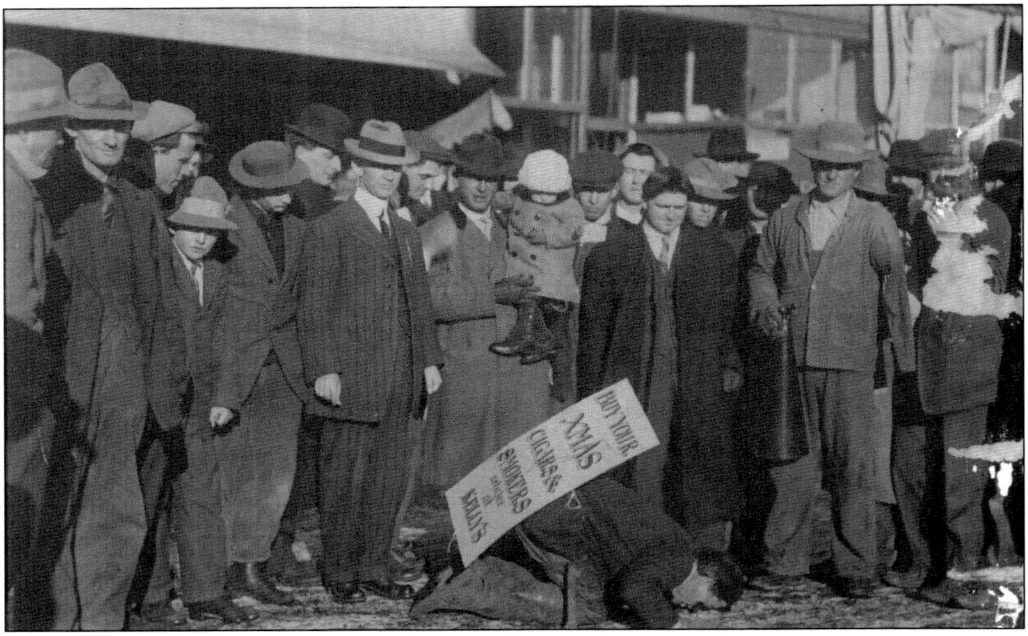

Sam Webb paid a wager to Jack Riddle by rolling a peanut across First Street with his nose on December 7, 1911. He had lost his bet that Socialists would win the election. Sam solicited advertisements to carry on his back, which netted him $25, and he sold photographs for $2 a piece. In the striped suit is Ruby Kelly, longtime owner of Kelly's Tavern.

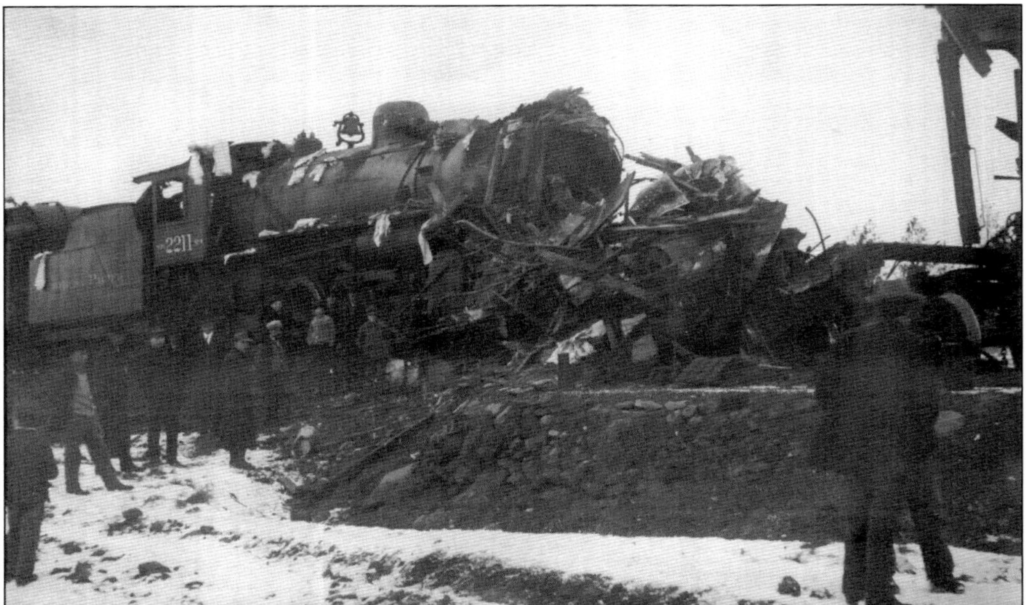

Train wrecks were all too common in the early days. This collision in 1916 was one of the worst. The engine of the North Coast Limited rammed six feet into a steel chair car which, in turn, was driven 50 feet into the wooden Pullman sleeper car behind it, killing at least four people. The hearing to determine the cause of the collision was held at the Cheney Normal School.

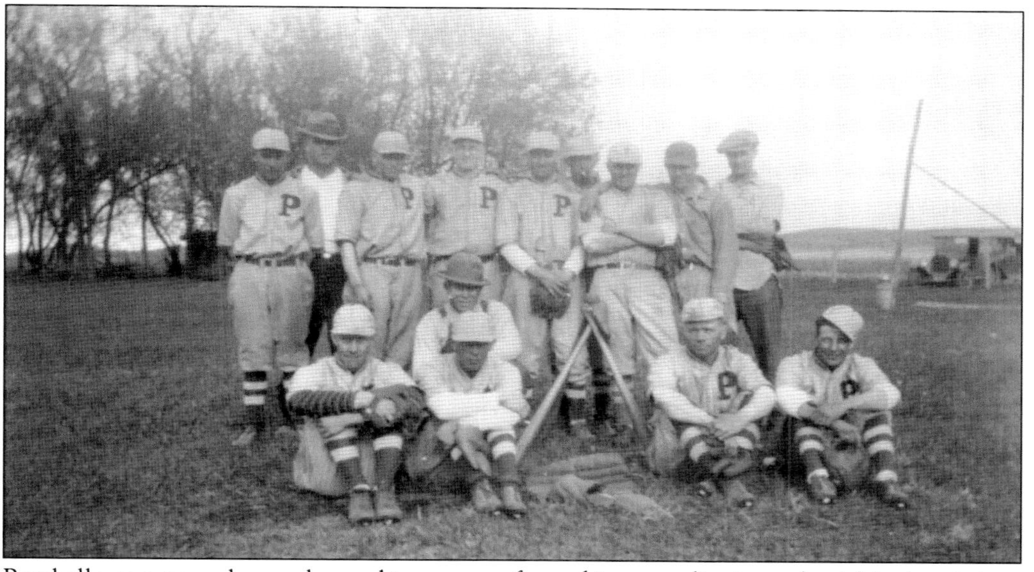

Baseball was extremely popular, and teams were formed in every district and neighborhood since 1882. Edwin Philleo (second from left in the back) had a team, posing here with his initial on their uniforms. Teams with names like Cheney Stars, Lance Hills Nine, and Cheney Baseball Club played against each other, as well as teams from Spangle, Sprague, Davenport, and Spokane Falls.

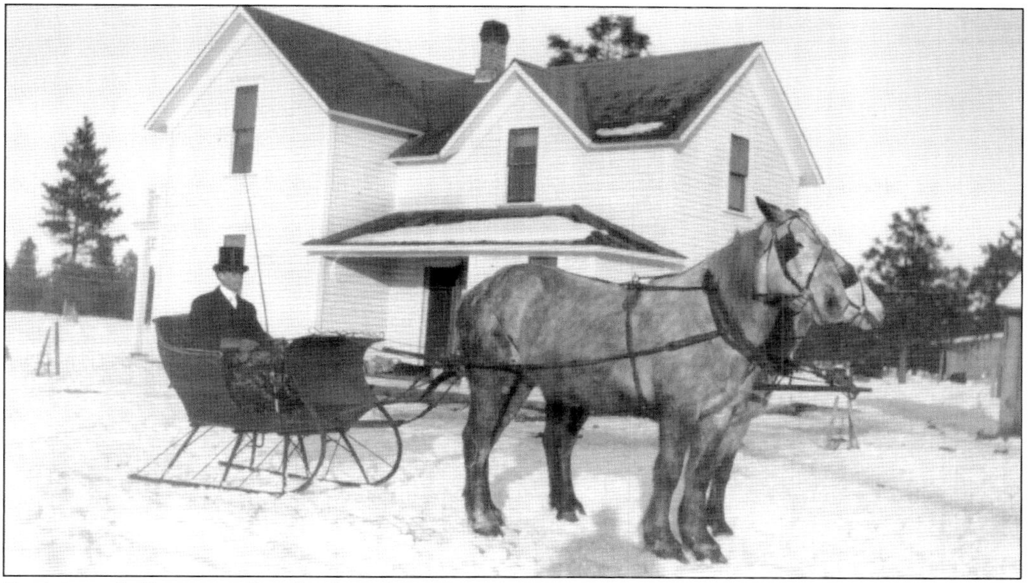

Fred Campbell poses in his sleigh in front of his home about 1900. Not just holiday entertainment, a sleigh or sledge was a necessity on snowy country roads, as well as in town. Winter pastimes included sledding, ice skating on ponds, hockey, backcountry skiing, and even ice fishing. Every generation had its favorite sledding hill and a field for building snow forts.

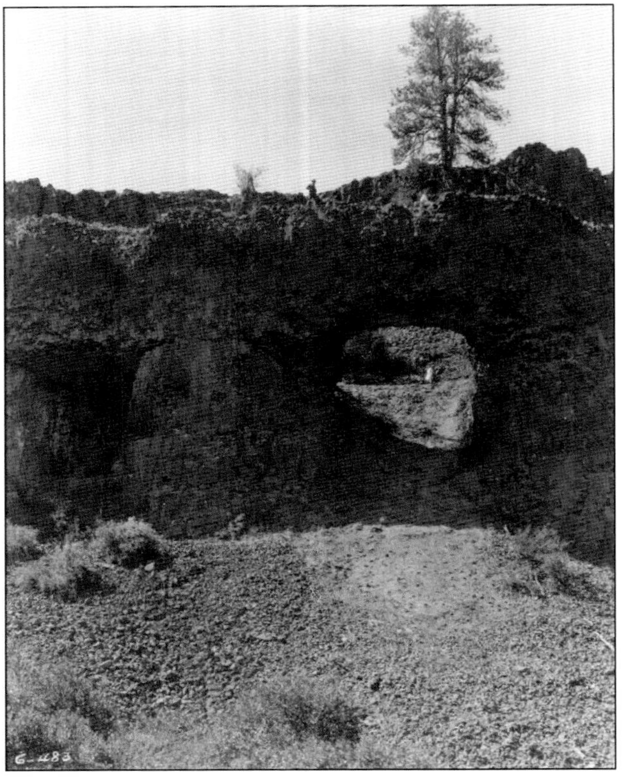

Hole in the Ground, a natural bridge about 10 miles south of Cheney, was a very popular picnic destination. Located in a canyon in the plateau with a creek and grassy meadow, it was part of an early homestead. This tourist attraction is on private land. Over time, the public became a nuisance and the owner cut off access to the site. (Washington State Digital Archives.)

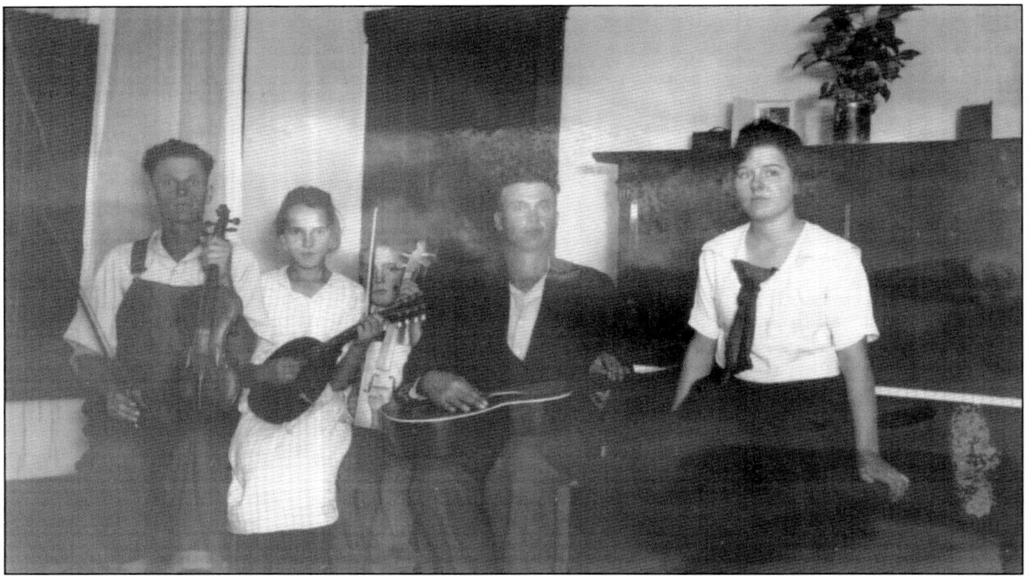

Families and groups of friends formed bands that were kept busy playing at township halls, granges, barns, and homes. When people held a dance, they rolled up the carpets and moved the furniture out. In this photograph from around 1918, members of the band are, from left to right, Fred Campbell, ? Mauretz, Fred Mauretz (holding a cigar box fiddle made by Fred Campbell), Clarence Campbell, and Maymie Mauretz.

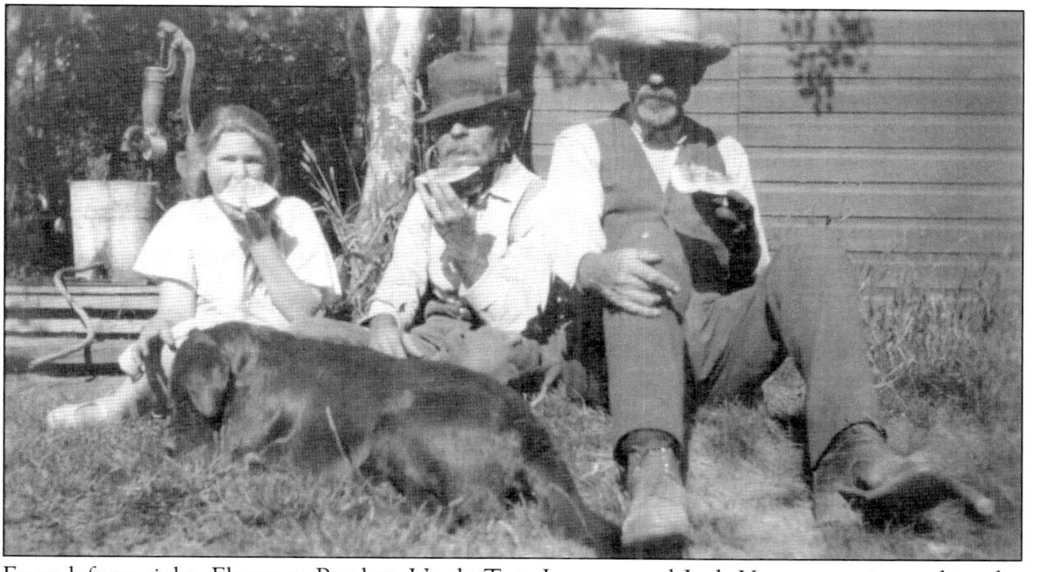

From left to right, Florence Bunker, Uncle Tom Lemon, and Jack Hume are pictured in the summer of 1914 eating watermelon outside the family cabin at Bunker's Resort on Williams Lake. The family dog keeps them company. Note the water pump on the porch behind them. Frank Bunker opened his resort in 1903, with his son later taking over operations. It was purchased by the McHenry family in 1953.

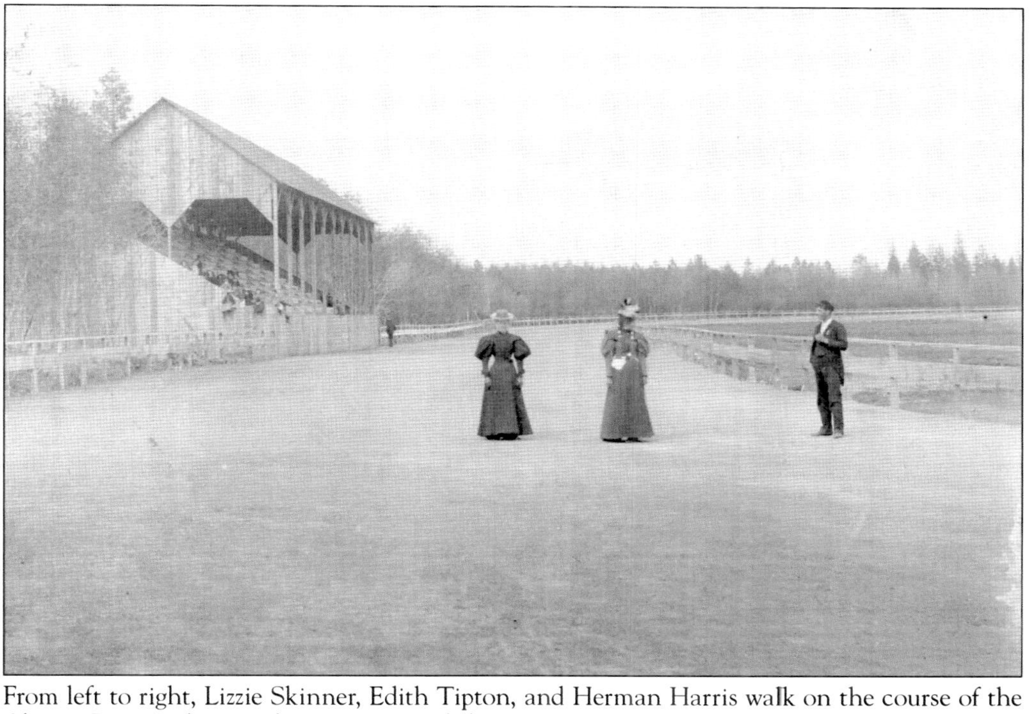

From left to right, Lizzie Skinner, Edith Tipton, and Herman Harris walk on the course of the Cheney Racetrack around 1900. It opened about 1895 just south of the railroad tracks, and was a popular site for the new bicycle racing craze. The grandstand could seat 1,000. Horse shows, ball games, foot races, and school sports were also activities at the track. (EWU 007-0584_3-14-1.)

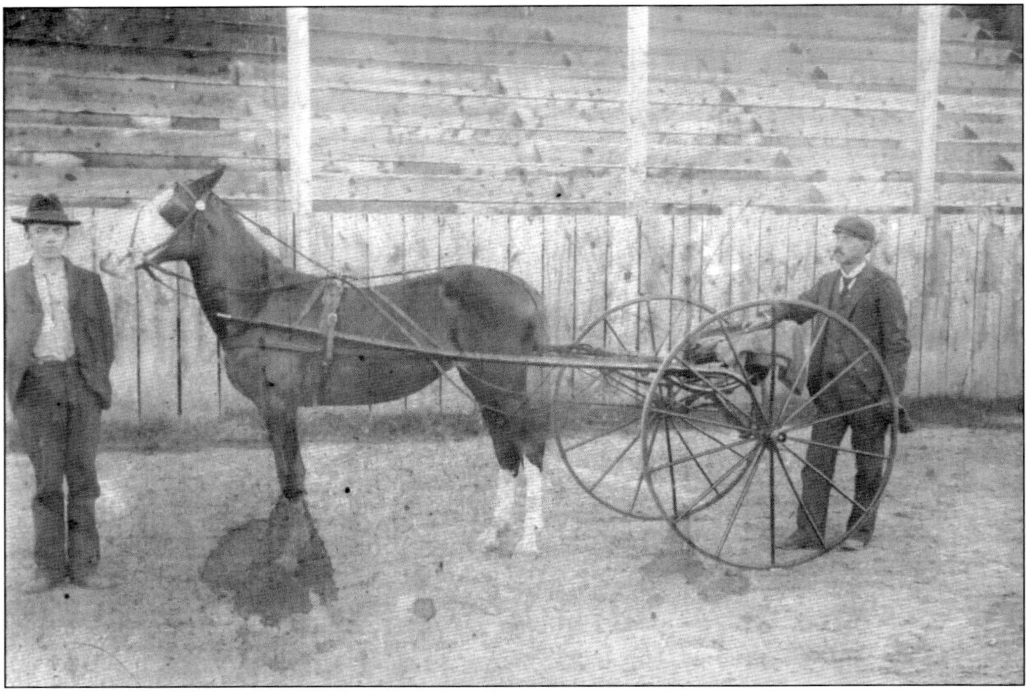

Dr. Wells, a local dentist (at right), stands with his racing gig and unidentified driver at the Cheney Racetrack around 1898. Pacing and trotting races were popular, along with horse and pony races. As automobile racing on streets and larger tracks elsewhere became popular in the 1910s, the Cheney track was used less frequently. It continued to be used for rodeos and community fairs through the 1930s.

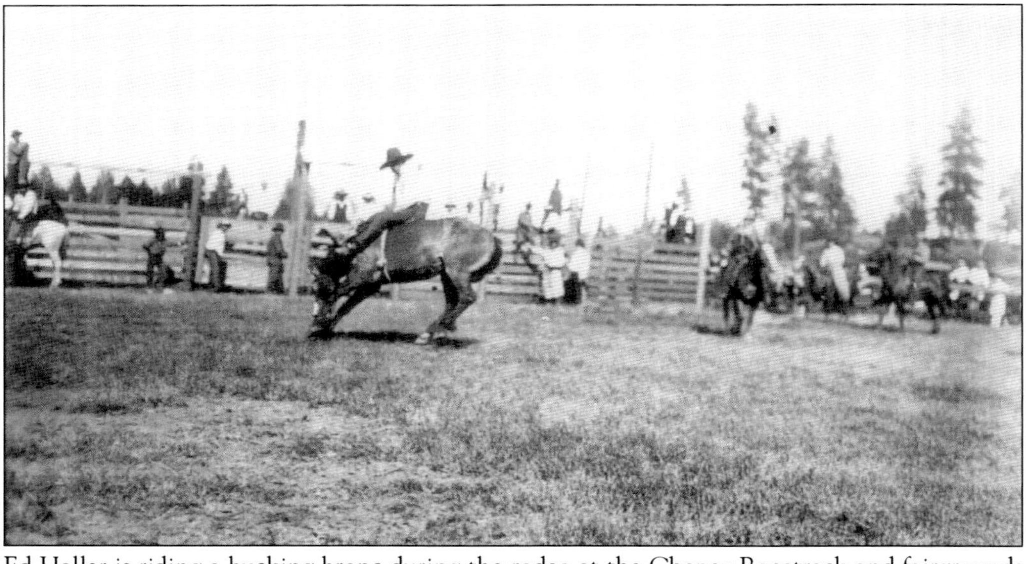

Ed Haller is riding a bucking bronc during the rodeo at the Cheney Racetrack and fairgrounds on July 4, 1927. There were numerous small rodeos held all around the region at Bonney Lake, Stubblefield Lake, Winona, and Plaza during the 1920s and 1930s. Ailene Warren was named the 1930 Cheney Rodeo Queen by an early version of the Cheney Rodeo Association.

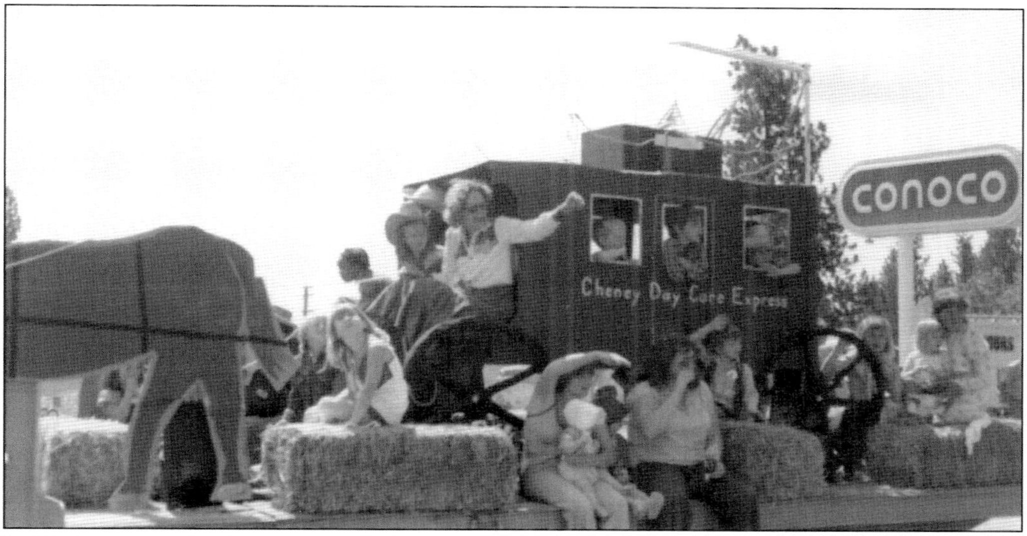

In 1967, a group of eight men passed a hat to collect money to start up a new Cheney rodeo. On land north of town, they set up chutes and held a drive-in style rodeo on July 12, 1968. Susan Patmore Vaughn waves to friends from the Cheney Day Care float in 1980 during the rodeo parade.

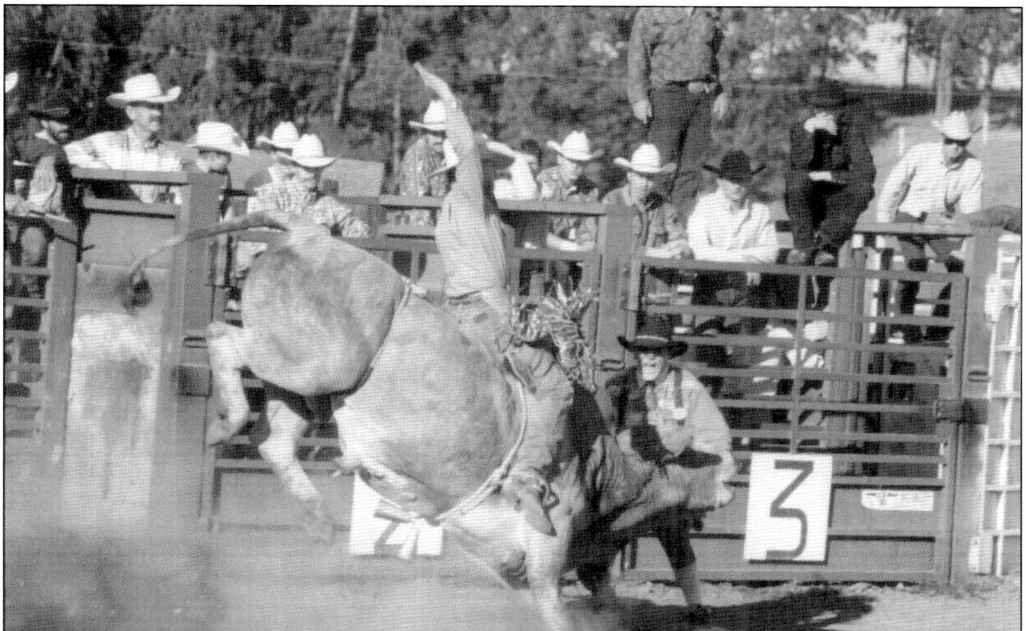

The Cheney Rodeo, with its downtown parade and street dance, continued to grow, and the volunteer association expanded and improved the rodeo grounds each year. Sanctioned by the Professional Rodeo Cowboy Association in 1990, the three-day rodeo brings professional cowboys from all over the Northwest. (Courtesy of Cheney Events Association.)

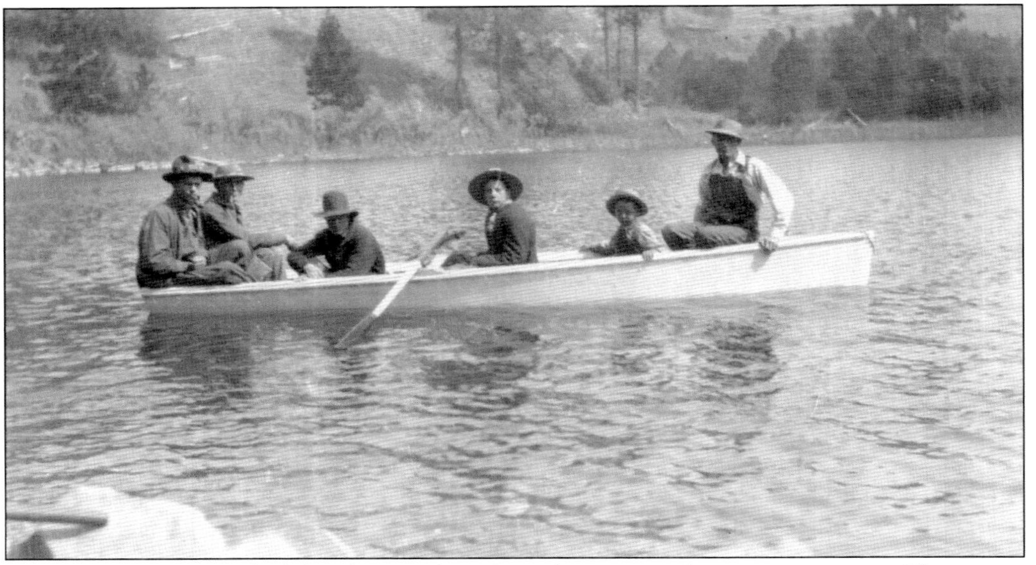

With a number of nearby lakes, boating has always been a popular summer activity. There were resorts with cabins or a hotel, camping sites, and boats for rent on Amber, Williams, Badger, and Fish Lakes. In this early 1900s photograph, Fred Campbell (at right), along with the Falter and Miller boys, takes the boat he built on its maiden voyage on Badger Lake.

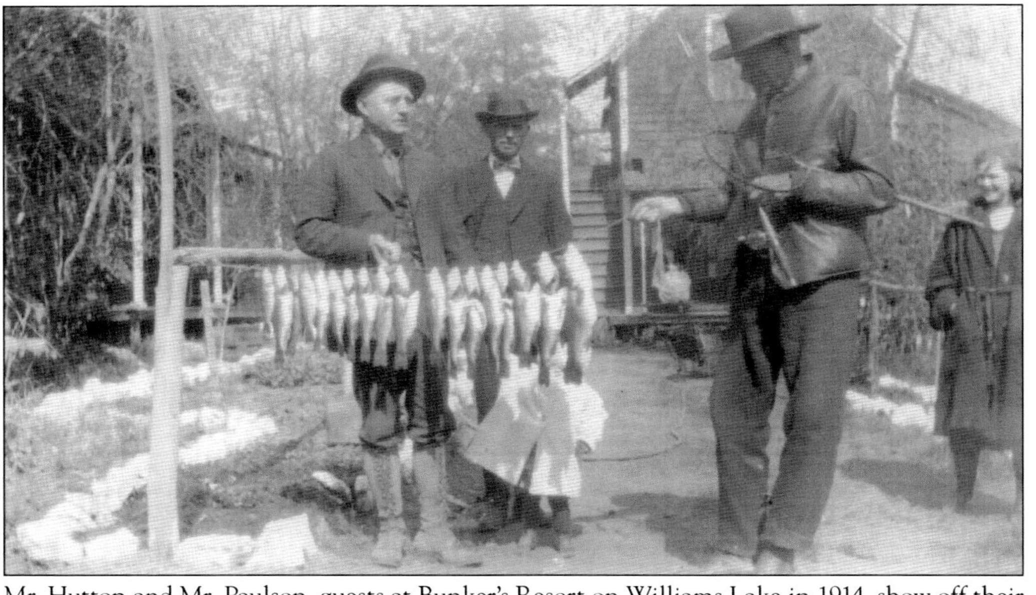

Mr. Hutton and Mr. Paulson, guests at Bunker's Resort on Williams Lake in 1914, show off their catch. Tom Lemon, holding the string of fish, acted as fishing guide on the lake, which was his home. His nieces, Betty (standing under the fish) and Florence Bunker (at right), spent their summers helping out at the resort.

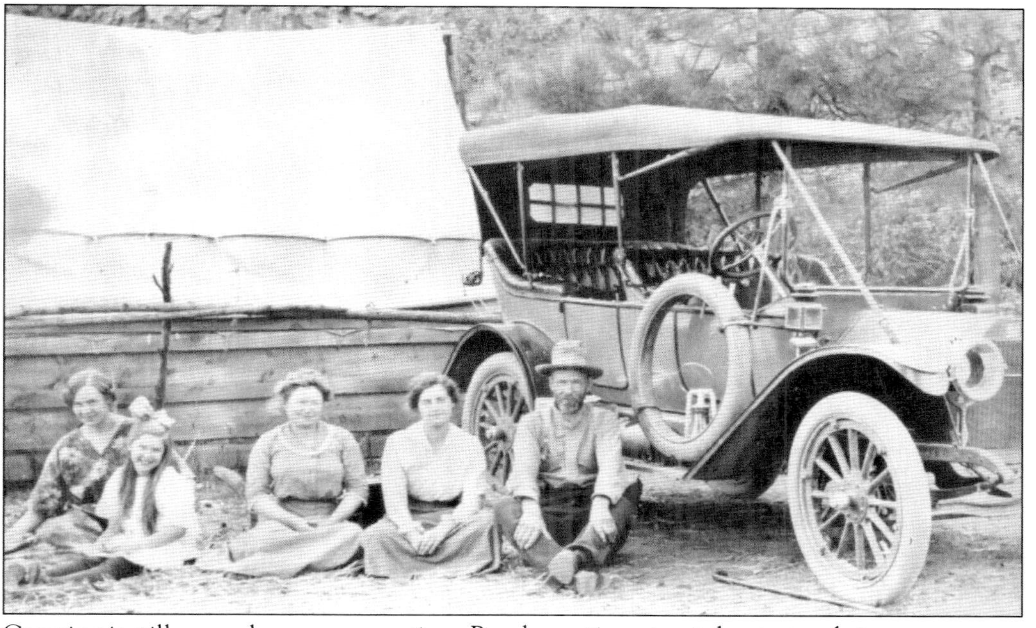

Camping is still a popular summer pastime. People continue to pitch a tent or bring a camper or RV to a lakeside campground for relaxation, boating, or fishing. From left to right, Rosella Lemon Bunker, Florence Bunker, unidentified, Milrie Coverly, and Tom Lemon show how a campsite looked in 1914.

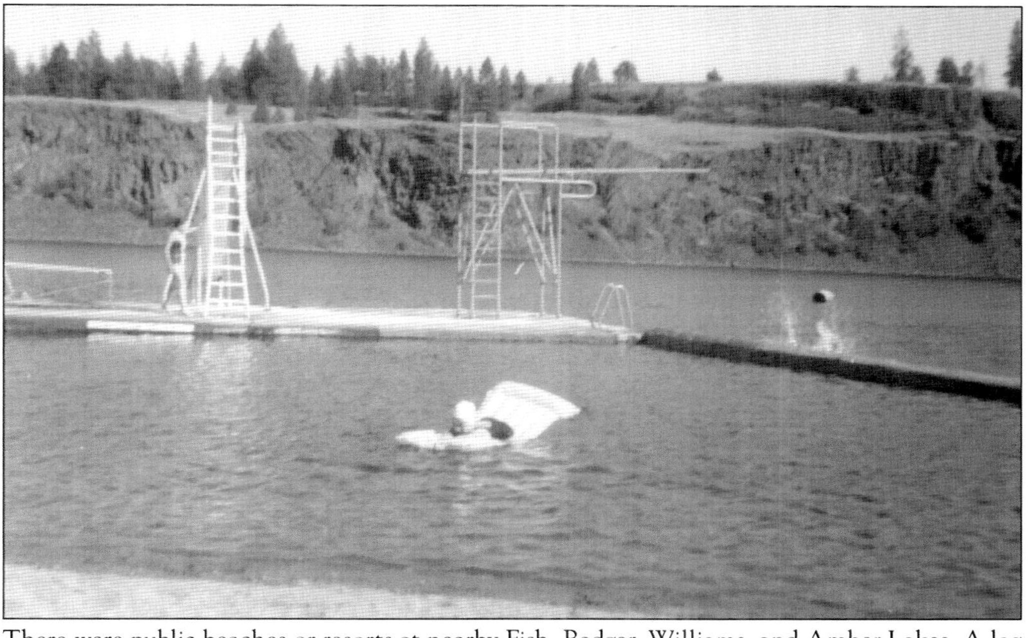

There were public beaches or resorts at nearby Fish, Badger, Williams, and Amber Lakes. A log boom with a dock surrounded the swimming area at the resort on Badger Lake, pictured here in 1964. Here, young people could spend an afternoon diving, swimming, going down the big slide, or floating on an inflatable raft. The resort store was cool inside and had an ice chest full of soft drinks.

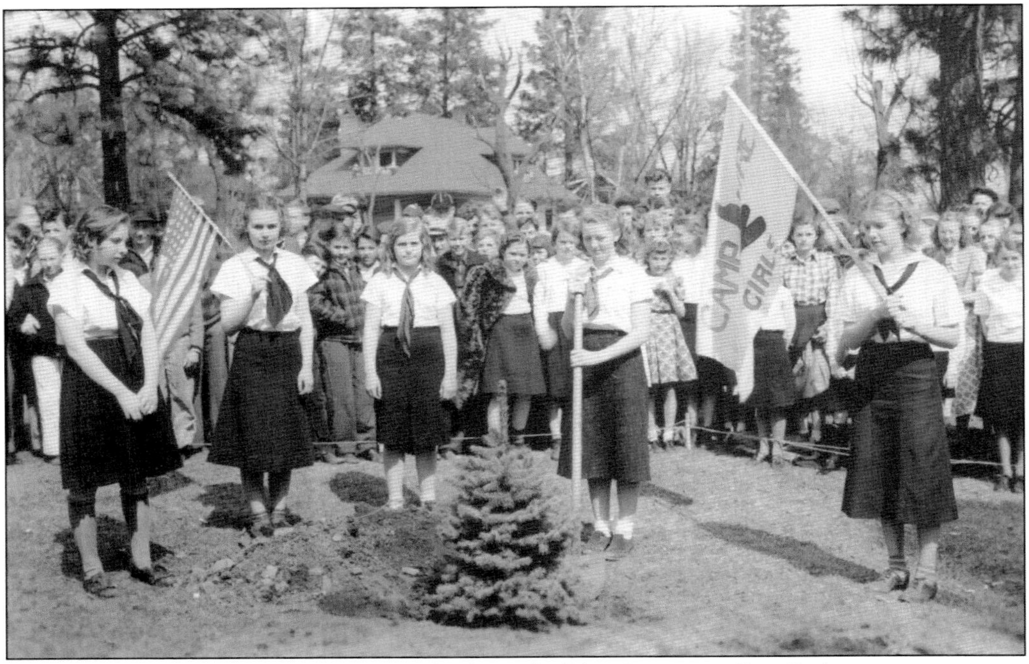

In a 1945 ceremony, the Camp Fire Girls planted a Blue Spruce in City Park to commemorate their organization. Planting memorial trees in parks and on the college campus was a tradition of the Tilicum Club, the women's organization that sponsored the Camp Fire Girls beginning in the 1920s.

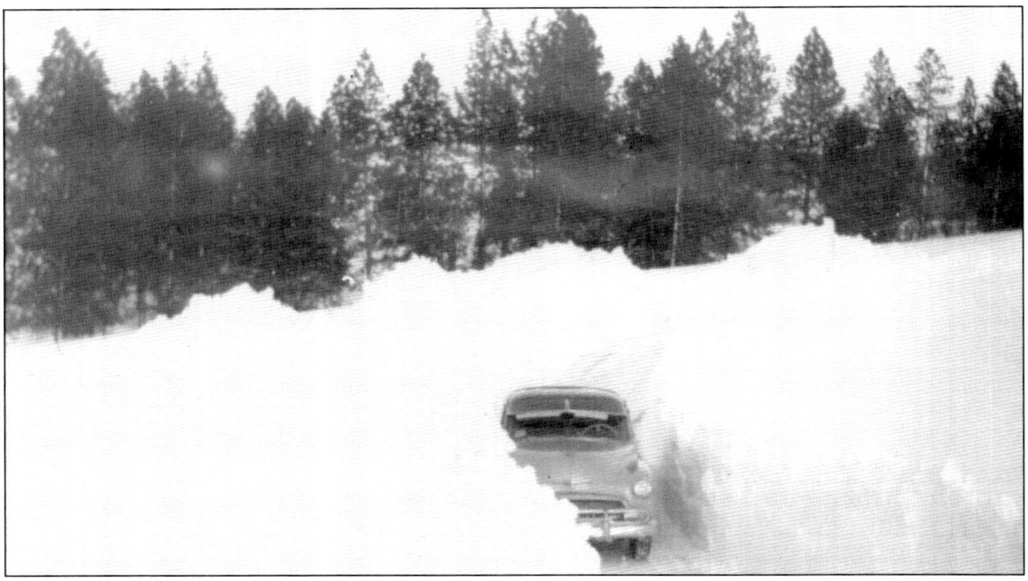

This photograph from January 1952 illustrates the remarkable winters that occur nearly every decade. The pioneers remembered the winter of 1887–1888, when the January temperature dipped to –30 degrees. Other memorable winters included 1909–1910; 1928–1929, when schools were closed for two weeks; 1942–1943; and the blizzard of January 1950. Later generations remember 1968–1969, 1974–1975, 1992–1993, and the winter of 1996–1997.

Pres. Harry S. Truman made a brief visit on May 11, 1950. The American Legion color guard marched with the motorcade up College Avenue. The Cheney High School banded played as the president passed by. Beverly Willms Lucas recalled that as she and Freda Brodin walked across the college lawn to see the president, he looked up and told them they should not cut across the lawn.

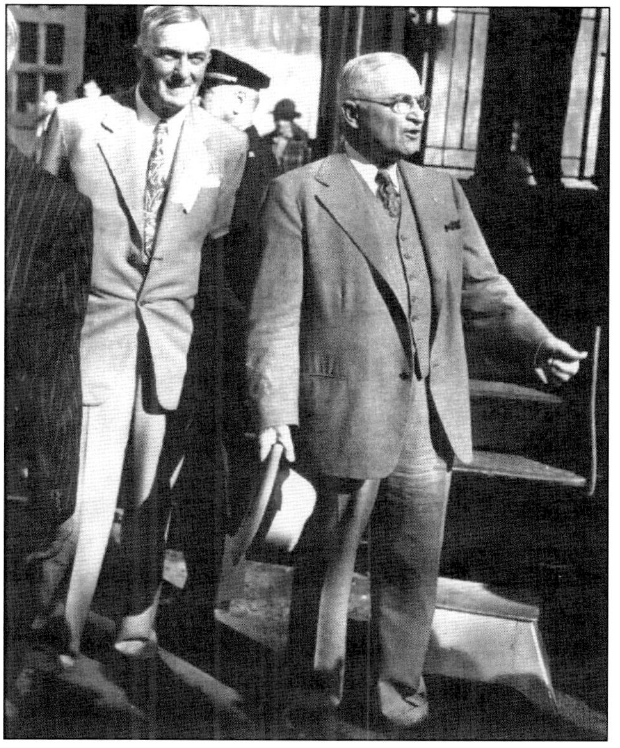

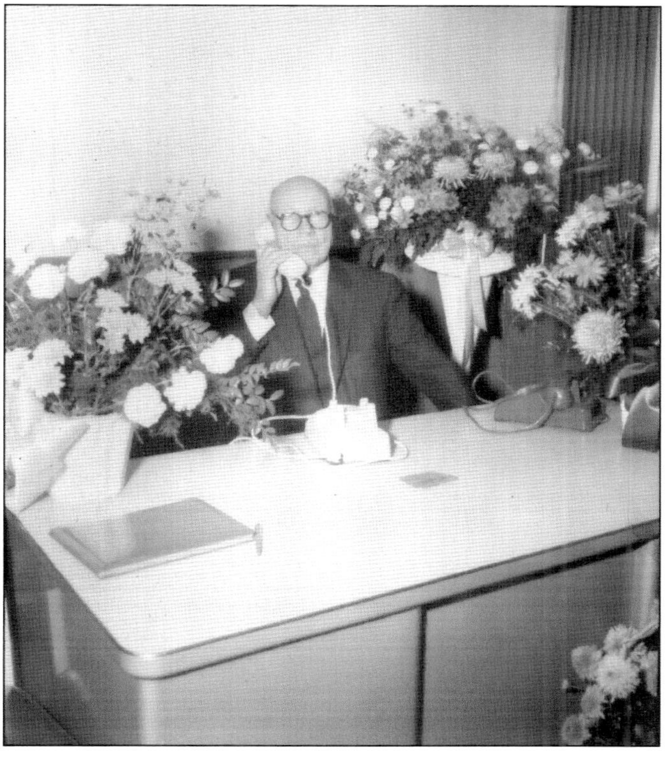

On October 16, 1956, an open house was held at the Masonic Hall to display new phones and demonstrate the direct dial system replacing the 66-year-old operator-based phone system in Cheney. John Lund, pictured here, and Beatrice Hilmer showed residents how to directly dial a neighbor or connect to the operator for a long-distance call on the new system.

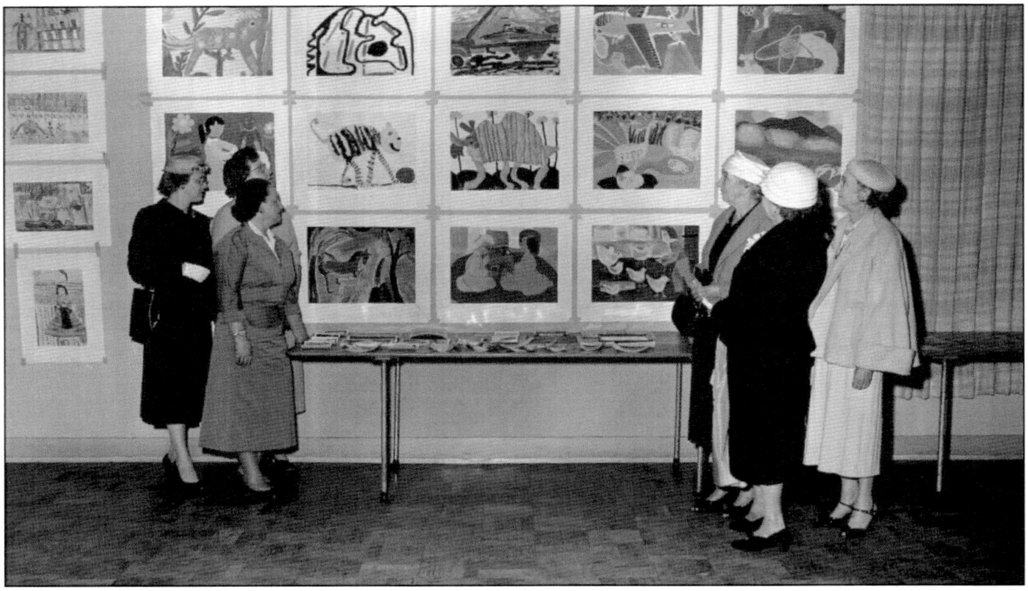

From the 1950s into the 1970s, the ladies of the Tilicum Club organized an annual art and hobby show in the auditorium of City Hall. Student and resident artists and hobbyists gave demonstrations and exhibited their work or displayed their collections. From left to right, Tilicum members Phyllis Hossum, Betty Schadegg, unidentified, Mildred French, Nell Dales, and Mattie Brown admire a display at the 1957 show.

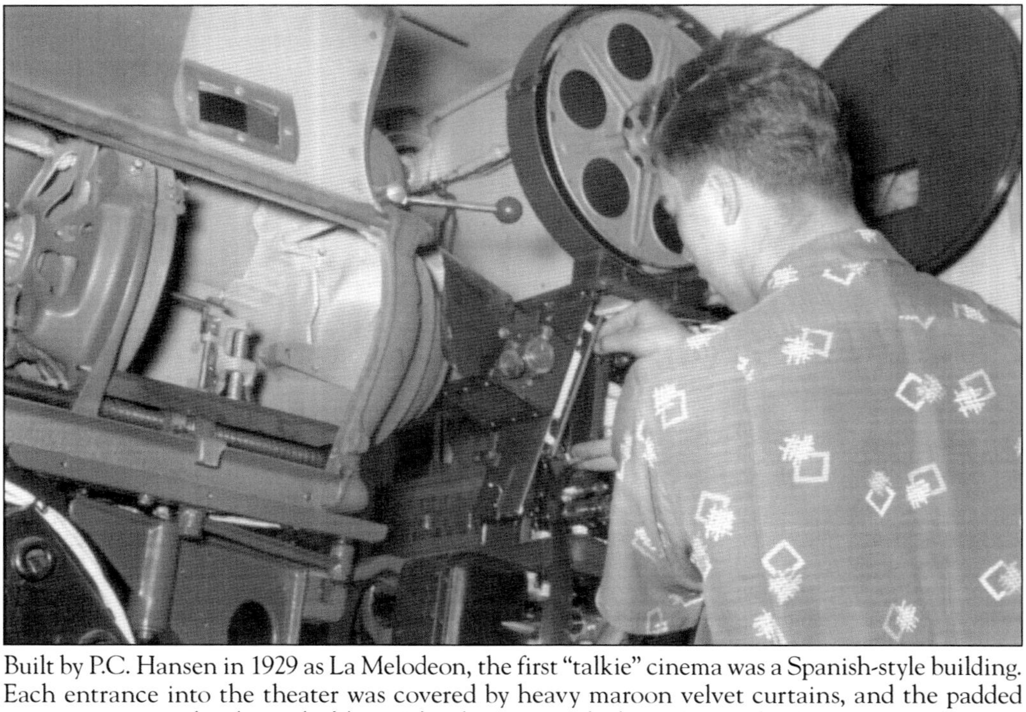

Built by P.C. Hansen in 1929 as La Melodeon, the first "talkie" cinema was a Spanish-style building. Each entrance into the theater was covered by heavy maroon velvet curtains, and the padded seats were covered in brocade fabric. The theater stood where the Bank of America parking lot is today. Here, Kyle Pugh Jr. threads the projector around 1954.

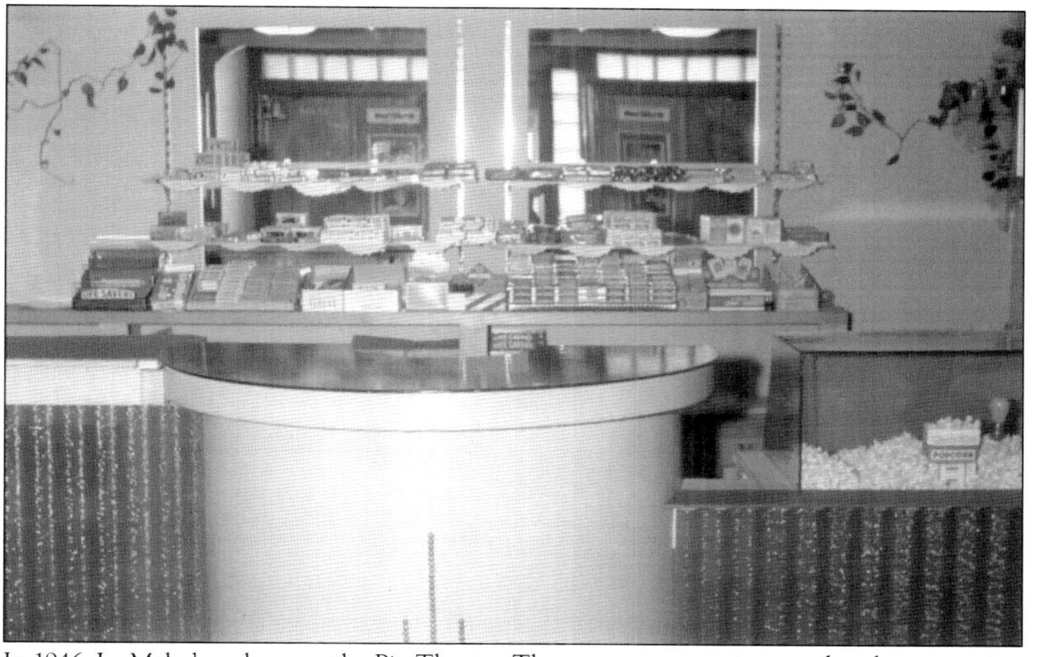

In 1946, La Melodeon became the Pix Theater. The postwar generation stood at the concession counter buying popcorn and candy before taking one of the 500 seats in the main theater or balcony. Through the mirror in back of the counter in this 1954 view, the other side of the lobby is visible. The final curtain closed on the Pix Theater in 1964.

The old 1891 Hotel Cheney at the foot of College Avenue was turned into apartments during World War II. On the night of April 7, 1956, the building erupted into flames. The Cheney Volunteer Fire Department kept the fire from spreading to the nearby Brown and Holter auto dealership and the Nabisco mill, but the hotel was lost. In 1971, the chamber of commerce had the foundation removed and the ground paved.

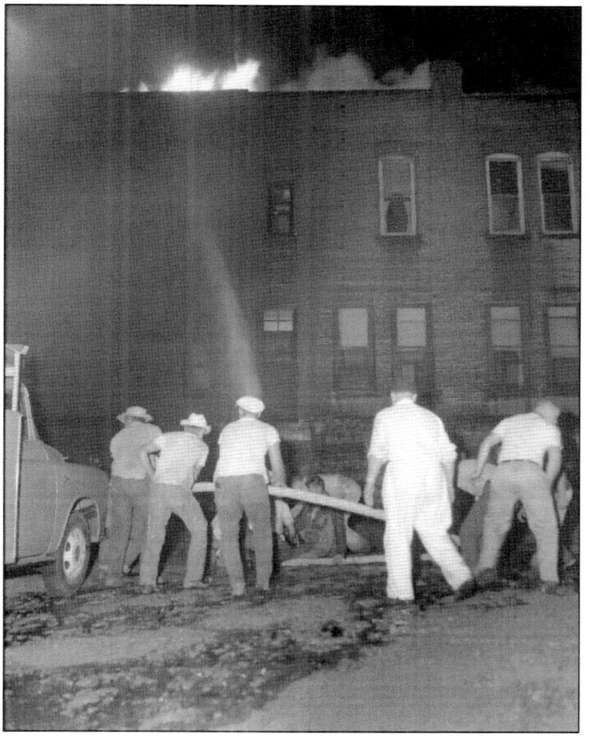

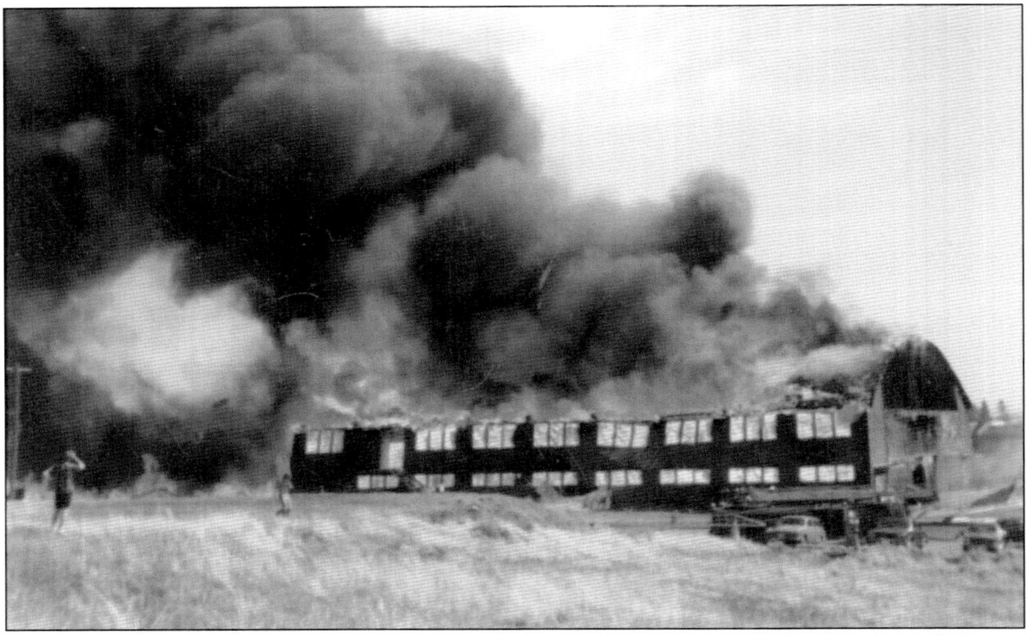

The old Memorial Field House went up in a spectacular blaze on April 25, 1977. A spark from a cutting torch on creosote soaked timbers started the fire as workers disassembled the building. Originally a drill hall from Farragut Naval Station in Idaho, it had been moved to the college campus in 1946.

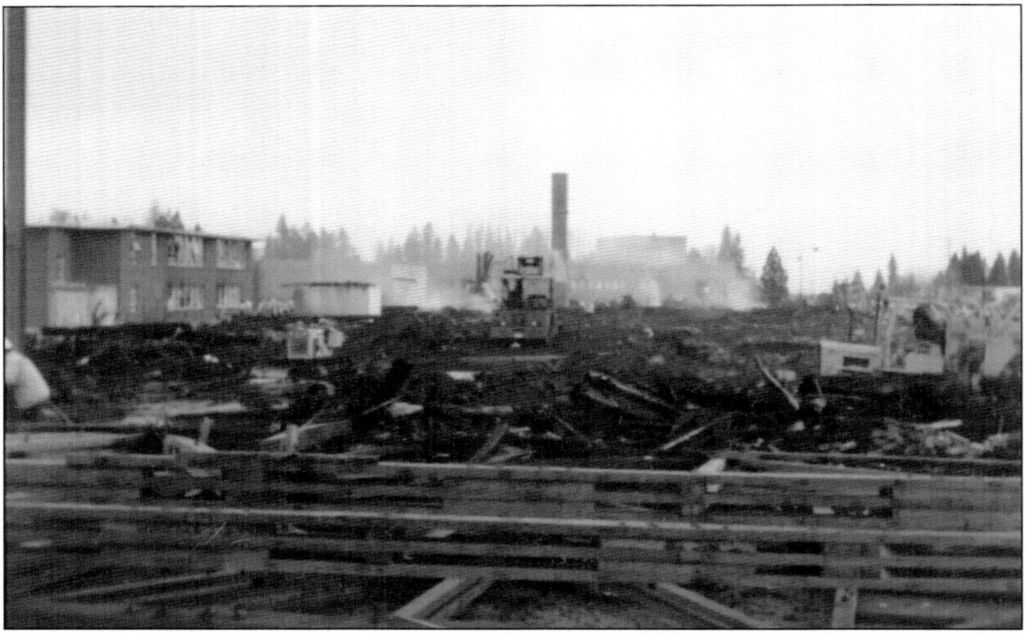

The intensity of the blaze melted power lines, as well as the paint and tires of cars parked on nearby Washington Street. Students and residents helped to push vehicles away from the inferno and sprayed water on nearby Cadet Hall and the fine arts complex to limit the damage to those buildings.

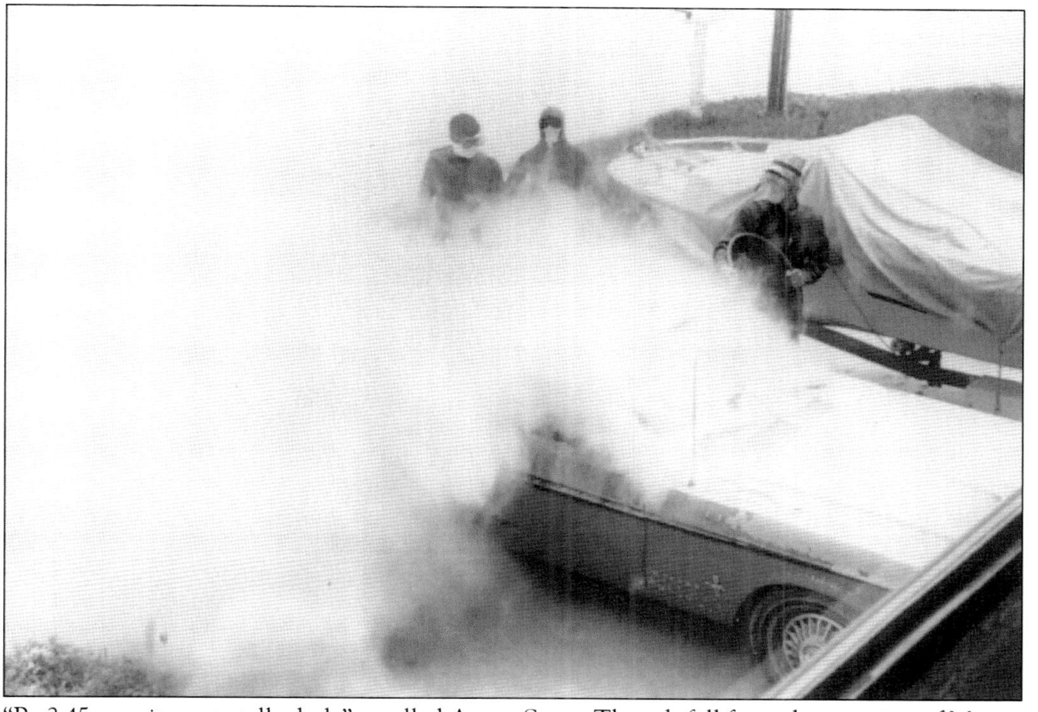

"By 2:45 p.m. it was totally dark," recalled Agnes Suess. The ash fall from the eruption of Mount St. Helens on May 18, 1980, left over a half inch of fine gray ash on everything. Roads and airports closed, and people were stranded for days. Randy, Steve, and Tom Davis used a compressor to blow the ash from their car the following day. The cleanup took weeks.

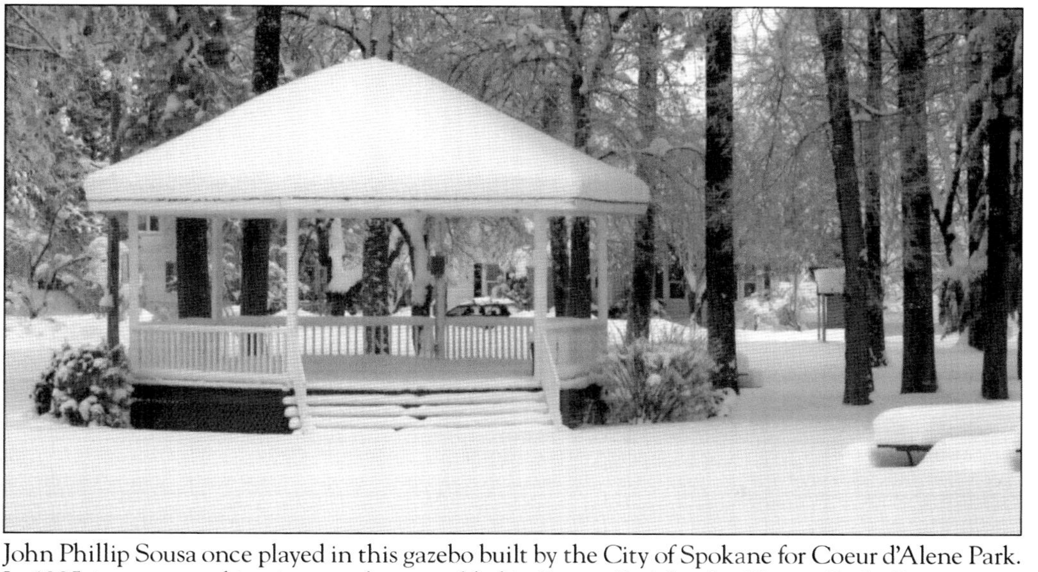

John Phillip Sousa once played in this gazebo built by the City of Spokane for Coeur d'Alene Park. In 1985, it was moved in pieces and reassembled in Sutton Park by the Cheney Parks Department maintenance crew. The electric department used its crane to lift the roof into place. The gazebo is popular for summer concerts, picnics, and weddings. This photograph was taken in 2008 by Claude Nichols.

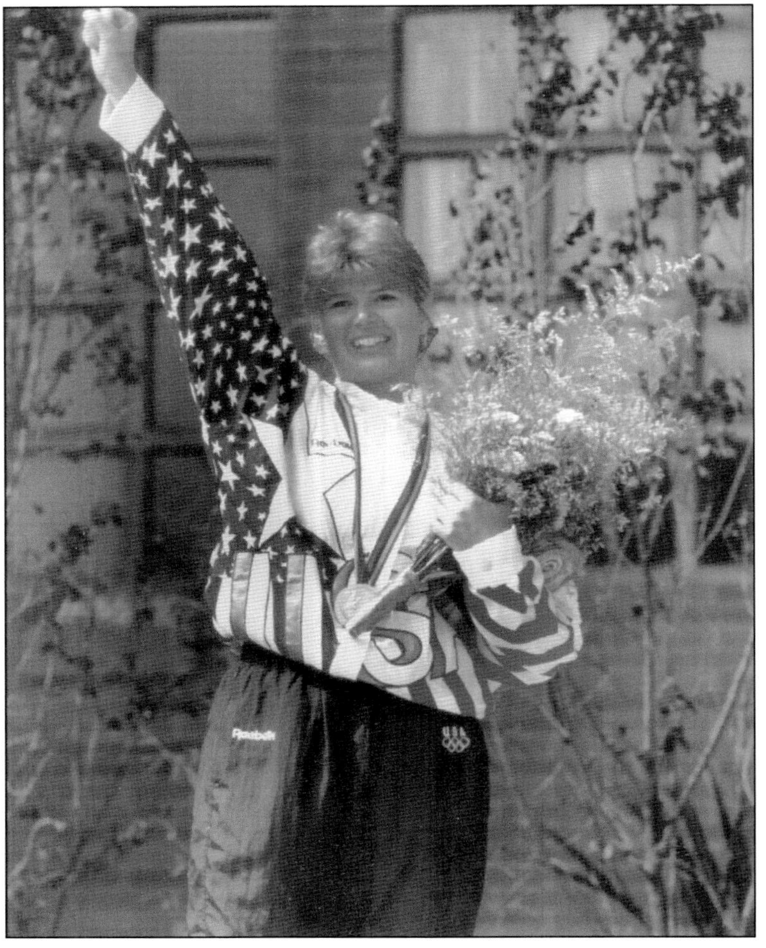

Olympic gold medalist Launi Meili poses at the 1992 Olympics in Barcelona, Spain. Launi began shooting a rifle in 1978 as a member of the Cheney American Legion rifle team, which was coached by teacher Wally Beard. During her competitive years, Meili won a number of national, World Cup, and world championship medals, as well as the gold medal in the women's three position small bore rifle event.

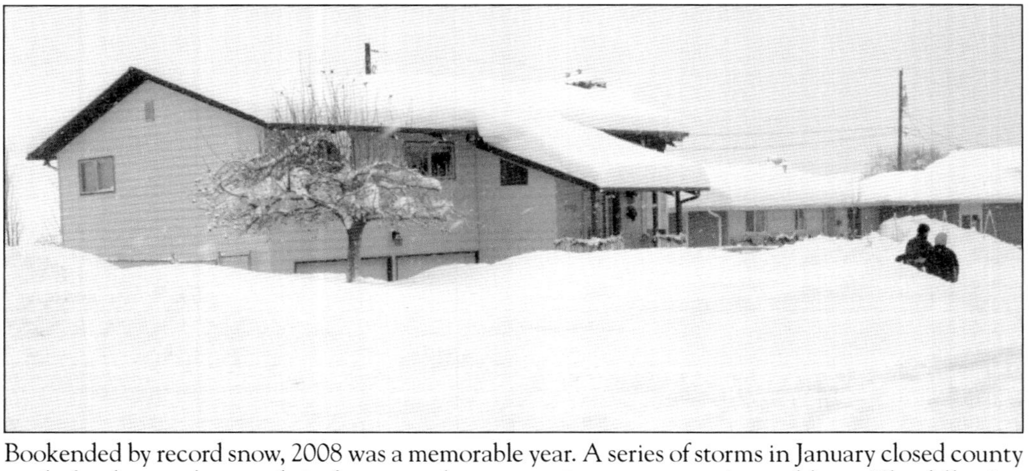

Bookended by record snow, 2008 was a memorable year. A series of storms in January closed county roads for days and created six-foot snow berms on city streets, as pictured here. The following winter, December saw 30 inches fall in 30 hours and a record 61 inches for the month. By April 2009, a new winter record of 97.7 inches of snow had been set.

About the Southwest Spokane County Historical Society

The Southwest Spokane County Historical Society is an all-volunteer organization dedicated to sharing the stories of our district's past.

Cheney's historical collection was born in 1935 when a group of pioneers and Women's Relief Corp members, an auxiliary of the Grand Army of the Republic, asked the Tilicum Club to preserve items from the early days. The pioneers were concerned that the younger generations would not know about the struggles and triumphs of their lives and the history of Cheney.

Established in 1903, the Tilicum Club was a women's social and service organization. The women were activists for improving the civic and social life of the community. Through the years, they cared for, and used, the growing collection in programs for school children and through the Cheney Historical Museum.

In 2011, the club reorganized into the Southwest Spokane County Historical Society, opening its membership to anyone with a love of history. The society continues to share, research, and preserve the history of the Four Lakes, Marshall, Cheney, Tyler, and Amber districts of eastern Washington entirely through volunteer efforts and donations.

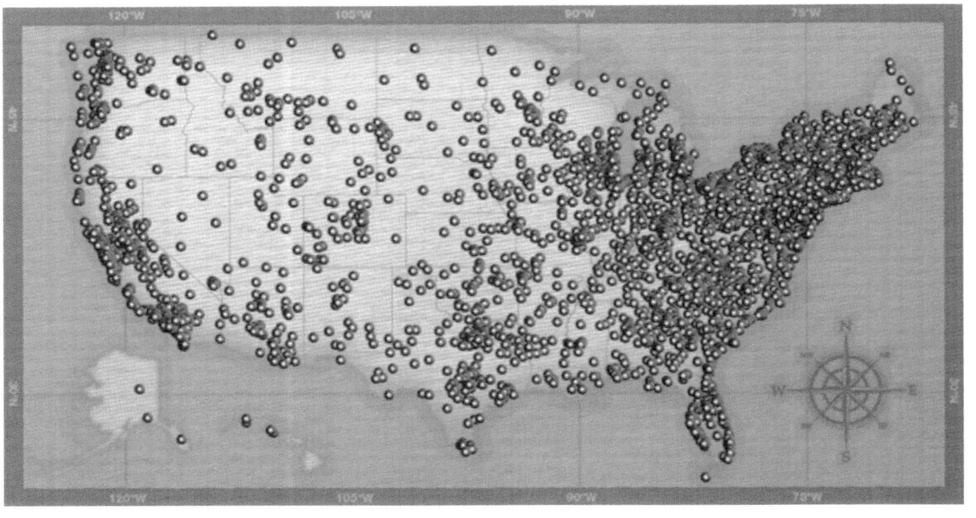